Henry Hunter

**Lectures on the Evidences of Christianity**

Henry Hunter

**Lectures on the Evidences of Christianity**

ISBN/EAN: 9783337163648

Printed in Europe, USA, Canada, Australia, Japan

Cover: Foto ©Lupo / pixelio.de

More available books at **www.hansebooks.com**

# LECTURES

ON THE

# EVIDENCES

OF

# CHRISTIANITY.

FOUR

BY THE LATE
REV. JOHN FELL,
OF *HOMERTON*;

AND

EIGHT
BY HENRY HUNTER, D.D.
MINISTER OF THE SCOTS CHURCH, LONDON-WALL.

*PUBLISHED AT THE REQUEST OF THE MANAGERS AND SUBSCRIBERS.*

London:

PRINTED BY BYE AND LAW, ST. JOHN'S-SQUARE;

AND SOLD BY

JOHNSON, St. Paul's Church-Yard; BUTTON, Pater-noster-Row; GOOD, No. 63, Bishopsgate Street Without; FLOWER, Cambridge; and COTTLE, Bristol.

1798.

# PREFACE.

THE first four Lectures, presented in this Volume, are the interesting remains of the late Rev. JOHN FELL. His expulsion from the office of Resident Tutor to the Academy at Homerton, and the situation to which he was thereby reduced, excited attention. His talents and virtues had procured for him an extensive reputation, and the warm attachment of many respectable and powerful friends, who considered that expulsion, and the treatment which he had previously received, as unmerited and unjust. Such friends were not disposed to permit a venerable minister of the gospel to sink under a load of years, of poverty, and reproach. The only difficulty was to find a proper channel in which their benevolence might flow. Mr. Fell's mental powers were still in full vigor, and might be employed usefully to the world, as well as honourably to himself. In deliberating on the subject, *A Course of Lectures on the Evidences of Christianity*, occurred to the mind of a gentleman of high respectability, Mr. Samuel Favell, who communicated his idea to those who were, in common with himself, the friends of Mr. Fell. It was eagerly embraced, as combining a variety of valuable and important objects. It would have a tendency to repel the poison conveyed in certain plausible tracts, lately published, against the religion of the Gospel: their friend's talents were peculiarly adapted to such an undertaking; and it would furnish them with an opportunity of ministring to his wants, without encroaching on his feelings. The plan was accordingly proposed, and adopted with a becoming spirit.

The

The Lecture opened at the Scots Church, London-Wall, in January 1797, under every auspicious appearance; and promised to be, in no common degree, acceptable and beneficial to the public, as well as profitable to the Author. But, alas, Mr. Fell's constitution had received a shock from which it was never to recover. The application of mind necessary to the composition of his Lectures, and the bodily exertion requisite to the delivery of them from the pulpit, overwhelmed a frame never very robust, and now considerably impaired by the recent attacks made upon it. He struggled through the four Discourses here given from the press, and then, from increasing indisposition, felt himself under the necessity of quitting the field. The rest need not to be told.

The Lectures being, from the first, intended for publication, a short-hand writer was employed to take them down as they fell from his

his lips. Mr. Fell's mode of study was singular. He carefully digested his subject in his thoughts, but frequently without committing a syllable to paper. Such, however, was his distinctness of arrangement, and power of memory, that his Sermons, when pronounced, had all the appearance of being read from a printed book. Had the art of short-hand writing been as perfect, as his delivery was accurate, no apology would have been needful for the blanks which appear in the following pages. But as his voice, not naturally loud, sometimes sunk too low for the ear, and was sometimes lost in the occasional stir of a crouded assembly, the writer was frequently incapable of catching the words; and who, but Mr. Fell himself, could fill up such blanks?

When it pleased God to remove this worthy man by death, our mutual friends requested me to preach his Funeral Sermon, and afterwards to print it. No choice was left me but

but to comply; and surely I have no cause to repent it. Unwilling to abandon all the objects of the Lecture, though they had lost a leading one, the Managers did me the honour to propose my undertaking a continuation of the design, by preaching eight additional Lectures on the same subject. In this, with fear and trembling I engaged. It was gratifying, to a high degree, to be thought worthy of filling a station to which Mr. Fell had been called; but it was a delicate and a difficult task to attempt to finish what such a man had begun. Had he left any regular traces of his general plan, they would have assisted me greatly, and I should have felt myself bound to follow his track. But not having that advantage, I was under the necessity of sketching a plan for myself, corresponding to the ground given me to occupy. Instead of my own church, it was deemed expedient to carry on the Lecture at the Old Jewry, and the use of that place of worship was granted, in the

hand-

handsomest manner, by the Rev. Dr. Rees, and the Trustees of his Church. The Lecture commenced on the Evening of the second Lord's Day of December 1797, and was continued on the fourth Sunday of that month, and on the second and fourth Sundays of the three following months; and it was attended by audiences numerous, attentive and serious. Many of my brethren in the ministry favoured me with their countenance and support; and both sweetened and alleviated the labour of the service, by conducting the devotional part of it.

The whole being completed, the Managers called the Subscribers together, who were pleased to express their satisfaction in the most flattering terms, and united in a request that I would accept of my worthy Predecessor's four manuscript Discourses, which Mr. Richard Sharp, his Executor, had generously given for that purpose, and prepare them, together with my own

own eight, for the press. This is a brief and simple account of the present publication, which I send forth, I can say with truth, under much greater solicitude about the reception of my friend's part of it, than of what is mine. When the circumstances, which have been stated, are impartially considered, the candid Reader, instead of being surprized at finding so many slips, in discourses digested and delivered under such disadvantages, will perhaps be disposed to wonder, that they should have assumed any form, or have possessed any energy at all. Many will view them with the veneration excited by the contemplation of a Raphael's outline, or a Michael Angelo's design; others, with a pleasing enthusiasm, considering them as the relics of a departed Saint. I would hope not, but I fear a few may feel an unworthy gratification in discovering defects in the posthumous publication of the thoughts of a man who, alive, was from his distinguished talents, the object

of

of their envy, and therefore of their diflike and perfecution; for even death difarms not the refentment of certain fpirits. Their cenfure, however, is more to be defired than their commendation, and their oppofition than their friendſhip. As to myfelf, the papers which follow, and which I produce not as a facrifice to vanity, but as a teftimony of my gratitude, will be a gratification to my heart as long as it beats, and they will tell pofterity with what manner of men I lived, and by whofe approbation and friendſhip I was honoured.

H. H.

Bethnal-Green Road,
6th *June*, 1798.

## To the Rev. Dr. Hunter.

*London, April 5th,* 1798.

WE the underfigned, Subfcribers to the Lectures delivered by you and the late Rev. John Fell, on the Evidences of Chriftianity, feeling a warm and unfhaken attachment to thofe principles which are the foundation of our Chriftian hope, a hope which folaces the heart through all the gloomy periods of the prefent ftate, and which affords it the moft triumphant profpect of a future life, at a time when the wit and talents of the age have been directed, with no common zeal, againft thofe principles, by men who, viewing them through the medium of their abufes, have traduced that excellent religion, which fpeaks peace on earth and good-will to men, as if it breathed nothing but war and peftilence.

At this time, with a confidence ftrengthened by the difcuffion of the fubject, we rejoice in the teftimonies of a Divine Revelation, perfuaded persuaded that the counsel is of God and cannot be overthrown, and we doubt not that He will overrule the spirit of Antichristian hostility which marks the present day, to destroy those superstitions which have so long debased and obscured its glory. We live at an extraordinary and eventful period. The dawn of that day of unfulfilled prophecies which predict the destruction of the man of sin, already appears. May it not cease to shine till it obtains its meridian splendour of universal peace and righteousness! May the turnings and overturnings which are in the world, prepare the way for Him whose right it is to reign, whose kingdom is an everlasting kingdom, and of whose dominion there is no end.

With these views, we beg leave to present you with the four Lectures delivered by Mr. Fell at your Meeting; and to whose memory and labours, we desire to pay this as our last tribute of affection and gratitude, requesting you will publish them, with those which you have delivered at the Rev. Dr. Rees's Meeting; begging you will also accept our most cordial acknowledgements for the readiness with which

which you undertook this service, and for the ability with which you have discharged it. Trusting a divine blessing will accompany all your labours,

We are, with great respect,
Sir,
Your obliged servants,
Ja<sup>s</sup> Davidson, Treasurer,

| | |
|---|---|
| Sam<sup>l</sup> Favell | Rob<sup>t</sup> Cowie |
| W<sup>m</sup> Dennison, M. P. | Nath Child |
| Sam<sup>l</sup> Moody | John Henderson |
| Tho Mullett | Nich<sup>s</sup> Phenè |
| John Maitland | Miles Burkitt |
| Ja<sup>s</sup> Dobie | J<sup>no</sup>. Paterson |
| Rob<sup>t</sup> Davies, Jun<sup>r</sup>. | A. Simpson |
| John Hoyes | James Pritt |
| William Dunbar | Sam<sup>l</sup> Lloyd |
| William Duff | John Edington |
| Ja<sup>s</sup> Baffington | W<sup>m</sup> Edwards |
| Rich<sup>d</sup> Lea | Sam<sup>l</sup> Nicholson |
| Joseph Howell | Jos: Jackson |
| John Fenn | Stephen Ponder |
| T. Addison | Edward Smith |
| Richard Sharp | James Collins |
| James Pearson | John Banister, Jun<sup>r</sup>. |

William

William Savill  Dav S. Hewſon
Caleb Talbot  John K. Hewſon
John Weſley  W$^m$ Reynolds
Benj$^n$ Shaw  J$^{no}$. Ja$^b$. Fehr
Tho$^s$ Savill  Ed$^d$ Reynolds
A. Harper  Joſ$^h$ Reynolds
G. W. Meriton  Alex$^r$ Shirreff
Daniel Alexander  Rob$^t$ Shirreff
Sayer Walker, M. D.  Ja$^s$ Turnbull
Nath Chater  David Stevenſon
William Kitchener  And$^w$ Wilkie
John Scott  Geo Fairley.
Geo Cowie

*To the Rev.* HENRY HUNTER, D.D.

London, June 1, 1798.

REV. AND DEAR SIR,

WHEN it pleafed God, in his all-wife, but myfterious Providence, to remove by death, the late Rev. JOHN FELL, foon after he had commenced a courfe of Lectures on the Evidences of Chriftianity, we were filled with folemn concern and pungent grief; while we humbly bowed before the unfearchable wifdom and fovereignty of the Moft High, we mourned that a veil was drawn over a defign, which to us appeared bright and promifing; and that fo rich a treafure of various, profound, and fanctified literature, fhould at once be fnatched from the world, at a time when confpicuoufly difclofing itfelf, in fupport of the moft glorious caufe, and amidft the moft encouraging omens of fuccefs.

Though we muft ever regret the lofs of a Friend whom we fo highly venerated, our anxiety for the important Lecture was in no fmall degree relieved, when, at the invitation

tation of Mr. FELL's judicious and generous Patrons, you, Sir, readily ſtepped forward to lift the ſtandard of Truth, which had fallen from his hand.

Having moſt of us enjoyed ſeveral opportunities of mingling with the intelligent and numerous Auditory, which, with high gratification and improvement, attended your progreſs through theſe Lectures, we now affectionately congratulate you on their completion; feeling peculiarly grateful emotions when we think on the kindneſs of our God, in removing a ſevere indiſpoſition, which, at one period, threatened a ſecond interruption of theſe labours. At a time when Infidelity hath attempted to reſume and to extend its gloomy triumphs, we cannot but rejoice in the united exertions of two ſuch able Advocates for the truth of that Religion whoſe origin is divine, whoſe evidences are inexhauſtible, whoſe diſcoveries are infinitely important, which lays the firm foundation of hope for Eternity, which diffuſes its benign influence through all the viciſſitudes of life, which ſwallows up death in victory.

Permit

Permit us, dear Sir, further to declare our satisfaction in the prospect of your exhibiting to the Public Eye, those Productions which have already charmed the Public Ear. The divine blessing, we trust, will accompany them to the instruction and consolation of many. We also take the liberty of expressing, how much we esteem it our honour to be known to the present age, and to posterity, as having enjoyed the acquaintance and friendship of the two respected Authors of this valuable work.

David Bradberry, Kennington Road.
John Reynolds, Camomile Street.
John Humphrys, Union Street, Southwark.
John Love, Artillery Street, Spitalfields.
William Maurice, Fetter Lane.
Frederick Hamilton, New Court, Carey Street.
Joseph Brookbank, Haberdasher's Hall.
James Steven, Crown Court, Covent Garden.
William Nicol, Swallow Street.
Robert Simpson, Evangelical Academy, Hoxton.
George Jerment, Bow Lane, Cheapside.

# LIST
## OF
# SUBSCRIBERS.

THE TREASURER, 12 copies.

### A.

ADDISON, T. Ludgate-hill, 2 copies
Alexander, Daniel, Newington, Surry, 2 copies
Allan, Grant, Clapham, 2 copies
Ancrum, J. S. Walworth
Anderson, ——, Helmet-row
Anderson, Thomas, -Pancras-lane
Angel, William, jun. Cornhill
Armstrong, Mrs. Poultry
Aston, Thomas, jun. Billiter-lane
Atkinson, Joseph, Bishopsgate-street
Austen, William, Tooley-street

### B.

Babb, John, Leadenhall-street
Backhouse, John
Badely, Samuel, LL.B. Temple
Baker, W. R. Fort-street, Spitalfields
Balfour, Rev. Robert, Glasgow
Ballantyne, William, St. Martins-le-grand

Banister, John, sen. ⎫
Banister, John, jun. ⎬ Broadmead, Bristol
Banister, Miss Ann, ⎪
Banister, Miss Eliza, ⎭
Bardwell, Miss, Tooley-street
Barker, Rev. John, Deptford
Barrow, John, Basinghall-street
Bassington, James, Smithfield, 2 copies
Beaumont, Charles, 5th Regiment of Foot
Beddome, B. Fenchurch-street
Beddome, S. Long-lane
Bell, Miss, Blackheath
Bell, Thomas, Dean-street, Soho
Benwell, Joseph, Battersea, 2 copies
Birch, Mr. Tryce, Peterborough
Bird, Richard Martin, Fenchurch-street
Bishop, Thomas, Enfield
Bishop, Samuel, Great Newport-street
Bliss, Mrs. Ann, Chipping Norton, Oxon.
Bliss, Thomas, Charterhouse-lane
Bliss, John, Hampstead
Bogue, Rev. David, Gosport
Borman, S. T. Fish-street-hill
Bosworth, Mr. Peterborough
Bowley, ——, Bishopsgate-street
Boyd, Matthew, Fountain-stairs, Redriff, 2 copies
Boyd, William, Paragon, 2 copies
Bradberry, Rev. David, Kennington
Brander, Alexander, Old Broad-street
Brewin, Robert, Leadenhall-street
Bridge, Stephen, Gainsford-street
Brookbank, Rev. Joseph, Haberdasher's-hall
Browne, Henry, Bristol

Browning,

( xxiii )

Browning, Thomas, Edinburgh
Brownley, James, Wych-street, 3 copies
Burkitt, Miles, Artillery-court, 3 copies
Butler, Mrs. Bethnal-green
Button, Rev. William, Paternoster-row, 6 copies
Buxton, Anthony, Brixton, Stockwell
Bye, Deodatus, St. John's-square, Clerkenwell
Bundy, William, Platt-place, Camden-town

## C.

Cairns, Thomas, Jerusalem Coffee-House
Cambridge Book Society, 2 copies
Campbell, Robert, Mary-bone-street
Campbell, William, Chertsey
Chalk, Charles, Red Lion-street, Clerkenwell
Chater, N. St. Dunstan's-hill
Child, Nathaniel, Bishopsgate-street, 3 copies
Clark, William, Tooley-street
Clason, Patrick, Cleveland-court, St. James's
Cockburn, Peter, Fenchurch-street
Collins, James, Spital-square, 2 copies
Collison, Mrs. Elizabeth, Stockwell
Cottam, Rev. J. Bristol
Cowie, Robert, Highbury-place, 6 copies
Cowie, George, Bury-court, St. Mary-axe
Cowie, John, Falcon-square
Cree, John, Addleston, Surry
Cunningham, James, Tench-street, 2 copies
Curtis, Timothy, Hackney

## D.

Dennison, William, Esq; M. P.
Davidson, James, Treasurer, Fish-street-hill, 12 copies

Davidson,

Davenport, John, Huggin-lane
Davidson, Mrs. Susannah, ⎫
Davidson, Miss Susannah, ⎬ Fish-street-hill
Davidson, James, jun. ⎭
Davidson, George, Fleet-market
Davidson, Ebenezer, Thames-street
Davie, James, Pitfield-street, Hoxton
Davies, Robert, jun. Shoreditch
Davy, J. Crediton, Devonshire
Dean, Edward
De Berdt, Dennis, Freeman's-court, Cornhill
Denflow, ———, Charterhouse-street, 2 copies
Deformeaux, J. L. Pearl-street, Spitalfields
Dick, William, Princes-street, Spitalfields
Dobie, James, Crane-court, Fleet-street, 3 copies
Dore, Rev. James, Maze-pond, Southwark
Duff, Archibald, Carburton-street, Fitzroy-square
Duff, Daniel, Salvador-house, Tooting
Duff, William, Charles-square, Hoxton
Dunbar, Rev. John, Dyke, N. B.
Dunbar, Robert, Billiter-lane
Dunbar, M. C.
Dunbar, Robert, Pentonville
Dunbar, Charles, ditto
Dunbar, Miss A, R. and J. R. Pentonville
Duncan, Peter, Grub-street, 2 copies
Durham, John, Enfield

### E.

Edington, John, Earl-street, Blackfriars, 4 copies
Edwards, William, Coleman-street, 2 copies
Edwards, Miss, Coleman-street
Elliott, Thomas, Bethnal-green

Ellis,

Ellis, ———, Primrose-street, 2 copies
Estlin, Rev. J. J. Bristol
Evans, Mrs. Castle-green, ditto, 4 copies
Evans, Joseph, Seething-lane

F.

Favell, Samuel, Tooley-street, 6 copies
Fairley, George, Islington
Falconer, Gilbert, Budge-row
Favell, Miss, Tooley-street
Fehr, John Jacob, Hoxton-square
Fenn, John, Cornhill, 2 copies
Fidler, Miss E. Snow's-fields
Field, Henry, Newgate-street
Field, Miss, ditto
Finch, Mr. John, Attorney, Cambridge
Fleeming, Dr. Charles, Irvine, N. B.
Flower, Benjamin, Cambridge, 6 copies
Flower, Richard, Ware, Herts.
Foreman
Forsyth, Mrs. St. George's, Jamaica
Foster, John, Horsemonger-lane, 3 copies
Fox, Joseph, Clement's-lane
Fox, William, jun. Finsbury-place
Fraser, Henry, Nightingale-lane
Friend, William, Newbury, Berks
Frost, Richard, Academy, Homerton
Fuller, William, Lombard-street
Fysh, ———, 170, Fenchurch-street

G.

Gastineau, Charles, Camberwell
Geikie, Alexander, Tooley-street

Gibson,

Gibson, Benjamin, Gosport
Gillespie, John, John Street
Gillespie, William, } Anderston, Glasgow
Gillespie, Richard, 6 copies
Gillman, William, Mile End
Glendinning, Thomas, Basinghall-street
Golloftanoff, Theodore, Bethnal-green-road
Good, Richard, Bishopsgate-street, 3 copies
Gray, Anthony, Artillery-street, Borough
Green, Mrs. Walworth
Gregory, O. Bookseller, Cambridge, 6 copies
Griffith, G. Homerton Academy
Grove, Rev. Thomas, Walsal, Staffordshire
Gurney, John, Serjeants' Inn
Gurney, W. B. Walworth

### H.

Hainworth, William, Falcon-square, 3 copies
Hamilton, Rev. Frederick, New-court, Cary-street
Harper, Alexander, Jerusalem Coffee-house, Cornhill, 3 copies
Harris, Wintour, Vice Chamberlain, Trinity-street, Bristol
Hardcastle, Joseph, Hatcham House, Deptford
Harris, Samuel, Islington, 2 copies
Hatt, Alexander, Fenchurch-street
Haweis, Rev. Thomas, M. D. Spa-fields
Haynes, Mrs. Wick, near Bristol
Hay, James, Islington
Heath, Benjamin, Fore-street
Henderson, John, Cornhill, 4 copies
Hendrie, Robert, Blossom-street, Spital-fields
Heron, Richard, Borough

Hoskins,

Hoskins, John, junr. Nailsworth, Glocestershire
Hewson, J. K.  }
Hewson, D. S.  } St. Mary-hill,
Hewson, Mrs.   }
Hey, Rev. John, Gloucester-street, Bristol
Hill, Rev. Noah, Old Gravel-lane
Hill, Thomas, Minories
Hills, ——, 53, Gracechurch-street
Holloway, John, Old-street
Holloway, Thomas, Newington-green
Houston, Samuel, Great St. Helens, 3 copies
Howell, Joseph, 2 copies } Newgate-street
Howell, Miss,            }
Hoyes, John, Nicholas-lane
Hughes, Rev. Mr. Battersea
Humphrys, Rev. John, Union-street, Southwark
Hunter, Patrick, Collett-place, Stepney
Hunter, Thomas, City-chambers
Hutchins, Rev. Mr. Bermondsey

J.

Jackson, Samuel, Lombard-street
Jackson, J. Newgate-street
Jacks, J. Cornhill
Jacks, John, Paternoster-row
Jacob, John, Newgate-street
Jay, Rev. William, Bath
Jennings, David, Chiswell-street
Jennings, John, Coleman-street Buildings
Jennings, Joseph, Queen-street
Jerment, Rev. George, Bow-lane
Ind, Edward, Cambridge
Inglis, John, Mark-lane

Inglis,

Inglis, Miss, Mark-lane
Johnstone, Andrew, } Pavement, Moorfields
Johnstone, Mrs.
Jones, Rev. Madgwick, Bristol
Jones, Thomas, Fish-street-hill
Jones, John, Bethnal-green
Jones, Thomas, Newgate-street
Jones, Miss Susannah, Bristol

### K.

Keith, Rev. Daniel, Bristol, 6 copies
Kershaw, James, Halifax, Yorkshire, 3 copies
Kitchener, Thomas, Bury, Suffolk
Kitchener, William, Princes-street, Lothbury, 6 copies
Knox, Miss, Circus, Minories

### L.

Langston, John, Newington, Surry
Law, Henry, St. John's-square
Lea, Richard, Old-jewry, 2 copies
Lea, William, Birmingham
Legg, Samuel, Fleet-street
Lloyd, Samuel, Thames-street, 4 copies
Love, Rev. John, Artillery-street, Spitalfields
Lowell, Rev. Samuel, Woodbridge, Suffolk
Lymburner, Adam, Fenchurch-street

### M.

Madgwick, Edward, Charles-square, Hoxton
Mair, John, Plantation, Glasgow, 6 copies

Mair, John, Junr. Friday-street
Mair, Hugh, Copthall-court
Mair, James, Fenchurch-buildings
Maitland, Robert, } King's-arms-yard
Maitland, Ebenezer,
Maitland, John, Basinghall-street
Mackay, John, Tooley-street
Marryatt,
Marshall, John, Gerard-street, Soho
Maurice, Rev. William, Fetter-lane
May, Thomas, Henley, Oxon
Meake, John, Princess-street, Lothbury
Meriton, G. W. Dockhead, 3 copies
Miller, William, Wine-office-court, Fleet-street
Moodie, Samuel, Queen-square
Mount, Mrs. Cross-street, Islington
Mullett, Thomas, 3 copies
Mullett, Thomas, Junr. } Broad-street-buildings
Mullett, Miss,

### N.

Narraway, ——, Bristol
Neale, Mrs. ——, Walworth
Neave, David, Threadneedle-street, 2 copies
Nicholson, Samuel, Cateaton-street
Nicol, Rev. William, Swallow-street
Norman, Thomas, Manchester
Norton, James, Fish-street-hill

### O.

Osbourn, Richard, Queen-street, Limehouse
Oswald, William, 2 copies } Deptford
Oswald, Mrs.

Palmer,

## P.

Palmer, Rev. Samuel, Hackney
Parker, ——, Ipswich
Parsons, Rev. Edward, Leeds, Yorkshire
Passavant, Luke, Devonshire-square
Paterson, John, John-street, 3 copies
Pearson, James, 4 copies ⎫
Pearson, James, junr. ⎬ Basinghall-street
Pearson, Hugh, ⎭
Pearson, Charles, Dockhead
Penman, Edward, Stamford-hill
Phené, Nicholas, 4 copies ⎫ London-Wall
Phené, Nicholas, junr. ⎭
Platt, Rev. W. F. Holywell-street
Plummer, Thomas, London-street
Polson, Major, Exmouth
Ponder, Steven, Houndsditch, 6 copies
Potts, Samuel, Golden-lane
Pritt, James, 12 copies ⎫ Wood-street
Pritt, James, junr. ⎭

## R.

Rapier, George, Bethnal-green
Reyner, Joseph, Shacklewell, 6 copies
Reynolds, Rev. John, Camomile-street, 4 copies
Reynolds, William, Hoxton-square
Reynolds, Joseph, Fenchurch-street
Richardson, David, ditto
Rippon, Rev. John, D. D. Grange-road, Surry

Robinson,

Robinson, Samuel, } Princes-street, Lothbury
Robinson, Mrs.
Roe, Edward, Blandford, Dorsetshire
Rose, Mrs. Tooley-street
Ross, Malcolm, Craven-street
Russel, James, Water-lane, Blackfriars
Rutledge, Rev. Thomas, Camberwell
Ryland, Rev. John, D. D. Academy, Bristol

S.

Stirling, Sir John Glorat, N. B.
Sabine, William, Islington
Sanders, ——, Fore-street, Spitalfields
Savill, Thomas, Aldgate-high-street, 2 copies
Savill, William, Haydon-square, 2 copies
Savill, W. Minories
Savill, Miss
Scott, John, Cornhill
Sharpe, William, Leadenhall-street
Sharpe, Richard, Fish-street-hill, 2 copies
Shaw, Rev. Mr. Enfield
Shaw, Benjamin, London-bridge
Shelton, Alexander
Shrimpton, Joseph, Bedford-square
Shuter, ——, Shoreditch
Simons, Rev. Mr. Rector of Paul's Cray, Kent
Simpson, Alexander, Bank of England, 6 copies
Simpson, Rev. Robert, Evangelical Academy, Hoxton
Simpson, Thomas, Nottingham
Sims, David
Smith, Rev. William, Dover

Smith,

Smith, Edward, Broad-street, 4 copies
Smith, James, Corn-exchange
Spear, Robert, Manchester
Steel, Robert, Islington
Stent, J. Bishopsgate-street
Steven, Mrs. Ely-place
Steven, Rev. James, Crown-court, Covent-garden
Stevenson, David, Brick-lane, Old-street
Stock, William, junr. Holborn
Stonard, Joseph, Tower-hill
Stonard, Nathaniel, Bromley, Middlesex
Strachan, Rev. John, ⎫
Strachan, Robert, ⎬ Enfield
Strachan, Miss Euphemia, ⎭

## T.

Talbot, Caleb, Smithfield-bars, 3 copies
Tate, John, Junr., 2 copies, Bucklersbury
Taylor, John, Upper Gun-alley
Teale, Miss Anne, Clapham
Thomas, Lemuel, Staining-lane
Thompson, John, Tooley-street
Thompson, Rev. R. Gate-street Academy, Lincoln's-inn-fields
Thorne, ——, Bristol
Thornthwaite, Thomas, Paternoster-row
Tod, Mrs. Canterbury-place, Lambeth
Townsend, Rev. John, Redriff
Trotman, Mrs. Clapton
Trotter, H.
Tulloh, Mrs. Gould-square, Tower-hill
Thomas, Rev. Mr. Devonshire-square

Turnbull,

Turnbull, James, Aldgate
Tute, Edward, Poultry

## U, and V.

Uffington, Salathiel, Lime-street
Vallantine, George N. Redriff
Vowell, Miss, Leadenhall-street
Vowles, ——, Bristol

## W.

Waldegrave, Rev. Mr. Bury, Suffolk
Walker, Sayer, M. D. ⎫
Walker, Mr. ⎬ Charterhouse-square
Walker, Miss, ⎭
Walker, ——, Chifwell-street
Warne, John, Long-lane
Waterstone, John, Liquorpond-street
Watt, ——, Southampton-buildings, Holborn
Weymouth, Henry, Junr. Battersea, 2 copies
West, Miss Margaret, Kingston, Jamaica
Wesley, John, Blackfriars-road, 2 copies
Wickenden, Joseph, Cornhill, 2 copies
Wilkie, Andrew, Wheeler-street, Spitalfields
Wilson, Joseph, Milk-street
Withey, Rev. Mr. Chapel-street, Holywell-mount
Wright, Robert, Prescott-street, Goodman's-fields
Wright, Michael, ditto
Wyatt, Robert, ⎫ Newington-green
Wyatt, Miss, ⎭
Westley,

Yallowley,

## Y.

Yallowley, Joseph,  } Whitecross-street
Yallowley, Joseph, Junr.
Young, Robert, Samson's-gardens.

# CONTENTS.

### LECTURE I.

PSALM XXXVI. ver. 9. *For with thee is the fountain of life; in thy light shall we see light* - - 4

### LECTURE II.

LUKE XXIV. ver. 44. *And he said unto them, these are the words which I spake unto you, while I was yet with you, that all things must be fulfilled which were written in the law of Moses, and in the Prophets, and in the Psalms, concerning me* - - - 29

### LECTURE III.

JOHN I. ver. 43. *We have found him of whom Moses in the law—did write* - - - - - 65

### LECTURE IV.

PHILIPPIANS IV. ver. 8. *Finally, brethren, whatsoever things are true* - - - - - 106

# CONTENTS.

## LECTURE V.

LUKE I. 1—4. *Forasmuch as many have taken in hand to set forth in order a declaration of those things which are most surely believed among us,*
*Even as they delivered them unto us which from the beginning were eye witnesses, and ministers of the word:*
*It seemed good to me also, having had perfect understanding of all things from the very first, to write unto thee in order, most excellent Theophilus,*
*That thou mightest know the certainty of those things wherein thou hast been instructed* - - - 133

## LECTURE VI.

JOHN I. 18. *No man hath seen God at any time: the only begotten Son, which is in the bosom of the Father, he hath declared him* - - - - - 161

## LECTURE VII.

GEN. XXII. 15—18. *And the angel of the Lord called unto Abraham out of heaven the second time,*
*And said, By myself have I sworn, saith the Lord, for because thou hast done this thing, and hast not withheld thy Son, thine only Son:*
*That*

## CONTENTS.

*That in bleſſing I will bleſs thee, and in multiplying I will multiply ſeed as the ſtars of the heaven, and as the ſand which is upon the ſea ſhore: and thy ſeed ſhall poſſeſs the gate of his enemies;*

*And in thy ſeed ſhall all the nations of the earth be bleſſed; becauſe thou haſt obeyed my voice.*

ACTS I. 7, 8. *And he ſaid unto them, It is not for you to know the times, or the ſeaſons, which the Father hath put in his own power.*

*But ye ſhall receive power after that the Holy Ghoſt is come upon you: and ye ſhall be witneſſes unto me both in Jeruſalem, and in all Judea, and in Samaria, and unto the uttermoſt part of the earth* - - 189

## LECTURE VIII.

LUKE XXIII. ver. 39—43. *And one of the malefactors, which were hanged, railed on him, ſaying, If thou be Chriſt ſave thyſelf and us.*

*But the other anſwering rebuked him, ſaying, Doſt not thou fear God, ſeeing thou art in the ſame condemnation?*

*And we indeed juſtly; for we receive the due reward of our deeds: but this man hath done nothing amiſs.*

*And he ſaid unto Jeſus, Lord, remember me when thou comeſt into thy kingdom.*

*And Jeſus ſaid unto him, Verily I ſay unto thee, To-day ſhalt thou be with me in Paradiſe* - - - 221

JOHN

## CONTENTS.

### LECTURE IX.

JOHN XVI. 33. *These things I have spoken unto you, that in me ye might have peace. In the world ye shall have tribulation: but be of good cheer; I have overcome the world* - - - - - 255

### LECTURE X.

MATT. VI. 10—12. *Thy kingdom come; thy will be done in earth, as it is in heaven; Give us this day our daily bread; And forgive us our debts as we forgive our debtors.* - 281

### LECTURE XI.

JOHN I. 1—5. *In the beginning was the Word, and the Word was with God, and the Word was God. The same was in the beginning with God. All things were made by Him; and without Him was not any thing made that was made. In Him was life; and the life was the light of men. And the light shineth in darkness; and the darkness comprehended it not.*
REV. I. 17. *I am the first and the last.*
ROM. XV. 13. *Now the God of hope fill you with all joy and peace in believing, that ye may abound in hope through the power of the Holy Ghost.* - - 303

LECTURE

## CONTENTS.

### LECTURE XII.

JOHN XI. 23—26. *Jesus saith unto Martha, Thy brother shall rise again.*

*Martha saith unto him, I know that he shall rise again in the resurrection at the last day.*

*Jesus saith unto her, I am the resurrection and the life; he that believeth in me, though he were dead, yet shall he live:*

*And whosoever liveth, and believeth in me shall never die: Believest thou this?* - - - - 333

LECTURES

# LECTURES

ON THE

# EVIDENCES OF CHRISTIANITY.

## LECT. I.

MY CHRISTIAN FRIENDS,

I FEEL myself placed in an interesting, and in somewhat an unusual situation; between a lively gratitude, and a deep sense of the importance of the undertaking before me. I wish it were in my power to express the sense which I have of the condescension and friendship of those gentlemen, who have engaged in forming and establishing, as far as lies in their power, this intended Lecture. They have conducted it with such dignity, and with so much delicacy, that even now, I know not the names of the major part of the persons concerned; and can truly say, this is my first appearance in this arduous business.

They

They have turned their thoughts to *me*, for this important purpose, and that in trying and interesting circumstances, which render their attention the more valuable. It will never be in my power properly to express my thoughts and reflections concerning their conduct. All that I can do at present, is to return them grateful and hearty thanks, with sincerity of mind. This is all I *can* do, more I might *wish* to do, were it in my power; but I must have recourse to the constant refuge of the weak and grateful, May the God of bounty and goodness, the Father of our Lord Jesus Christ, pour into their bosoms a ten-fold recompence, and fill their souls with those cheering consolations, and with that sweet peace, which he alone can give! I could dwell upon the subject, did time allow, and were it suitable to their desires. I trust, thus far they hear me with respect: I dare not farther urge their attention. Now I turn to the subject before us. And here, I confess, I tremble for myself, conscious of my own insufficiency for an undertaking at once so interesting, and so difficult; and I am not ashamed to ask the prayers of all good and faithful men,

men, that I may be affifted and inftructed, and enabled to fpeak fuch things as fhall be juft, edifying and ufeful to thofe who hear me, and more efpecially to the rifing generation. Perhaps my feeble efforts may be the means of exciting the attention of more powerful advocates for truth and religion; who may introduce the fame interefting objects with greater fuccefs. In fuch an event I fhall have much caufe to rejoice, and none to be afhamed. To the utmoft of my ability, and the wifeft and moft intelligent can do no more, I fhall purfue the important object of this Lecture, which reflects fo much honour upon its contrivers, and managers, and directors. One thing I muft farther obferve, that in a difcourfe of this kind, which muft be confidered only as introductory, I cannot turn my attention to particulars. I muft fpeak to the fubject in general, and perhaps be obliged to advert to circumftances not brought forward in ordinary affemblies. Yet, I truft, nothing fhall fall from my lips which can be deemed beyond the eafy comprehenfion of a common capacity. I am well aware that I fpeak in the hearing of many learned, many eloquent,

eloquent, many wife; and therefore have the greater reason to be timid, and humble, and cautious.

Upon this occasion I shall read to you, that expressive and interesting passage, full to our purpose, which you will find in,

PSALM XXXVI. VER. 9.

"For with thee is the fountain of life; in thy light shall we see light."

I do not feel any necessity to dwell long upon these words, but shall use them only as the occasion of entering immediately on my subject. I think it must be obvious to every one, that God, the maker of the world, the Father of our spirits, must be *the* fountain of life, or a fountain of life there cannot be. What that fountain is—how we are to be conducted to it—what benefits are to be derived from it, can never be known, but under the guidance of God's own light. And this I apply to all principles, that are connected with religion, of whatever kind. If I turn my thoughts to, what is called, the religion of of nature, it muſt ſpring here; and we can have no knowledge of it, but from the light which our Maker is pleaſed to afford; and which he has connected with the original conſtitution of all things, and particularly of mankind. And this is eminently true with reſpect to revealed religion, as muſt appear moſt evident to every candid mind.

The deſign of this undertaking is to vindicate revelation, in this untoward generation; when daring attacks are made upon every intereſting and important principle; and more eſpecially with a view to the benefit of youth, that is, of thoſe who are moſt likely to be ſeduced, whoſe hearts are the leaſt ſuſpicious, and who entertain generous ſentiments concerning men that affect openneſs and liberality, whatever their ſecret purpoſes may be.

I ſhall, at preſent, conſider the ſubject under a threefold idea.

Firſt. What is the object for which we are contending?

Secondly.

Secondly. What are we when considered as *destitute* of that object?

Thirdly. What are we, when considered as in *possession* of this supposed blessing?

The discussion of these three particulars will serve to reflect light upon the words, which I have read as our text, without pointing out any farther formal connexion of the passage.

I. What is the object for which we mean to contend? I answer, a divine Revelation, such as that which is contained in the holy word, emphatically called *the* Scriptures; which makes discoveries of things, that could not have been known by the mere light of nature and of unassisted reason—concerning the nature and perfections of the one living and true God—concerning his counsel and will, with respect to his creatures—concerning the state and condition of mankind in the present world—concerning the moral government and providence of God—concerning the purposes of his grace in the redemption of man

man—in the forgiveness of sin—in the renewal of our minds—in fitting us for a future and glorious state—in a word, concerning all those circumstances which contribute most to our well-being, and which will be found most efficacious toward our recovery and reformation in the sight of God—and concerning life and immortality beyond the grave. These, it must be allowed, are great and interesting topics, well worthy of the attention of every individual in this assembly. It cannot be expected, that I should enter, at present, upon particular doctrines to be found in the word of God—to these we shall be led in the farther prosecution of our plan.

II. Let us consider what man would be, considered as destitute of this supposed divine revelation.

He must be left, if he professes any religion; if he declares that he feels the power of any religion in his heart; he must be left to, what is called, the light of nature and reason, usually termed, the religion of nature; and commonly exhibited to the world in terms, and under ideas, which never were level to common capacities, that is to the generality of mankind, in some such way as this: (I follow a great and an accomplished master.) " It " appears," says he, " from nature, that the " common good of rational beings, is the " greatest good in the power of man; that " a diligent attention to this, will naturally " be recompensed with the greatest happiness " that individual men can obtain; that the " neglect of it will be followed with propor- " tionable misery and wretchedness."

From propositions of this kind, are reasoned out all moral duties; and they are supposed to be sufficient for our guidance in our passage through this vain life, and to answer all the purposes of religion. I dare not utter a syllable with respect to the life to come.

Now then what is man, left in this situation, and to these teachings, which in our day, are said to be preferable to what is called, a divine revelation? I wish to be guided by facts. The power and extent of natural religion must be gathered from the history of human

human nature, from what we know of former ages; and of those ages which had no higher guide, nor more sublime directions. And the moment that we look into their state and character, we cannot but be affected on reviewing the gross idolatries into which they fell: to such a degree that it would be a hard task to enumerate the number of their gods, and the objects of their trust and veneration; till, at length, they began to deify every thing which was supposed subordinate to the interests of mankind—to his welfare—to his conquests—to the gratification of his ambition —to the extension of his power. In the pursuit of these things, their external worship was of a kind suitable to the objects of it; low in itself, degrading in it's nature, accompanied with practices that cannot be recollected without pain, nor mentioned without shame; and these too constituted a part of their religion.

The history of mankind shows us, how little the efficacy of natural religion was. The ignorance, the barbarism of rude nations; the violation of all the solemn obligations of human

human life; the grossest immoralities that can well be conceived, appearing in their savage, low, coarse, abandoned actions, present a melancholy picture. I wish to represent things fairly and truly; and shall suppose that an advocate of, what is called, natural religion, in opposition to revelation, may say, " we must not reason from the rudest " and most barbarous nations upon this sub-" ject; but candidly take in the doctrines, " the maxims, the divine precepts of learned " and wise nations; more especially those of " Greece, which in literature and science, in " the estimation of the western nations, have " far surpassed all others." In the estimation of the *western nations*. I am speaking in accommodation to the reasonings and principles of other persons, not always to my own.

Now, you will give me leave to illustrate this by a quotation from an ancient Roman historian; speaking of the ancient Scythians, from whom our own ancestors sprang; he observes, " that they coveted neither silver " nor gold, as despising the things which " rendered their use necessary." He then follows

Lect. 1.   *Evidences of Christianity.*   11

follows it up with this reflection. " I wish
" other nations had shewn the same mode-
" ration, and discovered the same kind of
" abstinence from the property of their neigh-
" bours; for then destructive wars would not
" have been so prevalent and durable, in every
" part of the world; nor would a greater
" number of mankind have been cut off by
" the sword, than are cut off by diseases and
" death in the common course of nature."
And he afterwards expresses it as a matter of
just wonder, " that cultivated manners should
" yield, on a comparison, to uncultivated
" barbarism; and that those people should
" have acquired that which the Greeks, by
" a long course of literature pursued by their
" wise men, and by the precepts of their dif-
" ferent philosophers, never could attain:"
and he concludes with this remark, " of so
" much more avail was the ignorance of vice
" among the one, than the knowledge of vir-
" tue among the other." This testimony is
true.

I pass from the Greeks, and proceed to
the Romans; and will venture to say, that
                                           with

with all their literature, with their science, with their refinements, with their schools of philosophy and wisdom; they surpassed all the nations of the earth in a grovelling, gross, vulgar idolatry. The countries which they called barbarous never equalled them in this respect. The eastern nations, though mean enough as to the objects of their worship; yet, were never so degraded as Greece and Rome. While they professed the power of natural religion, they were estranged from the true God —they knew him not. And if I were to borrow the language of Scripture, I might say that, " they never glorified him as God, but " became vain in their imaginations;" they deified men of the vilest characters; and historians have charged them with worshipping human spirits as the highest objects of their adoration. I will not say quite so much: but even the wise and philosophical among them scarcely ever raised their thoughts above created deities. They violated every principle of morality; they taught vice by precept; they connected the most debauched practices with their worship, and made them a part of their religion; they were unfriendly to the common
bonds

bonds of society, they instructed their disciples in *many* vices, and encouraged them too often *in all*.

If we may credit the complaints of their own writers, they were unfriendly to the progress of mankind—to the existence itself, as well as to the refinements of human nature; and in no respect sought to ameliorate the condition of their fellow creatures. They frequently encouraged the practice of, nay they delivered precepts for, the exposing of their infant children, when it suited their convenience; that is, they delivered them up to be destroyed by ravenous birds and beasts of prey. And this was necessarily attended with very painful circumstances. Mothers were thrown into cruel anxiety for their infants when thus secreted. Many of them never could overcome their anguish, but expressed through life, inconsolable sorrow and bitterness of heart.

This inhuman conduct was countenanced by the wisest and most learned of their philosophers. Nay, the greatest man that Greece ever

ever produced, in a syftem of laws, recommends the putting children to death as foon as born, if they appeared to be maimed, or in any refpect defective in their limbs. He even goes farther. To prevent an undue increafe, he recommends in his laws, abortion, in the early ftages of pregnancy. Can fuch men be fuppofed to give a faithful reprefentation of the power and influence of natural religion? Can thinking perfons, in *our days*, wifh to be given up to the guidance of fuch a religion, if fuch be its effects?

Here, again, I wifh to be faithful to the fubject. Perhaps many advocates of natural religion, in our times, may fay, that " they " defpife fuch practices of the ancient Greeks " as much as we can do; and feek the promotion of benevolence, of humanity, of rectitude, and a proper regard to every individual and age of the human fpecies." I doubt it not. But whence did they learn this fuperiority of fentiment? How came they to a knowledge fo different from former ages? Were they guided by the principles of natural religion? Was not this the refult of revelation?
Yes;

Yes; and it may be proved from most decisive facts. Did not the heathen world oppose the introduction of the Christian religion, with all its purity, with all its sanctity? Did they not resist it, and preserve their own maxims, their absurd principles, and gross idolatry, for above three hundred years? Were not the most learned among them employed to crush, if possible, the growth of the Christian religion? I say then, that they derived these advantages from the holy Scriptures. Here is an instance in which true religion puts blessings into the hands of enemies, who use them as a sword to pierce her to the heart. But every effort of this kind serves only to point out her native excellence, and unspotted worth. She still smiles upon them with blessings. Being divine, she is incapable of being wounded; and will, in the issue, walk with a meek and godlike dignity over the graves of her opponents, and finally triumph in the complete blessedness of all her adherents.

In the disquisitions respecting the immortality of the soul, nothing certain could ever be suggested by them. And while their most learned

learned Philosophers laboured to convince their disciples of the immortality of the soul, they were never able to convince themselves. And there was a manifest indifference with respect to a future world. Nor could it well be otherwise. Think then of the condition in which mankind were left, as long as they were under the precepts and principles of natural religion, and while these were the highest sources of instruction.

But give me leave to consider this subject with regard to our fellow-creatures in another view. Without a divine Revelation, and the blessed prospect of immortality, What are mankind? Only consider how few our days are in the present state. And, of these days, How much is taken up in Childhood, in Youth, in attaining the knowledge of those things, without which we cannot pass through life with reputation. And how small a portion of time is allowed for the enjoyments of life, and for exercising ourselves to the advantage of others. When we consider the number of years in which nature usually is decaying, and coming to its final dissolution, the space left

is

is very short; and besides, if there be no hereafter, what is life to us? If there be no hereafter, I cannot so much censure, as I have done, those Ancients, who upon trivial occasions would put their infant Children out of the world. They must, at least, be indifferent about it. What must we say to Parents with respect to their Children, when they are afflicted; when they are oppressed with diseases; when they see them, as it were, expire in their arms? What are the Mother's consolations? What are the Father's prospects? What can afford him comfort in such trying circumstances? And those who are left under the power of, what is called natural Religion, have as strong, as interesting passions as the Jew or the Christian. What must be their reasonings with respect to the sorrows and distresses of the present life, which arise from a thousand circumstances? What light have they to guide them to a happy reverse? What views could they have of the compassion and benevolence of God, in turning these things to their advantage? Their days are not continued long enough, and they are cut off from future prospects. Shall we attend them to old age,

age, and see nature gradually decay; and those for whom we have had affection, for whom we have had veneration and respect, expire without hope, go out of the world in sullen silence, without any lively expectation or prospect of an hereafter? Surely, left to natural Religion, man must be considered as a wretched Creature. And if there be no hereafter, the condition of the brutes is better than that of man—their pleasures are more stated, and sincere, and less interrupted by accidental circumstances—their sufferings are without consideration beyond the moment.—*They* have no anxiety, no concern for family or offspring. *They* never felt the ties of faithful and affectionate friendship. *Their* views with respect to separation, in instances of the most important kind, never touched their souls for a moment. One blow finishes their existence, without their ever knowing that they were mortal. The knowledge of his mortality is a perpetual source of anxiety and distress to man. To one dying out of the world, what is the fair structure of the heavens, and the earth; what the produce of the earth, what the ornaments with which God hath embellished it; ornaments
which

which he hath rendered subservient to our comfortable subsistence and well-being? We can think on these things only as subjects of regret, but we cannot be interested in them. What can influence wise and prudent men to enter on the study of nature—to contemplate the motions of the heavenly bodies—to pursue the discoveries that have been made? What but the prospect of immortality? And give me leave to say, that the greatest things that have been done in this way, have been done by men who were under the influence of the hope of an immortal life. I do not pretend to say, that others may not have made great, and perhaps equal progress in the knowledge of nature, but it was only as matter of amusement; and, very often, was the effect of inattention to those great and interesting principles which belong to all men. But, let us go to the

Third thing proposed; and consider what man is, as possessed of a divine Revelation.

Here, almost every thing is reversed. We see the world, in general, with new appearances.

ances. We find no longer the adoration of stocks and stones—no longer the shrieks and cries of infants offered to Idols—no longer the sacrifices of our fellow-creatures—no longer obscene worship; which, in its nature, must pollute and corrupt society. I am not inferring from this, that the world, in general, is virtuous, and truly religious. No; but I do assert, that we have no such disagreeable appearances at present. Christianity extinguished idolatry, notwithstanding all the refined efforts of the friends of idolatry to resist the progress of the gospel of Christ. Are we, as a number of men, (pardon me for using such an expression in this stage of the subject,) I say a number of men, transformed in the renewing of our minds; restored, in some measure, to the image of God? Here in the Gospel are set before us well-grounded hopes of the forgiveness of sin, and of acceptance with God. Here we have just and authentic precepts for the worship of our Maker, and more especially, for the worship of God, as reconciled to man in Jesus Christ. Here we see him vindicating all the perfections of his nature, while he shows mercy and compassion to the chief of sinners.

sinners. Here we perceive men expressing their interest with God in the great blessings which he hath discovered—looking to a fellowship with Angels above, in a future state of existence; considering themselves as fellow-heirs with the Son of God, of "an inhe-" ritance incorruptible, undefiled, and that " fadeth not away." Here we see them reasoning, far beyond Philosophers, concerning the afflictions, the calamities, and all the trying events of the present life; and bearing up under these with meekness, with dignity, with unreserved submission to the holy will of God; and, in the midst of their distresses, extolling his wisdom, and acknowledging his mighty power with reverence and contrition.

Human nature, in its present depraved state, cannot possibly appear with greater dignity than that in which true christians often discover themselves. Under a divine revelation we are taught, in a divine and authentic manner, accompanied with the most decisive evidence, that " all things shall work together " for good" to the people of God—that our very sufferings and trials shall become the

means

means of the greatest and most important blessings. Such views could not be had without a divine revelation. Here we find heavenly succour in the midst of death itself—in the midst of *our own* death—in the midst of the death of *others*, which may precede our own. And I call the removal of every individual out of the world, which may be considered as a part of ourselves, the commencement of our own death—so far *we* die. The Christian can meet all these things with a calm countenance—with a peaceful heart. He can feel and be rational. He can be touched within, and, at the same moment, submissive to God. Consider, what consolation over his children, taken away by death! what pleasure he feels in his own heart, while he teaches them, when young, perhaps in childhood, in the midst of sickness, to look for a divine world; and teaches them to lisp out, as it were, their hopes and prospects. Here sweet comfort is diffused through the heart; and there are many instances of this kind, among others, a recent one known to myself, of a child leaving the world, and giving up its last breath with prayer to Almighty God;—and

this

this with no marks of enthufiafm, no traits of ignorant fuperftition attending it. Who can cenfure fuch things? No; the moft hardened enemy to the Chriftian religion will not open his mouth againft it. *He* might fay, " it was *well*, as it afforded prefent com-
" fort." *I* fay, it is *better*, as it carries the foul to a lively profpect of a future ftate. I know nothing to give fuccour to the human heart, like the truth—like the divine authority of that holy book, which is confidered as a revelation from God, and that too with the greateft truth.

Give me leave to add, that in the poffeffion of a divine revelation, every part of *nature* becomes more interefting to us. I prefume to affirm, that every blade of grafs or grain of corn collects new beauties and importance, confidered as the prefent fuftenance of rational and immortal beings. We may furvey the heavens with additional pleafure; and look with delight upon their regular and ordinary revolutions. We may put pleafant queftions to ourfelves—" Shall *I* be acquainted with
" fuch and fuch bodies hereafter, and better

" know their relative situation and depen-
" dencies one upon another; and altogether,
" upon the mighty God, whose infinite
" power gave them existence?" We cannot
doubt whether there shall be worlds to receive us when we leave the present. We see
numbers, and still greater numbers are unknown to us. I know not what may be the
purpose of God with respect to *them*; nor
what may be the final purpose and counsels of
God with respect to this, as to its inhabitants.
He has given us, at least, Christians, he has
given us ground to expect the greatest and
most sublime things that can be conceived.
Then let us indulge the subject. Strengthen
your hearts with a view of this divine revelation; apply it to all the incidents of your lives;
bring your sorrows and your distresses to it.
It will beam forth with new, fresh, brighter,
and more durable lustre than the rays of the
sun; and be accompanied with fresh discoveries to the latest period of your life.

I must, at present, draw to a close.

A far-

A farther reprefentation of the importance of Revelation, will be neceffary, and will fucceed in the procefs of thefe Lectures. Particular and interefting things will arife, in their regular order. Give me leave then to fay, it is our duty to examine the importance of a divine Revelation—whether it is not neceffary for the eternal interefts of men—whether God has given to men thefe inftructions, fuited to their feeble and deftitute circumftances in this life. I own my reafon will not fuffer me to confider the divine Being fo far deficient in benevolence, and a tender regard to his creatures, as to leave them deftitute in a matter fo important. The conceptions which I have of his high perfections, will not permit me to fuppofe, that man was created merely for the purpofes of fo fhort a life, as that which we fee, attended with circumftances fo deftitute of importance—fo little calculated to promote his real well being here, and far lefs to promote his eternal happinefs in the world to come.

Be not negligent upon this fubject. Let me reafon with you. I call upon you, on the

the principles of natural Religion, to attend to your own interest. Consider, I say, *your own* interest. When that is really discovered, it will be found the common interest of your fellow creatures. I have not set before you, what is of little worth, considered in itself. No; I have set before you, what is of the last importance. You are injurious to yourselves if you neglect the subject; you are injurious to the rising generation; you are injurious to your own families; you are injurious to your offspring, whose happiness you cannot but desire, and for whose welfare you feel every day. Only consider, what comforts flow to the affectionate mother, what consolations to the indulgent father, let the issue be what it may, with respect to his offspring. If there be excellencies, they shall never be lost. He shall find them all again, and his own well-being and happiness shall be enlarged. Put the question to yourselves, whether you know any precepts so holy, as those that attend the divine Revelation—any doctrines so consonant to the perfections of God—any maxims so rational in themselves, and so immediately conducive to our felicity?

Have

Have you ever found or heard of any system of Religion, better calculated to produce virtue, to extinguish vice, and to destroy those things that are contrary to God? Be faithful then, in what relates to others; and that fidelity will be found subservient to your own welfare and usefulness.

There is still another point I wish to mention. I cannot urge it upon the principles of natural Religion, because that is very faint with respect to a future state; and still fainter with respect to the Day of Judgment. You that have heard such things, trifle not with them, speak not reproachfully of them, left you should be found to despise your best interests. Give yourselves up to pure reflection, to faithful and honest examination upon the subject. I will say of natural Religion, that no one, under the influence of reason, can wish himself left under that, as his highest instruction—as his most extensive source of comfort. I would say of divine Revelation, from the short and infant sketch now given of it, every individual must wish it to be true, and

and see that his interest and his peace are connected with it.

May the God of peace guide your minds—give you patient and unwearied attention and fidelity, in the future investigation of these things! And may his truth beam upon your hearts; and you, in the end, taste all the heavenly and inexpressible consolations, that pour daily into the hearts of true Christians—that you may be filled with peace, and not only fitted for his presence, but enjoy it through everlasting ages! Amen.

# LECT. II.

MY CHRISTIAN FRIENDS,

I HOPE to be forgiven if I take notice of one particular circumstance, which, for certain reasons, may be better done now, than at the commencement of this Lecture. It is to express the obligations which I am laid under to Doctor HUNTER, the pastor, and the Trustees, for their ready and generous grant of the use of this place. The handsome manner in which it was conferred, is particularly worthy of my attention; and I hope, that my acknowledgments will be received, as they are sincere and grateful.

I now call your attention to an interesting passage of holy writ, which you will find in,

LUKE XXIV. Ver. 44.

" And he said unto them, these are the
" words which I spake unto you, while I
"  was

" was yet with you, that all things muſt be
" fulfilled which were written in the law of
" Moſes, and in the Prophets, and in the
" Pſalms, concerning me."

I beg leave to obſerve again, becauſe I apprehend I might not have been fully underſtood the laſt time I appeared in this place; that I did not conſider myſelf as offering any thing in that diſcourſe, which was to be conſidered as an argument in defence of divine Revelation. I feel myſelf under an obligation of delivering another diſcourſe of the ſame kind; but hope I ſhall have occaſion for no more of an introductory nature. I truſt that I ſhall not be conſidered now as attempting to offer arguments in ſupport of a divine Revelation; although the things which I ſhall have to deliver muſt be conſidered as the ground of various arguments.

That I may endeavour to meet the objection as fairly as I can, I now intend to ſhow, that ſuch is the inſeparable connexion between the Chriſtian Religion and the Old Teſtament Scriptures, that if the one falls, the other muſt fall

fall too—that if either of them stand, if either of them can be supported, (and I doubt not but that both may) the other must of consequence remain firm and immoveable.

In order to illustrate this position, I have read the words of our text; and beg leave to read them again, because I consider the speaker as the best judge of the Christian Religion, and fully as well acquainted with the design and intention of the holy Prophets, as any person in our days possibly can be. " And he said unto them, these are the words " which I spake unto you, while I was yet " with you, that all things must be fulfilled " which were written in the law of Moses, " and in the Prophets, and in the Psalms, " concerning me."

And you will be pleased to remember that these words were spoken after his resurrection from the dead, when they must have come with peculiar energy, and could not fail to reach the hearts of his disciples, to whom he spake them, and who were appointed to be
witnesses

witnesses of his resurrection, for the publication of his name among all nations.

    I would endeavour then, from these words, to show, that the descriptions which are given in the New Testament of the person and character of our Lord Jesus Christ, were not first invented, and brought forward, either by Jesus Christ himself, or by the Apostles; but that they were well known and understood among every class of the Jewish people, before the appearance of Christ; of which we have many decisive proofs, and from whence it plainly follows, that there must be some such person and character as the Evangelists and Apostles have represented the Lord Jesus to be; otherwise, there can be no light, no truth in the Old Testament Scriptures; nor can we perceive their real value, or what advantage could arise from them to the world in general. And that I may do this with effect, I shall in the

    First place, bring forward the sentiments and opinions of their own writers, the oldest that are extant, next to the Prophets themselves.

selves. And in order that it may be done to advantage, I muſt take the liberty to obtrude upon your ears the uſe of words and terms to which, perhaps, they are not familiar. I muſt particularly take notice of, what are called, the *Jewiſh Targums*. And, not to uſe the word in vain, I beg leave to explain it to you before-hand. The word *Targum*, ſignifies a *tranſlation* from one language into another, or a *paraphraſe* of thoſe parts that are ſo tranſlated, or both of theſe together.

There was an early neceſſity of tranſlating the Hebrew Scriptures into the Chaldee language; for from the long reſidence of the people in that country, they in ſome meaſure loſt their native tongue. This was done early; and of theſe things which were thus early performed, many are loſt. The oldeſt Targums that are extant, go by the names of Onkelos, and Jonathan Ben-Uzziel, or Jonathan the ſon of Uzziel. That of Onkelos ſeems to have been the moſt ancient. They were both diſciples, as it is ſaid, of the great Hillel, who was one of the moſt conſiderable men among all the Jews. He was of the ſeed royal by the mother's side, and exercised the authority of a magistrate and law-giver in many and various particulars; and was the head of the Sanhedrim. Perhaps, neither of them lived long before the appearance of Jesus Christ. Perhaps, they wrote about forty years before the incarnation of the Son of God.

There is another Targum or translation, called the *Jerusalem Targum*. Its age cannot easily be ascertained. There are various other Targums, but these three only are particularly worthy of our respect, and were regarded as authorities by the Jews themselves. From them we might endeavour to learn the sense of the Jewish Church before the times of Christ, concerning many remarkable prophecies which related to the coming of the Messiah the Son of God. I will take notice of a few. Their number indeed is great, but a small quantity will be sufficient for our purpose at present. The oldest prediction is this, that " the seed of the woman should break " the head of the serpent, and that the ser- " pent should bruise his heel." So it stands in the book of Genesis. These Targums express

press themselves thus, after they have given the text. "The sons of the woman them-selves shall bruise the heel in the latter days of the Messiah." And the other says, "they themselves shall bruise the heel, in the end of the heel of the days, in the days of Messiah the king." They seem to have had juster views of the character and office of the Messiah, than many of the Jews had in the days of our Lord's ministry. They bear a remarkable testimony to the sufferings of the Messiah, and to those sufferings as brought about by their own countrymen; who called themselves descendants of the promised seed, and heirs of that great and divine seed which was soon to make his appearance.

I shall next take the remarkable prediction of Jacob, in the forty-ninth chapter of Genesis, and the tenth verse; and shall notice the eleventh and twelfth verses, for the sake of the interpretations of these Targums. "The sceptre shall not depart from Judah, nor a law-giver from" the latter state of the people, "until Shiloh come." Onkelos says, "until the Messiah come." Jonathan, the son of Uzziel, says, "until the time in which the king Messiah shall come." And thus they paraphrase the eleventh verse; " Binding his " foal unto the vine, and his ass's colt unto " the choice vine; he washed his garments " in wine, and his clothes in the blood of " grapes:" Thus they express the patriarch's meaning. " How beautiful is king Messiah, " who shall arise out of the house of Judah; " he girdeth his loins, he descendeth, he sets " the battle in array against his enemies, and " slayeth many kings!" The next verse they thus explain. " How beautiful are the eyes " of the king Messiah, as the pure wine!" and so on.

These testimonies fully set before us their expectation, and the previous view which they had of the character of the Son of God, as the true Messiah.

I shall next take notice of the very remarkable prediction of Balaam, in the twenty-fourth chapter of the book of Numbers, and the seventeenth verse. " I shall see him, but " not now; I shall behold him, but not nigh;
" there

## Lect. 2. Evidences of Christianity.

"there shall come a star out of Jacob, and a sceptre shall rise out of Israel, and shall smite the corners of Moab, and destroy, (or rather, protect) all the children of Sheth;" for such is the meaning of the passage. " All the children of Sheth," are, undoubtedly, all mankind. Noah descended from Sheth; and from Noah, all the nations that are now upon the face of the earth. To *destroy* all the children of Sheth, would be to leave none to rule over—none to exercise the sceptre among men. Thus the Targums explain themselves: " A mighty Prince shall arise out of the house of Jacob, and the Messiah shall be anointed." Onkelos says, " There shall arise a prince, a king out of Jacob, and the Messiah out of Israel shall be anointed." In this respect, they agree with the most learned Christian interpreters of those very ancient predictions. I grant, some Christian writers seem to have set their faces against them. This shews the difficulty of the task which I have undertaken; since I cannot do justice to the sacred Scriptures without intrenching upon the principles which some men professing Christianity have advanced. Truth however is always stubborn in the estimation of the world—always graceful in the opinions of the wife—she must be obeyed.

I shall next go on to the words of David, in the twenty-third chapter of the second book of Samuel, and the third verse. "The God " of Israel said, the rock of Israel spake to me, " he that ruleth over men must be just, ruling " in the fear of God." Thus the Targums explain it. " He said that he would appoint for " me the king Messiah, who shall be revealed, " who shall be magnified, and who shall rule " in the fear of the Lord." Though I have passed over such large portions of Scripture, yet the number of passages are many wherein the Messiah is, perhaps, as fully, and as expressly represented, as in those which have been mentioned. I adduce first, such as I may have occasion to refer to, during the course of these Lectures.

I shall take notice only of two passages in Isaiah. The first is in the ninth chapter, where there is that beautiful description of the Messiah, " the mighty God, the everlasting " Father, the prince of peace." They express

press it thus, "The Messiah, the peace;" thereby confirming their applications of the passage to him that was to come. Again, in the beginning of the eleventh chapter of that prophecy; "And there shall come forth a "rod out of the stem of Jesse, and a branch "shall grow out of his roots." Thus they express it. "And a king shall come forth "from the sons of Jesse, and from his sons "shall the Messiah be anointed." There are several references in the Song of Solomon to the Messiah. I mention them for this reason, that they show the high estimation which they have for that book; and their opinion of its real worth and excellency. There are several in Jeremiah, almost repeatedly in the same terms. "I will raise unto David a righteous "branch;" according to them, "I will raise "unto David the holy Messiah," which is repeated several times. I must take notice of two passages in the prophecy of Zechariah, because of their importance, and of their intimate connexion with what is to follow. First, in the third chapter of the prophecy of Zechariah, and the eighth verse, "Behold, I "will bring forth my servant, the *Branch;*"

or, " the man whose name is the Messiah." Again, in the sixth chapter, and the twelfth verse, " And speak unto him, saying, Thus " speaketh the Lord of hosts, saying, Behold " the man whose name is the *Branch:* and " he shall grow up out of his place, and he " shall build the temple of the Lord." Thus they explain it, " Behold the man whose name " is the *Branch*, he shall be revealed, he shall " be magnified, he shall build the house of " the Lord." I pass by the prophecy of Malachi. Every one must know the strong expressions that are to be met with there upon this subject. I repeat, that the number of passages of this kind are numerous indeed. I know not a book in the Old Testament where there are not many decided references to the coming of the Messiah. I will just produce three passages of a different cast. Perhaps none of us would think of it in the reading of them. They are introduced for this reason, that you may perceive how full their minds and thoughts were of the future Messiah, and the glory of his kingdom. The first is in the thirty-fifth chapter of the book of Genesis, and the twenty-first verse. " And Israel journeyed, and
" spread

"spread his tent toward the tower of Edar." Now, the *tower of Edar* signifies, strictly and properly interpreted, *the tower of the flock*. Jonathan says, "from hence shall be "revealed the Messiah in the latter days." Here Jonathan refers to a remarkable passage in the prophecy of Micah, where the prophet thus expresses himself, after pointing out the coming of Christ in the fourth chapter and the eighth verse. " And thou, O tower " of the flock, the strong hold of the daughter " of Zion, unto thee shall it come, even the " first dominion; the kingdom shall come to " the daughter of Jerusalem." I beg leave to observe, it is no concern of mine, at present, though it may be hereafter, whether the Targum is strictly just in referring that passage to the other in Genesis: it sufficiently shows the reflections of the interpreters concerning it. And this farther it sufficiently proves, that he well understood it; for all the chapter is a remarkable prediction of the times of Christ, and begins thus, " But in the last " days it shall come to pass, that the moun- " tain of the house of the Lord shall be esta- " blished in the top of the mountains, and it
" shall

" shall be exalted above the hills; and people
" shall flow unto it. And many nations shall
" come, and say, Come and let us go up to
" the mountain of the Lord, and to the house
" of the God Jacob; and he will teach us of
" his ways, and we will walk in his paths;
" for the law shall go forth of Zion, and the
" word of the Lord from Jerusalem." This
prediction was accomplished in the things
that are related in the second chapter of the
Acts; where the Jews of all nations came together upon that occasion, and the law did
go forth out of Zion, and the word of the
Lord from Jerusalem; and there the Messiah
was first revealed. And the tower of the
flock is here considered by the prophet as the
defence of mount Zion; and as the word of
the Lord from Jerusalem; because of these
things the passage becomes remarkable.

I shall mention only one more, which we
find in the fortieth chapter of the book of Exodus, and the ninth verse. " And thou shalt
" take the anointing oil, and anoint the tabernacle, and all that is therein, and shalt
" hallow it, and all the vessels thereof; and
it

Lect. 2.   *Evidences of Christianity.*   43

"it shall be holy." It might be asked, what reference is there here to the Messiah? I answer, it was never in my power to see any. But the question is not, what can either I or you see in it? Nevertheless, the remark which the Targum makes upon it, and which runs in these strains, is very worthy of observation. " Thou shalt sanctify that, because
" of the crown of the kingdom, the house of
" Judah, and the king Messiah who shall re-
" deem Israel in the latter day." I do not pretend to say that it has no reference; for undoubtedly the priesthood, the purity requisite in the discharge of its office, the building of that divine intellectual temple, of which all the others were but so many types; in a peculiar manner belong to the Messiah; and between these two offices, to use the words of Zechariah, is, " the covenant of peace." However remote from the design of Moses, and the sense of the text, in appearance; we see the greater judgment in the application; and must own that these interpreters gave evident proofs of their skill and fidelity in explaining the word of God.

May

May I be permitted to mention only two more of this kind. The one is in the thirtieth chapter of the book of Deuteronomy, where Mofes is fpeaking of the probable future condition of the people, and fays, " it " fhall come to pafs, if any of thine be " driven out unto the outmoft parts of heaven, " from thence will the Lord thy God gather " thee, and from thence will he fetch thee." —" By the hands of his Meffiah," fays the Targum. By whom fhall they be fetched, unlefs by him? By whom have they been brought back to the Church of God, for nearly the fpace of eighteen hundred years? By whom fhall they ever be brought back in the true and proper fenfe of the terms, but by the king Meffiah, who is exalted for this purpofe, and whofe name is the anointed?

The other is in the fourth chapter of Zechariah, and the feventh verfe. " And he " fhall bring forth a head-ftone thereof with " fhoutings, crying, grace, grace, unto it." Thus the Targum; " And he fhall reveal the " Meffiah, whofe name is called from ever- " lafting; and the Meffiah fhall be anointed, " and

" and shall reign over all kingdoms." These, I think, afford abundant specimens of the sense which the Jews had of the coming of Christ, long before he did come.

Did time allow, I might produce some interesting passages from the book of Ecclesiasticus, written near two hundred years before the birth of Christ. And I know of no prophane writer, (as he is called) possessed of equal excellencies with the author of that book. And, I trust, I may be forgiven, if I recommend the reading of it, though it be confidered as apocryphal.

But I would farther observe, that we find the same doctrines current among the heathen. And surely their testimony upon this occasion, must be of some importance. I shall be as brief as possible in the notice which I take of what they have advanced to this purpose. Julius Marathus, who wrote the life of Octavius, his patron and his protector, tells us, that, upon a certain occasion, at Rome, about six months or less, before the birth of Augustus, it was foretold that nature was about

to

to bring forth a king for the Romans. This happened feventy-two years before the birth of Chrift. You will find the words of Julius quoted in Suetonius's life of Auguftus, in the ninety-fourth chapter. There is fomething remarkable in his terms. " Nature was " about to bring forth a king." Intimating, that his birth was not to be according to the ordinary courfe. Nature, in a fpecial manner, was to be exerted; or, in other words, the God of nature. He meant to fpeak of an operation great and extraordinary, for the production of a prince fo illuftrious, fo celebrated.

The next inftance which I fhall adduce is, the celebrated Pollio, of Virgil; one of the moft fingular poems in all antiquity. This was written about forty years before the birth of Chrift. Its contents are of importance, its language beautiful, its defcriptions highly finifhed and poetical. In that poem he fpeaks of the birth of a great prince, who is to have dominion over the world; and he thus defcribes his perfonal grandeur, and the grandeur of his kingdom. He fays, " a new
" feries

" feries of ages was to commence, and that
" the world was to be reftored to that ftate
" in which it was originally, and when all
" fhall again be perfect and complete." He
fpeaks of him as, " a Child, as a Son to be
" born." He fpeaks of him as, " a new
" race let down from heaven—as the glory
" of the age in which he lived;" and, indulg-
ing the warmth of his imagination, he ex-
claims, " O beloved offspring of the Gods!
" O thou, the great increafe of Jove!" intimating his fuperior excellence; as if it were
his firft-born fon, who fhould bring more advantages to the world than any who had ever
appeared in it before himfelf. He thus expreffes himfelf in general terms. I muft refer you to the poem itfelf. " The defign of
" his appearance was to redeem men from
" everlafting fear—to take away the remains
" of fin—to reftore a divine communication
" between the Gods, and good men, while a
" fimilar change was to take place in every
" part of nature—all animals are interefted
" in it—the fury and enmity that fubfifts
" between fierce animals was to be done away
" —the herds were no longer to fear man,

" nor

"nor flocks the ravenous beasts of prey." All were to blend together in perfect peace. The different parts of the universe were, at the commencement of his kingdom, to yield rich and alluring harvests. But with a kind of skill and foresight which could never have been expected from a heathen poet, he observes, that "the old vestiges of sin should remain; that men would continue to traffic, continue to build cities, and to carry on wars." But when this prince, and his kingdom, should arise to a mature and perfect state, then the sailor should depart from the sea, then the ground should not require its wonted toil, then the plough should not be wanted for the earth, nor the harrow for the field, nor the flocks need particular guardians to manage and to feed them. "All shall be at peace." The merchant shall not require an exchange of wares, because every land shall produce all that is needful. And he adds to these, many beautiful and poetic representations of the effects of this kingdom, upon the different parts of nature. Now I ask, Where could the poet have come by his materials, if not from the prophets? Where can we find, among all the

writings

writings of antiquity, any thing that can bear the leaft analogy to the language of the Roman poet, except in the prophets? In them indeed we find beautiful expreffions of the like kind. And I confider it as a decifive proof that the learned Romans, at leaft, were well acquainted with the Old Teftament Scriptures, through the medium of the Greek tranflation, which was introduced into the world feveral hundred years before the birth of Chrift.

I might quote another, and he alfo is a Roman hiftorian; Suetonius, who, in his life of Vefpafian, obferves, that an ancient and conftant opinion prevailed over all the eaft country, that it was in the decree of the fates, that about the times when Chrift was to be ufhered into the world, there fhould come men from Judea, who were to poffefs the empire of the world. And this, as might be expected, he applied to the conquefts of Vefpafian, who was proclaimed emperor while he was in Judea, before the times which he alluded to were paft.

I fhall appeal, once more, to another hiftorian; who is, I prefume to fay, fecond to none

none of that character, I mean the learned and accurate Tacitus; and who, perhaps, will help us to unravel much of the obscurity which overspreads this part of the subject. He says: "The greatest numbers were persuaded that it was recorded in the ancient books of the priests," (he does not say what priests,) "that the East should prevail," or the "rising sun," (call it which you please) "and that men coming out of Judea should obtain the empire of the world." You see how near the terms which he uses are to what Suetonius makes use of, in speaking of Vespasian. But there is this difference; Tacitus says, *Oriens*; meaning either the rising of the morning, or the rising sun.

I must now refer you to the predictions of Zechariah, "Behold my servant, whose name is *the Branch*." The Greek translators use a term which signifies, the dawning of the day, or the sun-rising. "Behold my servant, whose name is, "*the dawning of the day*." And in the sixth chapter and twelfth verse, "I will bring forth my servant, whose name is *the dawning of the day*." The evangelist Luke makes use of the same word,

word, in the firſt chapter of his goſpel, and applies it in the ſame manner to the true Meſſiah, the Son of God. "Whereby the "*day-ſpring* from on high hath viſited us." I think this will ſufficiently explain from what ſource theſe predictions were derived—through what hands they came to the Romans, and whence they were originally brought into their hiſtories. They were borrowed from the prophets. Tacitus could never have thought of uſing ſuch a term, "*the eaſt*; or *the riſing* "*ſun*, ſhall prevail;" had not the ſacred penmen led the way; and more eſpecially, if the tranſlators of the Old Teſtament Scriptures had not employed ſuch terms as theſe.

But enough has been ſaid to ſhow, that the ſame opinions, and the ſame doctrines, were well known in the Eaſt. I ſhall have the leſs occaſion to enlarge, in the next place, upon the repreſentations given in the New Teſtament Scriptures. I have only to glance at a few. At the birth of Chriſt, Herod ſent to enquire "where the Meſſiah was to be born." There were quoted to him the words of the prophet Micah, which preciſely ſay, "In

"Bethlehem," for thus it was written, "And thou Bethlehem Ephratah, though thou be little among the thousands of Judah, yet out of thee shall he come forth unto me, that is to be ruler in Israel; whose goings forth have been from of old, from everlasting." He who quoted the former part of that sentence, well understood the latter. And these words of Micah are thus expressed by the Targums: Speaking of Bethlehem in Judea, "From thee by me shall rise king Messiah, that he may exercise dominion." Had they given the interpretation of the Targums, Herod, perhaps, would not have been more alarmed than he was. They said enough to answer this question. They kept back enough to open the eyes of the multitude on some future occasion, if it should be requisite. And this, we see, was the constant opinion of the Jews in the time of Christ. Thus in the dispute mentioned in the seventh chapter of St. John, "Does not Christ come out of Bethlehem— Has not the prophet said, of the house of David, where David dwelt?" How often was he addressed by people in distress, "Thou Son of David?" They understood well this

cha-

character which he had fuſtained all along in their own records. And when he was uſhered into Jeruſalem, by a large concourſe of people, they ſing hoſannas to him as " the Son of " David," as " the king of Sion." But you yourſelves will recollect many inſtances to the ſame purpoſe. Similar expectations were like- wiſe found among the Samaritans; of which we have deciſive proofs in the fourth chapter of John, where the woman of Samaria, from the obſervations made by Jeſus Chriſt, from his unfolding her ſecret life, (for he had ſaid more than the Evangeliſt has thought fit to record, as is obvious from his own language) infers his true character. Nor do we find any ſuch imprudence in the narrations of the ſacred penmen as to ſuppoſe they ſaid all that might have been ſaid;—" She ran into the city, " and ſaid, Come ſee a man that told me all " things that ever I did, is not this the Chriſt?" She did not ſpeak of him as an unexpected perſon. The men of the city came to enquire for themſelves, and ſaid, " We believe, not " becauſe of thy word; but now we believe, " becauſe we ourſelves have ſeen, and know " that this is indeed the very Chriſt that

ſhould

"should come into the world." The Jews were frequently filled with perplexity, notwithstanding all their opposition; and often came and questioned him, for the fullest information, whether he was, or was not the Messiah. I must here observe one thing more. It is evident from the ancient Jewish writers, and much more so from the New Testament, that they considered it as a part of the Messiah's character, inseparably belonging to him, to discern the heart, and to know the characters of men by intuition. This they grounded upon the prediction of Isaiah, the eleventh chapter; "The spirit of the Lord shall rest "upon him, the spirit of wisdom and under- "standing, the spirit of counsel and might, "the spirit of knowledge, and of the fear of "the Lord. And shall make him of quick "understanding in the fear of the Lord; and "he shall not judge after the sight of his eyes, "neither reprove after the hearing of his "ears; but with righteousness and truth." Now, we have several proofs of this kind brought forward in the gospels; the great design of which is to show that he answered this part of the ancient description of his character.

Thus,

Lect. 2. *Evidences of Christianity.*

Thus, when he saw Nathaniel, he said, "Behold an Israelite indeed, in whom is no guile!"—" Whence knoweft thou me?" said the holy man. " Before that Philip called thee, when thou waft under the fig-tree, I saw thee." This was to Nathaniel a decifive proof who the perfon was; and he cried out, " Thou art the Son of God, thou art the king of Ifrael!" He knew him from this circumftance, from his quick difcernment of characters—from his knowledge of thofe things which no eye had feen, and which could not be known to mere created man.

We have another inftance, and a beautiful one, in the feventh chapter of St. Luke's gofpel; when the pharifee invited our Lord to dine with him. A woman of bad character came into the houfe, with a box of precious ointment, with which fhe anointed his feet; and then wiped them with the hair of her head. The pharifee faid, within himfelf, " If this man were a prophet, he would have known who, and what manner of woman this is that toucheth him: for fhe is a finner." That is, if he were the true Meffiah;

siah: for that kind of prescience and knowledge of things relative to him, was not at all essential to *a* prophet, merely as a prophet; but essential to *him* who was to come, as *the* great prophet, and the king promised of old. He immediately convinced the pharisee, that he was better acquainted with the secret thoughts of the pharisee's heart, than *he* was with the character of the woman. And this exhibited a full and complete proof of his own character. The woman of Samaria, " be-" cause of the things which he spake," with respect to her secret character and thoughts, " believed on him;" and many others of the Samaritans were convinced " that he was the " Messiah, the Christ, that should come into " the world." And to this I refer all those things, so often repeated by the Evangelists. " He knew what was in man; and, there-" fore, did not commit himself to them." And, in his answers, he generally made them feel that he was acquainted with the secret emotions of their hearts; and the hidden designs of their questions, and of their address.

Might

Lect. 2.   *Evidences of Christianity.*   57

Might I not *farther* take notice of the representation of our Lord himself upon this head? Indeed it would take up more than all my remaining time, to go through the assertions which he has made with respect to himself and his character, as spoken of by the prophets. I flatter myself, most of you here present are acquainted with that circumstance. Even his birth, his person, his origin, his character, his works, were all referred to by the prophets; and therefore they must have formed a judgment of him, and have understood to whom such things did belong. His sufferings, he again and again showed to his disciples, were the accomplishment of Scripture. Yea, the very manner of his sufferings, and the circumstances which attended them; such as the distribution of his raiment, and his garments; the piercing of his hands and his feet; his being numbered with transgressors, and the rest, all go to the same point. But I must sum them all up in the words of our text, " These
" are the things which I spake unto you, while
" I was yet with you, that all things must be
" fulfilled which were written in the Law of
" Moses, and in the prophets, and in the Psalms
                               " concern-

"concerning me:" Thus referring all to well known Scriptures. And in the middle of this very chapter we find that he began to open the Scriptures. He began at Mofes, and went from thence through the prophets, fpeaking of the things which related to himfelf; and obferves, that " it muft be fo;" otherwife, the " Scriptures cannot be true"—that " re-
" pentance ought to be preached to the na-
" tions"—and " falvation to the world, in the
" name of Jefus Chrift"—that there was a divine propriety in thefe things, and that they effentially belonged to his character. The fecond, thirteenth, and fifteenth chapters of the Acts of the Apoftles, with other circumftances mentioned in this chapter, will afford you abundant fpecimens of the manner in which the apoftles preached to the Jews—and difcover whence they drew their arguments, in order to fhow that " Jefus was the Chrift, the Son
" of God which fhould come into the world."

I prefume to hope that what I have now offered, will abundantly evince, that the great and important doctrines which Chrift and his apoftles delivered, were not new to the men
of

of Judea—were not their invention at the time; and that they fuppofed fuch a combination, and fuch intimate connexion between the Old and New Teftament Scriptures, that they muft ftand or fall together.

I conclude with a few reflections; and they fhall be fhort.

Firft; we fee the fingular wifdom of God, which runs through the whole of the Scriptures, from firft to laft; every thing is connected, every thing is confiftent, every thing is given to mankind by divine counfel and defign. Men born in ages diftant from each other, without feeing or knowing each other, are employed in carrying on the fame work. We may difcover the wifdom of divine Providence, in difperfing among the heathen nations, by means of the difperfion of the Jews, fuch early intimations of the coming of the true Meffiah. By thefe they were, in fome meafure, prepared for the publication of the Gofpel; and it would be unjuft to think of charging the facred penmen of the New Teftament, with the difhonefty of diffeminating

thofe

thofe things which happened before they were born, that they might give countenance to, what was called, the new fyftem of religion. Far from every candid mind be fuch thoughts! Here we difcover the wifdom of God. And I can never reflect on the fubject without admiring a divine order and regulation in this refpect. We may confider it as an epitome of the whole government of the fupreme Being. When the Jews introduced idolatry, they were feparated from all other nations—they were difperfed among all the different nations throughout the world; and thus they became the means, in their captivity and affliction, of diftributing that interefting information which they refufed in the days of their profperity to acknowledge. Their obftinate refiftance of Chrift, in defiance of their own Scriptures, which they maintained with the greateft zeal, is an affecting proof of the hardnefs of their hearts, and of the blindnefs of their minds. But God will make ufe of their infidelity to anfwer thofe purpofes which might have been obtained, perhaps, by their faith; their difperfed condition, their ftate among the nations, fo exactly anfwering prophetic defcriptions,

tions, are a complete monument of the truth and faithfulneſs of the things delivered by the prophets.

Again; I hope I may be pardoned for theſe ſuggeſtions, as I ſpeak them to ſuppoſed Chriſtians, and doubt not but I am ſpeaking to ſuch, It appears obvious from all the Scriptures, from firſt to laſt, that there is but one great "name, given under heaven, where-" by we can be ſaved;" that is, Meſſiah the prince of peace; the Meſſiah, the peace; the great king who was to deſcend from Jacob, from Judah, from David; and who is ſo often mentioned by the prophets under ſuch characters, and with ſuch marks, as could never fail of ſuggeſting the nature of that ſalvation which we have by the Son of God.

Let not the things which I have now advanced, in this reſpect, be loſt. O, do you treaſure up in your hearts the true ſource of this redemption of life and of peace. Let not our thoughts be carried away from things reſpecting the coming of Chriſt! The language of the evangeliſts, and of the apoſtles

is

is plain; calculated alike for us all; and muſt reach the heart of all who underſtand the beauty and energy of the holy word of God.

I have only farther to obſerve, that ſo far as I have proceeded, I have not conſidered myſelf as introducing arguments in defence of a divine Revelation, or of the divine authority of the Scriptures. I did not mean to renounce the intereſting circumſtances which I have mentioned, in that view, with a deſign to deprive myſelf of a fair opportunity, when a proper occaſion comes. I only ſay, I have not introduced them for that purpoſe at preſent. My next effort will be this,—

Firſt; to ſhow that the Pentateuch, or five books of Moſes, were really written by him whoſe name they bear, and that this is ſupported by authentic evidence.

Secondly; That all the ſingular and important incidents recorded, muſt, upon deciſive evidence, be conſidered as ſo many undeniable facts.

And

And laftly; That they carry indifputable marks of divine authority with them; that they were penned under the guidance and fanction of the Holy Spirit of God.

Perhaps, I fhall be thought to have propofed more than I am able to perform. Had I nothing to truft to but my own fkill—had I no other dependence but upon my own invention and contrivance—did I rely upon my own ability and management, I might truly and juftly tremble. I have no confidence in myfelf; but I have all confidence that my fubject will never fail me. It will open upon me, under his protection, who has been the guide of the Scriptures, from firft to laft; and fuch things will arife, I doubt not, and occur, as will encourage me in the purfuit of the work. Far be it from me to fuggeft, that fuch things will arife to me from a fupernatural fource. I pretend to no fuch thing. From no other fources do I draw but fuch as are open to you all. And I hope that you will perufe the Scriptures with fimplicity of mind—will mark their extent—will feel their importance—will rejoice in their contents, and look forward to that
refur-

resurrection and immortal life, which it is the highest honour of intelligent beings to attain. This is our hope. May the God of hope, and peace, confirm us in our expectation, that we may live with him to everlasting ages! Amen.

LECT.

# LECT. III.

MY CHRISTIAN FRIENDS,

I TAKE it for granted that moſt of you are acquainted with the ſubject to be diſcuſſed this evening; which is an attempt to ſhow that the books called the Pentateuch, and which go under the name of Moſes, were really written by that great and celebrated law-giver. And that we may, without further preface, enter immediately upon the ſubject, I would recommend to your conſideration, the following clauſe, which you will find in,

JOHN I. Ver. 43.

" We have found him of whom Moſes in
" the law—did write."

I have indeed omitted the word *Prophets*, becauſe the term *write*, belongs more immediately

diately to Moses in the construction of the words; and this, in a more pointed manner, refers to the subject before us. We have it here from high authority, that there was such a person as Moses—that he was a law-giver —that he wrote his laws, and that he added various predictions respecting the Son of God. Because no one is specified of whom Moses in the law did write, I am well aware that objections have been raised against this, plain and obvious at it is. And those who first raised the objections, never carried them farther than to certain short particular clauses, which they hastily supposed to have been added by some other hands. For myself, I am of a very different mind. A very late writer, still living, has picked out such objections as he himself thought best capable of management. These he has urged in such a way as to captivate the attention of the common people, and thus to disseminate pernicious errors, yet easily to be refuted.

I shall, upon this occasion, take notice of the leading arguments, before I enter on the proof that Moses wrote those laws which bear

his

his name; and shall then endeavour to refute the reasonings such as they are.

It is not my design, at least to any extent, to take notice of the unbecoming and scurrilous language of the writer alluded to, with respect to Moses, and the other sacred penmen. With regard to the Bible itself, after an introduction, where there is much of this kind, he begins in the following manner. " There is no affirmative evidence that Moses " wrote those books, nor any well-grounded " opinion that he wrote them, except a vain " one which has got abroad, nobody knows " how." This is undoubtedly a bold assertion in the face of the whole world; and clearly announces a person either without a rival in ignorance, or one totally regardless of his own character in the republic of letters. He enters upon his objections, and first states, what he calls, grammatical evidence, that Moses writes constantly in the third person, and does not speak in his own person; but, " God said unto Moses—the Lord spake to " Moses—Moses said to the people." But this is the manner in which all historians write and speak, when they are writing and speaking concerning themselves. I flatter myself, there are few in this assembly, that would wish me to enter upon a formal answer to such a weak argument as this; since it is well known that the best writers who have written their own lives, who have written their own actions, express themselves in the third person; nor do they appear in the first, where they were particularly engaged, so far as action is concerned. But, indeed, this he afterwards gives up, and says, " Supposing " Moses might be allowed to speak of him- " self and of his actions, in what manner he " pleased, yet his account is absurd and in- " consistent with itself; as when he says, " *now the man Moses was very meek, above all* " *men that were upon the face of the earth.*" Here, says he, " if Moses wrote this, he was " one of the most consummate coxcombs; " and if he did not write it, the books are " without authority. If he was the author, " the author is unworthy of credit." It is scarcely possible for one sentence to contain more absurdities. I shall wave it, with other things of the like kind, by observing, that

he

he muſt feel ſomething like a degradation who has firſt noticed what could never be urged with decency, or without diſgrace. Many paſſages of that kind before me, ſhall be buried in oblivion. The character of Moſes, as it may be ſeen in his own writings, ſtands far ſuperior to ſuch little attacks as this.

But the next thing produced as an argument is this, " That he writes an account of " his own death and burial, which is totally " inconſiſtent with his being the author of " the preceding books." I have only to ſay here, if there ever were, if there are any perſons who believe that Moſes wrote the account of his own death and burial; they ought to be claſſed with him, who can urge the writing an account of Moſes's death and burial, as an argument againſt the genuineneſs of his books. Their names ſhall ever go together. Let them contend; there is no difference; as combatants, neither ſide will ever diſgrace the other. I never met with a writer in my life, nor with any perſon whatever, who ſuppoſed Moſes to be the writer of the account of his own death and burial. The abſurdity is too grofs to be admitted for a moment. Let this matter then be brought to fome decifive point. What is there wrong here in the account of Mofes's death and burial? There can be no defect, unlefs in two refpects. Either, firft, that the account of his death and burial ought never to have been written; or elfe, if written, it ought to have been placed in a different fituation. Will any one fay, that no account ought to have been written of the death and burial of Mofes; a man whofe life was fo remarkable, and whofe death was attended by fuch fingular circumftances? Surely not. Then it muft terminate here, Whether the account of Mofes's death ought to have been added at the clofe of his laws and life; or ought to have been made the preface of the life of fome other perfon; or have been placed at the clofe of the jewifh hiftory; for inftance, at the end of the fecond book of Chronicles. And I fhould imagine, every one will eafily perceive the folly of fuch an idea. But then again it is urged, "Who fhall write that account, if *no man knows of his fepulchre to this day?* How fhall the writer tell where he was buried?" There is no inconfiftency here. There were feveral several persons capable of doing it, without the supposition of its being done above four or five hundred years afterwards. Joshua was capable of writing the account. Eleazar, the successor of Aaron, was capable of writing the account. Phineas, the son of Aaron, as eminent a person as any in those times, was capable of writing the account. And, I suppose the account to have been early written. But this is a point upon which some men are not to be pleased. It is not wrong that it should close the laws. It would have been wrong to have prefixed it to the book of Joshua; still worse to have deferred it to the close of other books. And the same persons who ask, How shall any one, at such a distance of time, know any thing about the death and burial of Moses, know what the account expressly says, he was buried in such a place in the land of Moab; but where his grave was, (nothing more is intended than his sepulchre there) but where his grave was, no one knew, even in that day. And if not so soon afterwards, there was no ground for any knowledge in that matter in after times. Therefore, I think, we may fairly dismiss this point, as no argument againſt Moſes's having written the Pentateuch. Such an idea would be altogether abſurd with any man who is accuſtomed to inveſtigate writings, and to reaſon for himſelf.

The next objection is, that there are certain alterations in the book of Deuteronomy, which are inconſiſtent with the things written elſewhere; particularly with reſpect to the ſabbath; where it is ſaid ſo and ſo in the twentieth chapter of Exodus, but a different repreſentation is given of the commandment in the book of Deuteronomy, in the fifth chapter. Now this I beg leave poſitively to deny. The commandment is the ſame in both places. And in the fifth chapter of Deuteronomy, Moſes does not introduce any new commandment, or inſtitutions. He refers to what was ſaid in the twentieth chapter of Exodus, " Remember to keep the ſabbath " holy, as the Lord thy God hath com- " manded thee." He does not ſay, *does* command thee, or *commands* thee, but refers to the former inſtitution. It weighs nothing, that in the twentieth chapter of Exodus, there is no reference to the coming out of Egypt; and

and that in Deuteronomy, there is no reference to the creation, and the original inftitution of the fabbath. That is nothing to the purpofe. There is no alteration whatever as to the command. It is the fame in both places. And in the beginning of Genefis Mofes adds an *additional*, not a *different* reafon. They were brought out of Egypt with a view to a church ftate, where they fhould enjoy a divine reft. Hence the argument drawn from the beginning of Genefis was pointed, and to the purpofe; and hence the additional argument in Deuteronomy, which puts them in mind of the purpofe for which they were delivered out of Egypt, is an additional reafon for the obfervance of the fabbath. All is confiftent, orderly, well-connected, without any apparent difference, without any injury whatever to either paffage. And furely Mofes, as well as any other writer, might refer to what he had formerly written, without being confidered as a different writer.

The next things mentioned are, what he calls, his hiftorical and chronological evidences. The firft is taken from the fourteenth

teenth chapter of Genefis, where it is faid that Abraham purfued the kings to Dan. This he takes hold of in order to fhow that Dan was originally Laifh; an account of which we have in the book of Judges. He alleges that there was no fuch place as Dan in the time of Abraham; Mofes therefore could not be the writer of the book, becaufe Laifh had not the name of Dan till after this. Here now you will give me leave to obferve; before this writer had any right whatever to draw fuch a conclufion, he fhould have proved the following particulars: Firft, that by Dan, in that paffage, fome city or town was undoubtedly intended. Next, that Laifh had really been built, and was in exiftence at the time when Abraham purfued the kings. And thirdly, that Laifh and Dan were, undoubtedly, the fame places, as evident from geographical defcriptions. But he has not attempted any one of thefe; nor any one of thefe will he ever be able to prove, fhould he recommence his enquiries. It will be enough to fay, that no intimations are given by Mofes, in that part of the hiftory of Abraham, of Dan's being any town; far lefs of Dan's being the
fame

same with Laish. But some geographical enquirers have added, what reconciles the account in both places: he recommenced there his action against them, and in their flight pursued them to the valley of Hobah, which was on the left hand of Damascus, a part of the valley of Damascus. All writers speak of its beauty, and of its delightful situation. Dan, that was called Laish, was situated between Jordan and Tyre, towards the west of Judea. Hobah was on the other side of the mountains of Antilibanus, near the junction of the ridge of mountains called Libanus, and lay in a corner. The term signifies *covered* or *hid*. And, I think, it is clear, that Abraham pursued them upon the east side of Jordan, not upon the west, nor was ever likely to come near such a place as Laish, did Laish exist at that time, which I think not very probable. All this, therefore, must be rejected, as inapplicable to the subject, till it has been proved that Laish did exist at that time; till it has been shown, that Moses there refers to some city or town; and till it has been shown that the city of Laish was the Dan, the name given to Laish, according to this writer, long after

by

by Joshua. We must not receive things urged in such a manner as this. But this argument seemed to him so powerful, that he presses it with great eagerness, and turns it into a chronological evidence, as if he had a mind to push it home. I shall therefore endeavour to follow him, though, perhaps, not with equal steps. Thus he expresses himself; " according to " the chronological arrangement, the taking " of Dan, and the changing of its name, " was twenty years after the death of Joshua; " and by the historical order, as it stands in " that book, three hundred and six years after " the death of Joshua; and three hundred " and thirty-one years after that of Moses." This is as bold as his first assertion. Let me endeavour to open this point. He lays great stress upon the chronological dates in the Bible, and says, " I will bring nothing to " refute the Bible, but from the Bible. I " will therefore take the chronology of the " Bible, and show that it is a heap of ab- " surdities." Who is most absurd? The chronological dates upon the top of the leaves of our common Bibles, and in the margin, were first introduced by a Rev. prelate of our

own

own country, about the year 1701, and the marginal references were the result of his industry. So that Moses is to bear the supposed errors of chronologists who lived between three and four thousand years after he wrote. Does this carry with it any appearance of candour? Will this support any just evidence in reasonings of such importance? Surely not. But let us take another view of the subject. He says, " that Laish was taken, and its " name changed, according to the historical " order, as it stands, three hundred and six " years after the death of Joshua, and three " hundred thirty-one years after the death " of Moses." Now, according to the chronological dates in the margin of our common Bibles, there was only forty-five years between the death of Moses and the taking of Laish; and between the death of Joshua and that event, twenty-one years. But in truth and fact, Laish was taken, and its name changed, several years before the death of Joshua; and the account is given in the nineteenth chapter of his book. So that according to true chronology, Laish was taken, not more than about ten years after the death of
Moses.

Moses. The reasons why a more enlarged and particular account was afterwards given of that event, in the book of Judges, are too obvious to need to be stated at present; and the rather, as I may have occasion to consider them afterwards. Now, here let me observe, this writer either did, or did not know, that Laish was taken, and its name changed, in the days of Joshua. He either did, or did not know, that a particular account is given of it by Joshua himself, in the nineteenth chapter of his book. Now, if he did not know, his ignorance was such as excluded him from meddling with the subject at all; if he did know these things, his dishonesty renders him unworthy of any credit or attention whatever. Calm and considerate men are not to be deceived with such kind of reasoning as this.

The next argument which he urges is of a different kind; it is taken from the thirty-fifth chapter of Genesis. "And these are "the kings that reigned in the land of Edom, "before there reigned any king over the "children of Israel." This he draws out at large,

large, and fuppofes that no reafon could be affigned for the remark but this, that it was written after kings did reign in Ifrael; and therefore carries it to the days of Saul or David. Some very learned men have fallen into, what I call, an error in this particular, and therefore you will allow me to open it. God appears in perfon to Jacob, and promifes him that nations and people fhould fpring from him, and that kings fhould come out of his loins. Mofes then gives an account of the defcendants of Efau; and in order to illuftrate the faith and patience of God's holy people in this matter, he makes the following obfervation, that " thefe were kings in Edom, " before there was any king over Ifrael;" that he might fhow how great their patient expectation was for the accomplifhment of the word of God. He gives us an account of feven dukes that defcended from Efau; four of them were the fons of Eliphaz, grandfons of Efau himfelf, and the youngeft of the four was Amalek; whofe people was become a powerful nation when Mofes came out of Egypt. He then gives an account of the fons of the two others, and then of Aholibamah,

Efau's

Esau's last wife, of whom came three dukes; and she was the daughter of one duke of the family of Seir, and the grand-daughter of another duke of the family of Seir; and these fourteen dukes reigned nearly at the same time. I say, fourteen, because so many dukes of Seir, by their various intermarriages, and other circumstances, will show that they were all dukes at the same time. There were, moreover, above three hundred and forty years between the time of Esau's marrying into the family of Seir, and the death of Moses. He then gives us an account of the kings. And here, I would not have you imagine they were such kings as David or Solomon, or such kings as might be found in different parts of the east, in after times; by no means. They were kings created, or appointed, for a special occasion. And there is great reason to believe, that not one of these kings died a king; he laid down his office before his death. Not one of those kings was the son of a preceding king. But I would endeavour to explain this from other circumstances of those very times. And first, in the twenty-second chapter of the book of
                                    Numbers,

Numbers, look into the history of Balak sending for Balaam. Balak was the son of Zippor, king of the Moabites. It does not appear that Zippor was ever a king, or that Balak was a king to his death. There are circumstances against it. Balak was king of the Moabites at that time. It might be rendered, " he was king of the Moabites upon that oc-" casion;" because of the appearance of the people; such a vast multitude covering the countries round about; he said to the Midianites, " Now shall this company lick up all " that are round about us, as the ox licketh " up the grass of the field." And then his name is mentioned as acting officially; for it is evident, that the elders of Moab and the elders of Midian were the managers of this business, and followed Balaam. They applied to each other, to these elders of Moab and Midian; here, in a verse or two after, called the princes of Moab, and the princes of Midian. At the close of the business they are stiled *kings*. They are mentioned afterwards with their plain names, and with titles of an inferior kind. Thus in the thirty-first chapter of Numbers, and the eighth verse,

where

where there is an account of the slaughter made of the Midianites, on account of the artifice which they used in order to draw Israel into idolatry, according to the secret advice of Balaam; Moses thus expresses himself, besides the rest that were kings, "they slew the kings "of Midian, Evi, and Rekem, and Zur, and "Hur, and Reba, five kings of Midian; "Balaam also, the son of Beor, they slew "with the sword." Joshua happily gives us an account of these same men, and of this battle. It would be interesting to compare his account with the other. Joshua xiii. 21. "And all the cities of the plain, and all the "kingdom of Sihon king of the Amorites, "which reigned in Heshbon, whom Moses "smote with the princes of Midian, Evi, and "Rekem, and Zur, and Hur, and Reba, "which were dukes of Sihon dwelling in "the country." Literally it would run thus, "whom Moses smote with the heads of "Midian, Evi, and Rekem, and Zur, and "Hur, and Reba, anointed princes of Sihon "dwelling in the country." I think we may fairly infer, when we consider the accuracy of Moses, that these same men were not then kings.

kings. And, indeed, nothing was so common in those times as a person named *king*, for a particular purpose. And the same custom came round through the east into the north, and was found among our ancestors in Germany. It would be interesting to discuss these titles fully, but that belongs not to our present object. Moses, in Exodus the fifteenth, says, " The dukes of Edom shall " be afraid." And, accordingly, we see it came to pass. For Moses sent to the king of Edom, as he was called then, to let Israel pass through their land, but Edom refused; but Edom would not suffer it. Edom gathered together an host.

Having now stated these particulars, let me bring the whole together. There were, undoubtedly, kings in Edom, before the ministration of Moses. It is an undoubted truth, that there was no king over Israel before the days of Moses. Might not then Moses, with as great propriety, say, those were kings in Egypt before there was any king over Israel; as say, these were kings in Egypt before his own time? And this was,

undoubtedly, the meaning of his language, as I ſhall farther ſhow, from the thirty-third chapter of Deuteronomy, where it is expreſsly aſſerted that Moſes was "king in Jeſhurun;" aſſerted in the ſtrongeſt, and moſt deciſive language, verſe the fourth, "Moſes com-
"manded us a law, even the inheritance of
"the congregation of Jacob; and he was
"king in Jeſhurun, when the heads of the
"people, and the tribes of Iſrael were gathered
"together." And at the giving of the law at Sinai, in the preſence of God he was made king, he was made firſt magiſtrate, by the approbation of the people under the ſanction of God. And I ſhould wiſh to know what higher ſanctions any king could ever have; or what juſter ſanctions, unleſs you ſhould ſuppoſe, that this is a bold invention of my own. But I obſerve that our own countryman, the very learned Selden, has clearly proved that Moſes was king in the higheſt, ſtricteſt, and moſt extenſive ſenſe of the word.

Now, then, to what amounts all this mighty objection? Moſes muſt be writing concerning what happened before his own time, or elſe

Moſes

Moſes muſt contradict himſelf. But it is abſurd to ſuppoſe that he contradicted himſelf in this matter. No, by no means.

The next circumſtance which he lays hold of, is the eating of the manna, in Exodus the ſixteenth, with the ceaſing of it, in the fifth chapter of Joſhua, and the twelfth verſe; where Moſes is charged with a great impropriety; nay, with advancing an abſurdity; as if he had ſaid, "The manna ceaſed as ſoon " as he came with them to the borders of " Canaan, to a land inhabited." But Moſes ſays no ſuch thing. He ſays that manna continued till they came to the borders of Canaan, to a land inhabited and cultivated. Moſes came to that land. Moſes was a witneſs of its continuance. Moſes drops not a ſyllable of its ceaſing. Moſes had a right to ſay what is there attributed to him, without any impropriety whatever, far leſs any great impropriety. After they had eaten of the old corn of the land, ſome time after the death of Moſes, Joſhua ſays, that manna ceaſed, and they had it no more. What is it that ſuch kind of reaſoning may not affirm?

The next thing is the bedstead of Og, mentioned in the third chapter of Deuteronomy, and the eleventh verse, "Is it not in the city of "Rabbath?" The reasoning upon this is somewhat curious. "How should Moses "know what was in the city of Rabbath? He "could never have taken Rabbath. That "the bedstead of Og was there could not "be known above four hundred years after- "wards." So the bedstead of Og was supposed to be continued there all the time. Thus we are forbidden to credit things probable, and to swallow the most improbable things. That, indeed, is too often the case. Moses took the city of Og, and plundered it of so much of the spoils as he could. If the bedstead and other things that were thought curious and valuable were conveyed away, who could have a clearer view of that circumstance than Moses? Who had opportunities of better information? Look into the transactions of neighbouring nations upon the occasion. No one could say, "Is it not in the "city of Rabbath," but Moses. After Og was destroyed, and the valuable things taken away, it could not be in the power of Joshua to affirm it.

I will

## Lect. 3. Evidences of Christianity.

I will take notice of another circumstance. I apprehend this writer did not know what this bedstead of Og was. He supposed it made all of iron, like such bedsteads as we lie on. The term does not signify *bedstead*. And Mr.* , in his two volumes of observations upon divers passages, has shown that the words run literally thus; " Now the " *mattress* of Og was a *mattress* of iron." They had no such a thing as a bedstead in that country; nor do I suppose there is such a thing to this day. The mattress was filled with round pieces of iron, in the manner of a coat of mail, sufficient to show the hardy and rough nature of Og, king of Bashan. Men should make themselves acquainted with subjects before they take them up, and urge them without any sort of propriety.

Such are the arguments brought, in order to show that Moses did not write the Pentateuch. And I have some right to affirm that these arguments are inapplicable. They fail in every instance to support the position for which they are brought forward.

* The name escaped the ear of the Short-hand writer.

Now you will give me leave to proceed to what he calls positive evidence. The book of Genesis is first laid hold of. " Moses " does not speak there. We find no such " terms, that the Lord said to Moses. Moses " is never once brought forward. The " transactions in the book of Genesis were all " finished." Why then should that be urged as an objection which before was urged in a contrary way? I shall not, however, investigate this matter, but proceed to the following observations.

First; it will not be in any man's power to understand one chapter in the book of Exodus, who has never read the book of Genesis. To him it must be all darkness and confusion. But if we proceed regularly with the history, every thing opens upon us with the greatest consistence. Genesis is the foundation of all the Mosaic dispensation. Genesis contains, not only the history of the original of nations—not only of the original of the world, and of mankind, but of all true religion whatever. To the book of Genesis we must have recourse for the first commence-

ment

ment of the great and interesting transactions of the jewish dispensation. In Genesis we find the first sacrifices. In Genesis we trace the first instances of prayer: In Genesis, the first laws respecting civil society, and the preservation of men. In Genesis we find the first father of a Church fearing and worshipping God. In Genesis, we have the origin of circumcision: In Genesis, the first instance of tythes, and we have them repeated in the prayer of David. Moses is not to bear the weight of these things, as matters of his own institution; though they were matters which he very probably considered as an introduction to the law which God communicated by him. I mentioned *tythes*, because of an ill-natured observation of a person in this country. I am no more a favourer of tythes than other men; but Moses, I say, was not the author of them. " Thou shalt not " muzzle the ox that treadeth out the corn." Tythes are not once glanced at by Moses in the chapter, nor in the contents of the chapter. I would never call in, as an objection to tythes, the aid of low, vulgar, and

malicious

malicious objections. Such things have nothing to do with the Christian religion.

I would observe farther; the book of Genesis is a part of the law of Moses. I know no book that contains more commands, more statutes, more judgments, not even Exodus itself. There we find the ground of all the Laws respecting marriages among the Jews. Moses, as the writer of the book of Genesis, was never known among the ancient Jews, separately from the writing of the book of Exodus, Leviticus, Numbers, and Deuteronomy. I might as well take any book of the history of England, separate from the first, and say, the received author of the whole, did not write that particular book. I am sorry that ideas of this kind should have made their way even into the breasts of Christian ministers. The whole of Moses's writings are called the Pentateuch, not because they are five different books; but, to give it you literally, *the five-fold volume*. The Jews never knew the book of Genesis as separate from the rest. The ancient heathen never knew a book of Genesis separate from the rest of the laws

laws of Moses. They went together. Unskilful distinctions, when they gain ground, often become the source of ridiculous observations. The sacred penmen make use of these terms as synonymous. " The law of Moses; " the book of the law of Moses; the law " of Moses, the man of God; the book of " the law of Moses, the man of God." And under these forms of expression are they urged. The book of Genesis is quoted for arguments, in order to inforce the observance of the law by the jews, before the times of Christ; for in the first book of Maccabees, Judas Maccabeus calls his children together, and exhorts them, when he was about to die, to defend their law and principles, in these words, " Now, therefore, my sons, be " zealous for the law of God, and the cove- " nants; lay down your lives for the law of " God; and consider the works of your " fathers, what *they* did. Call to mind " Abraham, who was faithful, and it was " counted to him for righteousness; and the " covenant of God was in his flesh. Re- " member Joseph; who, in his afflictions, " kept the commandment; and he was
" faithful

"faithful, and made lord of Egypt." Would he have thus spoken of the law, had he not confidered it as a part of the writings of Mofes—had it not always been cuftomary with him fo to receive it?

Shall I defcend to an inftance, perhaps, which fome may confider as more decifive—it is in the Epiftle to the Galatians; where the Apoftle calls upon the Chriftian zealots, "You that obferve the law, hearken to the "law. Abraham had two fons, one by a "bond-maid; the other by a free woman." Would the Apoftle have fetched an argument from thence, had he not known the book of Genefis to be written by Mofes, as it is faid to be, (for I ftill except to the ridiculous cuftom of making it a diftinct book,) and the authority of the Apoftle is great. I have faid, that heathens themfelves never knew it feparate from the writings of Mofes. And in this particular, I will quote an expreffion from one of the moft celebrated of heathen writers; the eloquent Longinus upon the Sublime. He pays a compliment to Mofes, and expreffes himfelf in this manner. "The
"law-giver

" law-giver of the Jews, a man of no com-
" mon genius, having conceived in his mind
" the power of the supreme Deity, in a
" manner worthy its dignity, thus expresses
" it. He says,—*God spake*. What did he
" speak? *God said, Let there be light, and
" there was light. Let there be earth, and
" there was earth.* This he said, writing in
" the beginning of his law." Which, I think, is a decisive testimony so far as the heathen are concerned; and takes in the whole of this important subject. Are we now, for the sake of such frivolous arguments as have been mentioned, to set aside some of the most important and interesting truths? Far be it.

I now proceed, from the Holy Scriptures themselves, to show, that Moses was the writer of his law. I begin,

First; with the seventeenth chapter of Exodus. In the first battle which the Israelites had with the Amalekites, verse the fourteenth, " The Lord said to Moses, write
" this for a memorial in a book, and rehearse
" it in the ears of Joshua." It does not follow
from

from hence that Moses wrote all his laws. No; but it follows from hence that Moses kept a journal, and that he recorded transactions that happened. But we have more complete and full evidence. Thus, in the twenty-fourth chapter of Exodus, and the fourth verse, "Moses came and told the "people all the words of the Lord, and all the "judgments; and all the people answered, "with one voice, and said, All the words "which the Lord hath said, will we do. "And Moses wrote all the words of the "Lord, and rose up early in the morning, "and builded an altar." This evidently takes in all, from the beginning of the twentieth chapter of Exodus, and comprehends a large extent. Again, in the thirty-fourth of Exodus, and the twenty-seventh verse, "Write thou these words, for after "the tenor of these words, I have made a "covenant with thee and with Israel."

I would observe with respect to the book of Leviticus, which, if any could, upon the principles that have been urged, might be called in question; though not justly; that in
the

the course of this book Moses expresses himself thus, " This is the law of the burnt-offering;" and then gives an account of it. " This is the law of the meat offering;" and then gives an account of it. " This is the law of the sin-offering;" and then gives an account of that. " This is the law of the trespass-offering;" and then gives an account of that. All which you have before the end of the seventh chapter of Leviticus. And when it is said, they were to observe all the laws, and statutes, and judgments, who dares to say that these were not included? Undoubtedly they were.

We have other proofs in the book of Numbers, towards the close; where Moses states his conduct, and that in obedience to God; and asserts that he had written an account of all their journies from the very first to that time. Consult the thirty-third chapter of the book of Numbers, the first and second verses; " These are the journies of the children of " Israel, which went forth out of the land " of Egypt, with their armies, under the " hand of Moses and Aaron. And Moses
" wrote

" wrote their goings out, according to their
" journies, by the commandment of the
" Lord; and thefe are their journies accord-
" ing to their goings out." I do not know
what more decifive evidence there can be.
And the book of Deuteronomy gives us additional inftances, and that too with refpect to
peculiar characters; particularly in the
feventeenth chapter of Deuteronomy; where
he has let them know, that when they came
into the land promifed them, they would
have a king; inftructions are given for his
conduct. " And it fhall be when he fitteth
" upon the throne of his kingdom, that he
" fhall write him a copy of this law in a
" book, out of that which is before the
" priefts, the Levites." That is, the copy
which Mofes himfelf wrote, and delivered to
the priefts and Levites, to put into the place
provided for it at the fide of the Ark. And
other circumftances of this fort are farther
mentioned in the thirty-firft chapter of Deuteronomy, and the twenty-fourth verfe. " And
" it came to pafs when Mofes had made an
" end of writing the words of this law in a
" book, until they were finifhed; that Mofes
                              " commanded

"commanded the Levites, which bare the
"ark of the covenant of the Lord, saying,
"Take this book of the law, and put it in
"the side of the ark of the covenant of the
"Lord your God, that it may be there for
"a witness against thee."

In the first chapter of Joshua we see that the writing was transmitted faithfully to the next generation. Read the seventh and eighth verses, "Only be thou strong and very courageous, "that thou mayest observe to do according to "all the law which Moses my servant com- "manded thee; turn not from it to the right "hand or to the left, that thou mayest prosper "whithersoever thou goest. This book of the "law shall not depart out of thy mouth; but "thou shalt meditate therein day and night, "that thou mayest observe to do according to "all that is written therein." There are other passages in the book of Joshua as full to the purpose, which it would be needless to quote now, as I may have occasion to introduce them hereafter. Only observe, that this same testimony went through future ages and generations, to the times of David, four hundred and eighty years after the Exodus out of Egypt. David thus charged his son Solomon, saying, "I go the way of all the "earth, be strong, therefore, and shew thy- "self a man, and keep the charge of the "Lord thy God, to walk in his ways, as it "is written in the law of Moses." So they went down to the close of Malachi, when the canon of the Old Testament scriptures was finished; I leave you to read it at your leisure, where he refers them to the law of Moses, as written, with the statutes, and with the judgments.

Now then, what must I say to the person who dares to use such language as this, "There is no affirmative evidence that Moses "was the author and writer of these books; "an unfounded opinion that got into the "world no one can tell how." It is singular, that such an opinion should run through all the gentile nations. Their most capital historians bear testimony that Moses did write laws; and those, I would observe, among the Jews. Diodorus Siculus says, "Moses, a "man of great genius, first persuaded the
"people

Lect. 3.   *Evidences of Christianity.*   99

"people to use written laws, and to live by them." And he not only represents his writing of laws, but declares who he was that did so, and publishes it to the world.

But I shall now conclude with a few remarks; which I address to my young Christian friends. Suffer not yourselves to be carried away with unsupported insinuations. Always entertain suspicion when arguments are rested upon the names of ancient cities and titles; things little understood in modern times. They are generally fallacious—they often deceive the man who grounds arguments upon them; and still more effectually betray those that receive arguments against the reality of the Holy Scriptures, founded upon such delusive circumstances. Search for yourselves. Examine the word of God. Are we likely to give up such an important point as this, that Moses wrote his own laws, because of such frivolous objections, in defiance of all the repetitions of the fact by Moses himself, by successive leaders, princes, and kings, to the end of the Jewish dispensation—in opposition to the uniform testimony of all great

H 2    writers,

writers, even of the heathen themselves? Surely it is something like insolence to demand any thing of the kind. Hold fast the truth of God. I have given you sufficient instances of fallacy and deceit; or, of the most gross ignorance, either of which disqualifies the testimony that may be so given.

But again, you need not be surprized, that such an attack should be made upon the books of Moses, for if they are overthrown, the Christian religion must fall of consequence. Indeed, I am sensible, some eminent men have suggested, that the Christian religion will stand, independent of the Jewish dispensation. But I deny this, because it supposes, that in the Christian religion there is no reference to the Jewish dispensation. But who can then vindicate the language of the evangelists, and of the holy apostles? Take away that dispensation, and a cloud of darkness is thrown over the fullest and strongest expressions of the Son of God himself. Take away that dispensation, and the first source of our hope is dried up, and all the prospects of immortality will be destroyed. O, do not suffer yourselves

selves to be beguiled by infinuations of this kind. And here I would obferve, that it is not at all to be wondered at, that men fhould fuggeft, that whatever the other parts of the book of the law of Mofes might be, there are no decifive proofs that Genefis was written by him. There *are* decifive proofs. I have brought them. There is the fame reafon for perfuading you into the non-neceffity of the difpenfation of the Gofpel. Becaufe, take away that book, and the firft fpring of all is gone; nay, the fountain of life, if I may fo fpeak, is fhut up. For it is a part of the conduct of God in his government of the world, and efpecially of the moral world, to act, as at the commencement of the world *itfelf*—out of darknefs he commanded light to arife; from *the* darknefs came all the glories of the day. Out of darknefs and obfcurity he hath brought forth the moft important light and knowledge, with refpect to a future world. And the Chriftian religion, as delivered in the New Teftament, throws back the moft illuftrious beams upon all preceding difpenfations; while, with a never-fading light, it conducts our eyes and our hearts to the fair profpects of a bleffed immortality. You have, undoubtedly, fomething worth contemplating—you have things that are the ground of all morality—of all virtue, if there be fuch a thing as virtue; while, at the fame time, you have to contend for all the great and interefting doctrines that refpect our redemption and eternal life by Jefus Chrift. I may fpeak in the language of a holy apoftle, and fay, " This is the faith formerly contended for " by the faints," and the people of God. Let it be contended for among you. But again.

Let me recommend it to you to open your hearts to conviction every way; to weigh deliberately whatever may be advanced for or againft. Ponder impartially. I am not afraid you fhould ever be injured. Conduct yourfelves with modefty. Do not prefume that you know all things, when the wifeft, perhaps, will find that he knows nothing. He that comes with the moft extenfive knowledge, may end in the greateft ignorance.

May

May I recommend to you what the voice of nature suppposes. And I repeat it again, though it is what men are not now very fond of—may I recommend to you what the voice of nature supposes; humble, solemn, sincere, unreserved prayer to Almighty God, the father of our spirits, the fountain of light and knowledge, that he would be pleased to assist you; and, through his own word, to guide and direct you to the most important truths. "O! "that is to make enthusiasts of us!—that is "to suppose we are to have special and divine "revelations!" Do not credit, as I have said before, bold assertions. I intend no such thing. But this I will repeat again and again: It would be absurd to deny the power and influence of God over the human mind, which we evidently see is pervading the whole of the material world. Are his intelligent creatures the only part of creation that is forsaken by the fountain of goodness and mercy? Surely not. It would be irrational to suppose this. Do we not cry to men for assistance in necessity? does not this vindicate our looking for assistance from God? If we look for aid from the less, surely much more from the greater.

I never heard of a man, whatever his thoughts might be with refpect to the holy Scriptures, but in the extremity of his diftrefs would call upon God for his mercy, to deliver him—to fave him. Then we fee the undifguifed voice of nature. Our eternal happinefs is at ftake. Offer up prayer and fupplication to God, that you may be able to repeat the language of the text, and fay, " We have found him, of " whom Mofes in the law — did write." Amen.

# LECT. IV.*

THE subject for this night, my Christian friends, is this; an attempt to unfold those evidences which tend to shew the truth and reality of the important objects exhibited in that part of the Mosaic Pentateuch, which is called the book of Genesis. In this piece of history there is greater variety of matter, and a detail of more important incidents, than perhaps can be found in any other historical composition; wherein Jews, Gentiles and Christians are alike interested—wherein all mankind have their respective concerns. For, extinguish this book, and we shall lose the first fountains of religion, the sources of history, the commencement of those arts which are of the greatest use to society; as well as

---

* A particular apology is necessary for the inaccuracy and defectiveness of this Lecture. It is the last that Mr. Fell composed and delivered; and it was delivered under the pressure of that bodily infirmity which terminated in his dissolution. Hence his voice sometimes sunk so low that the ear of the short-hand writer could not catch the words. The candid reader will make proper allowance; and will consider this piece not as the fabric, but as the fragments of a great mind.

those

those which are calculated to promote the entertainment and instruction of mankind.

I shall, upon this occasion therefore, select the following passage, as a text, whereon to ground this important subject, which you will find in

PHILIPPIANS IV. first clause of Ver. 8.

" Finally, brethren, whatsoever things are
" true."

If no scheme is proposed, if no labour is exercised in laying the foundation, the superstructure cannot last long. He that builds for duration, must lay deep the basis of his building, otherwise he will come short of his purpose. I apply similar principles to our instruction in every species of knowledge; in every art, in every science. And perhaps in the present time, the rudiments of things are too much neglected; especially those which concern true religion. Hence it is, that men rush into the most important parts of its practice, without being at all acquainted with its first principles. Hence it is, that many things are advanced, which bring no honour to the

prophets

prophets and apostles; but are the occasion of objections groundless and injurious to the characters of the sacred penmen.

Unless men be well acquainted with this book of Genesis, they never can understand the ground and foundation of true religion. Perhaps I ought to beg pardon for so bold an assertion; yet still I am confident of its truth.

In opening the subject I propose to myself two things—only one of which I can overtake this evening.

> First; To consider the general evidences in support of the contents of the book.

> Secondly; To discuss particular evidences connected with particular events, as they present themselves to our view. And,

First; As to the general evidences in support of this book; which, indeed, are of a peculiar kind, and arise out of itself. I would here observe, that the writer himself appears not at all in this piece of history. We have no no such expressions as these, "The Lord spake unto Moses, saying, bid the Patriarchs, or bid Israel, or the children of Israel to do so and so." Nothing of the kind. Nor could it be in the very nature of things. Because all the transactions recorded in the book had passed a considerable number of years before the writer was born: therefore he could take no part in the transactions recorded. This I mention with pleasure, as an important truth. No prejudices derived from the supposed character of the writer can be urged with the least propriety.

I would again take notice of a similar circumstance; which, if it be not, yet ought to be as thoroughly understood. There is not one single instance in the whole book of Genesis, wherein God ever speaks to any one, saying, "Go, speak to such a one—command such an one." No, not one. No one person is ever employed to carry a message, or instructions, or commands from God to others. Moses was the first person that was ever called to this important and arduous task, accompanied with so many difficulties, as are

at

at all times sufficient to press down the soul with grief and anxiety.

I now open to you the true reason why Moses expostulated with God upon this matter, when he was sent to the people of Israel. He never heard of such a thing. He had no conception of such a thing. I grant, indeed, that Moses considered himself early in life as ordained of God to rescue the people of Israel out of Egypt. And when he slew the Egyptian, as it is expressed in the seventh chapter of the Acts of the Apostles, he thought they would have understood that God meant to deliver them by his hand. So he did. But Moses never dreamed of being employed to carry a message, either to Pharaoh, or to the elders of Israel. It was altogether unprecedented. Read the account at your leisure—compare it with the contents of this book. Suffer me to make a remark upon it, which I consider of very great moment. Two thousand four hundred years elapsed, before God ever employed any man to carry a message from him to other men. And yet there was religion in the world during all this space of time.

time. God was worshipped—God was feared —God was trusted—God was honoured. My friends, through this whole duration, I defy any man to say, and bring a proof of his saying, that religion was the invention of priests, together with the collusion of oracles, and to be considered as the tricks of that class of men. No such thing can be affirmed. No one instance can be adduced. No circumstance of the kind can be laid hold of. Religion sprang up in the world, or, if you prefer the expression, was introduced into the world, under the common government and providence of God; without force, without effort. All we can say of the matter, *it is* there. And in this book we have the first rudiments of religion as practised among the Gentile nations, through the various scenes of idolatry. I do not speak as to the objects of worship, but as to the rites themselves. We have no examples of a combination to force men to be holy and good against their inclinations. No; what God chose to communicate during this lengthened period of time, was to individuals; and it concerned the individuals themselves; and seldom went farther
than

than to their children and defcendants; and to them only as a matter of choice and of approbation. I fay again, it is all clamour, it is all falfe reprefentation, which has fo often beguiled the minds of uninftructed perfons, that the priefts were the inventors of religion, and of the worfhip of God. You may fee for yourfelves. You may examine for yourfelves upon this occafion. And it is worth your while to do fo. But again:

In no one part of this book does the facred penman ever attempt to introduce any evidence, any direct proof of the truth of what he fays. Indeed, it would have been abfurd. I am not, my brethren, talking paradoxes. The evidences arofe out of the very contents of the book. And you will forgive me when I affert, that the facts recorded in this book, were as well known, for the moft part, to the whole world, as they were to the writer. It would have been foreign to his purpofe, therefore, to have introduced evidences, and to have urged them in form. It could have anfwered no end. Perhaps I may be confidered as fingular in this affertion. I fhall here

here then more immediately enter into the general proofs. And you will give me leave thus to reason—That Noah, and his three sons, must have obtained exact and decisive information with respect to what happened at the commencement of things—at the commencement of this world—at the commencement of human life—Under the first state of mankind, they were the most competent to report the occurrences in the world before the flood; at least, to give a general representation of them, without entering into a detail of particulars. They knew what they said when they asserted the necessity of sacrifices—of a divine worship—when they recorded the testimonies of approbation from God. They knew what they said when they gave a representation of the manners and characters of leading men before the flood—of the commencement and progress of arts, which are particularly mentioned. Noah himself was a striking example of this kind of knowledge; and his sons could not be destitute of the same knowledge. Methuselah was contemporary with Adam for several hundred years, and died not long before the flood. Therefore, I say
again,

### Lect. 4. *Evidences of Christianity.* 113

again, Noah and his sons were undoubtedly competent to judge of the facts which they handed down to their posterity, and which are recorded in the book of Genesis. Perhaps this will be admitted, and the rather, that we are not supposed to have so much concern in the transactions of men before the flood as in those which followed it. But with respect to this point, I am of another mind. However, I accept of the concession— greater attention *may* perhaps be due to the transactions which followed the flood, among the descendants of Noah. Then I must reason in this manner. Fix upon individual persons, and take specific dates. I would observe, that according to the order of narration in this book, Shem and his descendants lived together in the upper part of Mesopotamia, near those districts which run up to Armenia, and to those tracts which are at no great distance from where the ark rested; for such is the description of the places specified in the history, if we trace them as we should. And it is clear that the patriarchs were very attentive to all those incidents which led their minds to the coming of the promised seed;

I and

and which made a grand and capital figure in the progress of mankind. God said to Noah, "I, even I, do cut off the world with a flood; "but my covenant will I establish with thee." What covenant? He had made none with Noah. He had made no promise to Noah at that time of any covenant—he had entered into no agreement with the patriarch. No other covenant or promise could be understood than this, "that the seed of the woman "should bruise the head of the serpent." That covenant must fail, if all mankind were cut off—that covenant must stand, if Noah and his sons were saved. Hence we see that Noah himself propagated among his sons the expectation of this great blessing. And even in the tenth chapter of Genesis, particular notice is taken of Shem, as the father of all the children of Edom—of those that were more immediately interested in the covenant.

Now, I suppose, that these holy patriarchs lived together for a considerable time—came not into the plains of Shinar, nor into the borders of Babylon, nor had any thing to do with that extraordinary undertaking; and that they

they continued together till the days of Abraham.

Here then, I muſt again obſerve; Abraham was born three hundred and fifty-two years after the flood. He lived ſeventy years among his own kindred and anceſtors. He then left his kindred and his country, and went into a land he knew not where, which God was to point out to him, and which he afterwards found. He truſted the promiſe that a numerous offspring ſhould deſcend from him, though as yet he had no child; and that ſuch a particular country ſhould be aſſigned to that offspring, by the righteous governor of the world, and be bleſſed with his more particular and ſpecial preſence. In connexion with this we muſt conſider the hiſtory of Abraham. Iſaac was born four hundred and fifty-two years after the flood. Here we muſt fix our dates. Noah died three hundred and fifty years after the flood; that is, only two years before the birth of Abraham. Shem died five hundred and two years after the flood; that is, about the fifty-third year of Iſaac. Eber died five hundred and thirty-one

one years after the flood; about the eighty-fourth year of the age of Isaac, and the twenty-fourth of Jacob, and Esau; so long was the life of that patriarch extended, to nearly ten years after the death of Abraham; and he lived some hundreds of years along with Shem, and therefore was competent, as a witness; and was eighty years contemporary with Isaac; and there can be no doubt that they must have had many interviews, from a variety of circumstances which might be mentioned.

Now then, I say, with respect to the particulars related in the book of Genesis, subsequent to the flood, they may be stated thus: As to the persons between that period and Moses, Eber lived   \*    \*    and Moses himself   \*    \*    I know of no records respecting the affairs of Europe that can pretend to such transactions as these do.

But I observe farther; if things were so minutely observed, on account of the length

---

\* Mr. Fell's statement of the facts is for ever lost.

of their age, in the family of Shem; they were not lefs fo among the defcendants of Ham, nor among the defcendants of Japhet. In all their various collateral branches, even to * * * * which were the defcendants of Shem's fecond fon. And we find, that the defcendants of Shem particularly were eminent for marking events. Thus Eber called his fon Peleg, "becaufe in his days "the earth was divided," which was an hundred and one years after the flood. There muft be the fame kind of knowledge among all other nations as among the defcendants of Abraham, as intimate and as exact. It would have been in vain for Mofes to have attempted any deception. Here he could not have fucceeded, but muft have been detected at once. The very Egyptians would have been the firft to have done it, who defcended from Ham, by his fon Mizraim, and who perhaps might think themfelves marked out in an unfriendly manner, and excluded from a fhare in that promife, which made a great and extenfive * * * *.

But I would still farther observe upon this head; that I have no reason to suppose that the ancient patriarchs did not keep records, or that there were no writings in those days. I believe that writing was made use of long before the days of Moses. Moses himself glances at a common practice, that of writing upon stones; and commands Joshua after he should be dead, and the people should have crossed the Jordan, to erect an heap of stones, and upon them to write certain laws. For my own part, I suppose there were engravings upon the heap of stones, set up to denote the covenant made between Laban and Jacob; and I am disposed to think, that the pillar which Jacob anointed had an inscription upon it, at least, this word, BETHEL, the house of God; and that from hence arose the custom among the Phenicians of erecting pillars, which they called * * * * a very little variation from the term Bethel. All these things clearly prove, that Moses could have no thought of deceiving. He had no visible end in view. It could answer no purpose to him. It could make no alteration with respect to preceding events. And he was well aware of the exact

know-

knowledge which the rest of the world had of the facts he recorded. And he has given us frequent intimations that he wrote under a consciousness that others understood the Scriptures as well as himself. I will produce some instances. " Tubal Cain's sister was " named Naamah." This is all that is said. It has afforded ground for various conjectures among learned men, none of which are worth mentioning. Her history was well known— all the peculiarities of her character were understood in those times. It was needless for Moses to say more, and it might be proper to observe so much; for we find he is never fond of deviating into subjects which are not interesting in themselves, and which afford no advantage with respect to future times. We have the same things said after the flood. Speaking of Nimrod, " Therefore," it is said, "Nimrod was a mighty hunter " before the Lord." This was given as a proverb. The circumstances of his character, pointed out by the proverb, were then well known—all nations understood the things thus intimated. More was not necessary. Moses wrote under an extensive knowledge of

the

the times. Indeed, the same thing occurs with respect to the history of Abraham himself, at least of Sarah. It is supposed, that Sarah is a name by which she was known in Ur of the Chaldees, among her ancestors; and which glanced undoubtedly at some peculiar circumstances of her history. More was not requisite. There are, as I think, in the thirty-sixth chapter of Genesis, two very remarkable instances where Moses writes in a full consciousness how well the men of his times, understood the history of the facts which he was recording. "This is that " Anah which found the mules in the wil- " derness, as he fed the asses of Zibeon his " father." We understand not these things, but they were undoubtedly well known in those times. Some read the passage now quoted, " he found mules;" thus, " This is " that Anah who found hot-baths, or warm " springs in the wilderness;" or " This is " that Anah who found giants in the wilder- " ness, and of himself cut them off." Or again, " This is that Anah who found the plant " Jemma." What this plant was—what were its excellent properties, as they are not

indi-

indicated, who can tell? And yet I am inclined to fuppofe, that this is neareft to the true fenfe of the paffage. The thing was well underftood in thofe times. At the clofe of the fame chapter, fpeaking of the kings who reigned in Edom, he fays, "Baal-Hanan died, and "Hadar reigned in his ftead, and his wife's "name was Mehetabel, the daughter of Ma- "tred." Who thofe perfons were we cannot tell. She muft have been of a renowned character, elfe fhe would not thus have been mentioned. Her character was then well known, and therefore farther particulars are not given.

I mention thefe things only to fhow that Mofes wrote with a confcioufnefs how wellinformed the world was, with refpect to the things which he delivered. Now give me leave to bring thefe matters home. I have already afked, could not Noah and his fons give a fufficient and authentic account with refpect to the tranfactions before the flood? Could not Noah and his defcendants give as exact an account of the tranfactions that followed the flood? Mofes in the tenth of Genefis, nesis, has marked out the limits of every nation then in the known world; limits which continue to this day; and which have been pointed out by great and eminent men. Any nation would have corrected him had he been mistaken. Many nations would have rejoiced to have done it, had he committed any error. Could they not inform us, that at such a time the earth was divided, when Eber called the name of his son, " Peleg, for " in his days was the earth divided." By the division of the earth I understand the allotments of the different parts of the then known world among the descendants of Shem. By the division of the earth, I do not understand the dispersion at the building of Babel; that was another thing; and I suppose, could not be less than above an hundred years after the former. The earth is spoken of as very distinct and different. Could not they tell as well as Moses, and Moses as well as they, who were the founders of such and such cities, and such states; who were the law-givers of such states; what was the commencement of history in such countries? These were things in which the whole world was concerned.

These

These things bear some relation to our own capacities as rational beings; nor should we think of charging Moses with absurdity, of which he was never guilty.

I will now take notice of a few things with respect to religion. Was Moses the inventor of offering the firstlings of the flock, and the fat thereof to God? No; this was practised before the flood. Was Moses the person who first drew the line between beasts clean and unclean; and birds clean and unclean? No; God himself enumerates them in general to Noah, previously to his entering into the ark. Was Moses the author of erecting altars? No; the first we ever read of was set up by Noah. Was it Moses who forbad the eating of blood? No; it was handed down to him in a regular progression through the posterity of Noah. Was Moses the author of consecrating such and such things to God, by pouring out oil and otherwise? No; Jacob set the example when he consecrated a place to God with oil, and called it Beth-el. Was Moses the author of the custom of paying tythes? No; Abraham gave tythes of the spoil to Melchisedech.

Jacob

Jacob vowed the tenth of all that he should acquire to God; and he laid the foundation of that custom. Was Moses the inventor of the distinctions which respected marriage, and were they peculiar to that dispensation? No; they were found and practised among the Pagans. Was Moses the inventor of that odious rite, and so very singular in itself, circumcision? No; it was practised by several nations before the birth of Moses. Why then should Moses be loaded with all the supposed religious absurdities that can be collected together?

Now I call upon the advocates of natural religion to ascertain what they mean by natural religion. Whether or not does it include the offering of sacrifice? The ancient heathen connected sacrifices with religion. They made that a part of natural religion, and attributed the practice to the instruction of their gods. It does not belong to Jews particularly, it does not belong to Christians particularly, to account for these things. It belongs to men of all nations, to men of all persuasions. Then let us not deceive ourselves.

Now

Now I wish to state the objection as fairly as it lies in my power. I will suppose it to run in some such manner as this. Perhaps, sir, what you have said with respect to the commencement of religion, kingdoms, arts, sciences, &c. even down through the lives of the patriarchs themselves, may be true.

But some one will say, "What say you " to this? Here is an odd circumstance,— " such a man as Abraham, pretending to " divine communications, taking it into his " head to leave his country and kindred, " supposing that God would give him some " land he knew not where."

Now I would speak, my friends, with all honesty upon this head. So far as I know myself, and the modes of reasoning I have been accustomed to in private investigation; it is most likely I should have said, that Abraham was a man of a singular turn of mind—there was something odd in his head, and peculiar to the family. I doubt not that the world thought so. He and Lot both
left

left their country in queft of a foreign land, where they propofed only to dwell as ftrangers and fojourners; vainly hoping, I would fay, that God would put their pofterity into the poffeffion of it. And they kept up this idle pretence for about four hundred years. I fhould have faid, had I lived in thofe days, "It is a ftrange affair." And perhaps fhould have admired the conduct of Pharaoh, who received with fo much calmnefs Jacob's anfwer to a fimple queftion, ". How old art thou?" "The days of the "years of my pilgrimage are an hundred "and thirty, and I have not yet attained "unto the days of the years of the life of "my fathers." Perhaps I fhould have faid, Pharaoh acted like a gentleman. He refpected Jofeph, and took no farther notice—he knew the man and his family, and was well acquainted with all the defcendants of Heber; both thofe who lived in the eaft, from whence Balaam came; as well as thofe few wanderers who ftraggled about the land of Canaan. He paffed the matter by as a gentleman. Probably I might have thought in this manner. But what fhould I have done in the

iffue,

issue, had God given me the life of Methuselah, and I had lived to see all the power of heaven awake to bring the people out of Egypt—to lead them and to feed them in desart and barren lands; and at length, give reality to all their dreams, by putting them into the possession of the land they so often spake of. This issue, my brethren, forbids me to treat any part of their history with ridicule or contempt. The facts are before you. Reason upon them as much as you please. I will grant all your reasoning. If nothing be fallacious, then there must be a foundation for it.

But I have another circumstance to open, and with it I shall draw to a conclusion. It is this. I have taken notice of the prediction that " the seed of the woman shall bruise the " head of the serpent." This must at last terminate in some particular family. We see how reserved Scripture is on the subject. No mention of it is made before the flood: nor is it limited to any nation. Nor till three hundred years and more after the flood was it first intimated to Abraham, who doubtless
bore

bore the reproach, and his fon and grandfon bore the reproach, as did their defcendants, of appropriating it to themfelves: which made the writer of the Epiftle to the Hebrews look back when he uttered that expreffive fentence, " Wherefore God was not afhamed to be " called their God, for he hath prepared for " them a city." Now tell me how this could have been done in a gentler way. Abraham, while he talks about his communications from God; and the covenant God had entered into with him;—forced not other men to receive his religion. He did not come pretending meffages from God to other men; never once. I repeat it, never once. Hence we fee all open, all clear, all without effort; and we can affign no other reafon for fuch events than the immediate interpofition of a divine Providence; otherwife they could never have reached our ears, much lefs have been left upon record.

But I would obferve farther, this led the way, by degrees, to other great and interefting changes. Difputes arofe among the heads of the holy families themfelves, on
account

Lect. 4. *Evidences of Christianity.* 129
account of the promised seed. Hence the enmity between the Moabites and the descendants of Jacob; between the Amorites and the descendants of Jacob; between the Edomites, the offspring of Esau, and the descendants of Jacob; between the Ishmaelites and the descendants of Jacob. They all maintained their share in this promise, and were not willing to be excluded. Do not you perceive how this operated in keeping up the most decisive evidences in support of the truth? Their mutual jealousies forced them all to be faithful in their records, and in what they published to the world. Let us discuss these things in the light of divine truth, and see the hand of God through all; and attend to the openings of true Religion through these events. I consider myself as having only entered upon its surface. I conclude with a short improvement.

First, We see clearly that religion was not the invention of men—not originally forced upon the world by any human art—that it carries all the marks of divine authority. And is it nothing to alledge in its support, that

that even false religions, through all their corruptions, as found among the gentile nations, are to be traced from the first traditions hence derived, and handed down to their posterity. True religion is not obliged to account for those corruptions, which are the result of human passions. By no means. The nations ceased to be so exact in their records after the people of Israel came out of Egypt. And we see this circumstance affected all the patriarchs. It naturally begat silence, where they could not refute; and hence we may trace out a variety of other occurrences in the world.

Further, I hope, my young friends, you will perceive the necessity of reading, of sifting the word of God—of trying it—of bringing it to the light of your own minds—of doing the same justice to it that you would to other books—of examining without prejudice. It is a great misfortune when men sit down, particularly to the sacred Scriptures, not with any view to be convinced, but if possible to find something through which to attack those holy books. Let all such things

things be removed from your minds. May you find the seed of the woman to your everlasting happiness. Through him may you discern the destruction of death, and the discovery of an immortal life. Through him may you be enabled to collect all the lines, in their various and nice dependencies, which run through the whole of the sacred Scriptures till they terminate in the New Testament! May light open gradually upon your understandings, as it did upon the world with respect to those great and wonderful things. While you are zealous to maintain the truth of the Scriptures, put this question to yourselves, " What advantage is it to me if the " Scriptures be true? What objects do I pro- " pose by maintaining their authority? Have I " any interest at stake?" Ah, my friends! the greatest interest: That interest, without which your very beings could not be a blessing: That interest, without which all your hopes must be swept away: That interest, without which every thing beyond the grave must be awful and horrid darkness, while we are in the present state: An interest which, if lost, we are robbed of every comfort—of every confolation—of every joy—of every peace.—May you find, and bind it to your hearts, and live for ever in the fight of God! Amen.

*This was Mr. Fell's folemn farewell to the world.*

# LECT. V.

### Luke i. 1—4.

*Forasmuch as many have taken in hand to set forth in order a declaration of those things which are most surely believed among us,*

*Even as they delivered them unto us which from the beginning were eyewitnesses, and ministers of the word:*

*It seemed good to me also, having had perfect understanding of all things from the very first, to write unto thee in order, most excellent Theophilus,*

*That thou mightest know the certainty of those things wherein thou hast been instructed.*

THERE are subjects of which a man may be innocently ignorant; and there are others with which he must be acquainted at his peril. Every one is not obliged to be a mathematician, nor to cultivate a taste for music, for painting, or for poetry. Many are born with a total incapacity to acquire those

those sciences, as some are born blind, some deaf and dumb. But an indispensable necessity is laid on all men to study, to know, and to practise morals and religion, and all are endowed with the capacity of attaining proficiency in these. In some cases a vague, partial, defective knowledge may serve the turn; and there may be, and frequently is, very accurate and extensive knowledge, laid up, like so much useless treasure, to be only occasionally displayed and reckoned over, but never turned to any good account. But in matters of duty toward God, our fellow-creatures, and ourselves, knowledge must be clear and distinct, and it must have a constant and a commanding influence upon the heart and life. Morality and religion are in their nature so closely interwoven, that every attempt at separation, aims at destroying the whole texture. Morality is the well-organized body, and religion the quickening spirit. Morality is religion brought down to the perception of sense, and religion is morality sublimated into pure intellect. Nevertheless what God has thus intimately joined together, man is too frequently endeavouring, with impious hand,

Lect. 5.  *Evidences of Christianity.*  135

hand, to tear asunder; and the effort ever did, and ever will, produce infinite mischief. A religion without morality formerly kindled fires in Smithfield, and burnt the bodies of men to ashes for harmless, often for well-founded, opinions. A morality which affects to supersede religion is a well-constructed time-piece from which the main-spring has been withdrawn, or which hastens to a state of rest for want of being wound up. It contracts the period of human existence, it narrows the sphere of human usefulness, it diminishes the sum of human happiness.

We assume it, therefore, as an axiom, a primary, self-evident truth, that to such a being as man, a moral rectitude, animated by a religious principle, is of essential importance. He may want, or he may lose an arm or an eye; he may be slow of speech, dull in apprehension, of cold affections, have an unretentive memory, yet still be a man, and good, and happy; but withhold or extinguish the principle of conscience, and the *man* is annihilated.

K 4  But

But where are we to search for this precious treasure, destitute of which man is poor indeed? "Where shall this wisdom be found, "and where is the place of understanding? "The depth saith, It is not in me; and the "sea saith, It is not with me. It cannot be "gotten for gold, neither shall silver be "weighed for the price thereof:"—" It is "not hidden from thee, neither is it far off. "It is not in heaven that thou shouldst say, "Who shall go up for us to Heaven, and "bring it unto us, that we may hear it, and "do it? Neither is it beyond the sea, that "thou shouldst say, Who shall go over the "sea for us, and bring it unto us, that we "may hear it, and do it? But the word "is very nigh unto thee, in thy mouth, and "in thy heart, that thou mayest do it." Every man *has* this treasure, *is* this treasure, in himself. To unfold to a man what he is, what he wants, what he ought to be, what he may become, is to furnish him with the completest evidence which can be given of the truth, importance, and divine origin of the religion of Jesus Christ: and such is the nature of the evidence which we mean to adduce

adduce in the course of the following Lectures.

Christianity, as an appeal to the understanding of mankind, has triumphed over all opposition, and is established upon " a rock " against which the gates of hell shall never " prevail." If there be still infidels in the world, it is not that the proofs of the gospel are either feeble, or few in number; it is because the spirit of this world is predominant, it is because habits of acting wrong have been unhappily acquired. " This is " the condemnation, that light is come into " the world, but men love darkness rather " than light, because their deeds are evil. " For every one that doth evil hateth the " light, neither cometh to the light, lest his " deeds should be reproved." If, therefore, the influence of a present world could be moderated, and the powers of the world to come impressed; if men could be persuaded that it is their highest interest to subdue their corrupt affections and forsake their vices; that by " doing the will of God, they shall know " of the doctrine, whether it be of God," then

every

every purpose of this institution were fully answered, then a service acceptable to God and beneficial to man shall be rendered, and we shall enjoy mutual satisfaction in having made the attempt, and in contemplating the success of it.

In this awful undertaking I engage with fear and trembling. I feel the ashes of my departed friend yet stirring under my feet. I behold his labours arrested by the hand of death. I feel my own strength how small, my charge how weighty. I hear an Apostle exclaim, " And who is sufficient for these " things?" But another voice cries, " Fear " not, thou worm Jacob, for I am with thee: " be not dismayed for I am thy God: I will " strengthen thee; yea I will help thee; yea " I will uphold thee with the right hand " of my righteousness." If the Lord give the word, as he did to Cyrus, for the purpose of a temporal deliverance to his church, " the " two-leaved gates shall open before him, " the crooked places shall be made straight, " the gates of brass shall be broken, and the " bars of iron shall be cut in sunder."

It

It is impossible accurately to clafs the perfons who may find themfelves difpofed to give attendance on fuch occafions as thefe, nor is it needful. There is a goodly proportion, we truft, who have actually attained what the Evangelift in the text, propofes to communicate, the knowledge of " the cer- " tainty of the things wherein they have " been inftructed," and who are holding " the beginning of their confidence ftedfaft " unto the end." There may be others who, it is to be feared, have been inftructed in the truth as it is in Jefus, have admitted it without fcruple, without enquiry, and never ferioufly believed, becaufe they took every thing for granted. How many have " a name to live " and are dead," hold " the truth in un- " righteoufnefs," attempt to eftablifh an impracticable union between Chrift and Belial, Chrift and Mammon, Chrift and Moloch? There is a lukewarm tribe, continually halting between two opinions, living and dying in a ftate of indifference and indecifion, and a tribe, ftill more numerous, that of the idle, of the curious, who muft at any rate get rid of that heavy commodity, their time; and, incapable

of

of difpofing of it in wholefale, find themfelves reduced to a petty traffic in variety. Thefe hunt after novelty, however frivolous, while it is a novelty, and abandon it, however ufeful, interefting and important, as foon as that charm is loft. Determined, inveterate enemies of the gofpel do not frequent places of public worfhip, and have given over reading the Scriptures, except in the view of finding food for their fpleen and malevolence, and therefore may be confidered as having no place in this enumeration: but there is a clafs which prefented itfelf to my mind, the moment that the idea of fuch a lecture was fuggefted, and which, in the profecution of it, engroffes almoft all my thoughts: it is the clafs of ingenuous, well-defcended, well-difpofed, well-inftructed youth, entering on the perilous voyage of life, in a diffipated age, in a corrupted metropolis, where the fyren fong is heard at the corner of every ftreet, and Circe's ftupifying cup is conftantly replenifhed from a thoufand fountains. Have youthful modefty, fimplicity, candor, fenfe of fhame, fenfe of duty, been preferved? O how defirable to tranfmit thefe amiable qualities

qualities unimpaired, improved, into the maturity of manhood, the purfuits of active public or private life, and the dignified tranquillity of refpectable old age. Has the tempter deceived, has the young heart been betrayed, and made to tafte the bitternefs of fhame, of remorfe? O how defirable to extricate the thoughtlefs bird from the fnare of the fowler, to prevent inconfiderate error from degenerating into habits of vice, to reftore compofure to the troubled confcience, and confidence to the abafhed countenance. If we cannot melt, convince, reclaim the hoary libertine and unbeliever himfelf, we will at leaft difpute with him the poffeffion of yet unpoifoned minds, yet undegraded faculties, yet unperverted powers. This is the arduous purpofe which we have formed. And with what armour are we furnifhed for the accomplifhment of it? " The weapons of our war-" fare are not carnal." We mean to make a fimple appeal to your hearts and confciences, in behalf of the religion of Jefus Chrift. Without giving up one iota of the external evidence of Chriftianity, confifting of the diftinct accomplifhment of innumerable ancient predictions

refpect-respecting the person, character, offices, actions, sufferings and death of Jesus of Nazareth; and of the performance of innumerable miracles by himself and his apostles, which were as certainly wrought as any other facts transmitted to us through the channel of history, we mean to take up Christianity as it is, and as it must appear to every candid enquirer, and to attempt a demonstration of the following propositions, in so many successive discourses:

1. That the religion of Jesus Christ is entirely conformable to all the ideas of Deity which we are enabled to form by the exercise of our own reason, on a serious contemplation of the great universe; in other words, that it is the true, and only, religion of nature:

2. That it is universally congenial to the constitution and frame of the human mind:

3. That it is most happily adapted to the feelings, necessities and expectations of the human heart, at every successive stage of man's existence:

4. That

4. That it is our most infallible guide, and our securest guard, amidst all the vicissitudes of this transitory life:

5. That it is the strongest and sweetest cement of human society:

6. That it is the only satisfactory interpretation of the mystery of Providence: and

7. That it constitutes the grand proof of immortality, and exhibits the only rational display of a life to come.

If these things should be, I will not say demonstrated, but rendered probable, presumable; should but a few of these good effects, and in an inferior degree, appear to be produced by the gospel, surely malignity must be disarmed, and a little credit given to Christianity, for the little good it does, though not to the full extent of its pretensions. Nay, supposing us totally to fail in our attempt; supposing no one of our positions made good, and that none of those benefits have resulted, or are likely to result from the belief and reception

ception of Christianity, we have still one modest plea to urge with its opposers. Why, what harm hath it done, or is it likely to do? Why hate the thing you affect to despise? Why this rancorous opposition to what were more effectually crushed by neglect? Why form cabals to run it down, when you have only to let it alone, and waste itself? Does not this zeal to subvert the religion of Jesus, excite suspicion, and betray a consciousness on your part, that there is more in it than you are willing to avow?—But this is only scattering words in the desert air. Persons of this description we commend, with a prayer of earnest heart, to the great Teacher who is able to remove mountains of prejudice, that he would open their eyes, and soften their hearts; and bestow on them the consolations of that religion which they now set at nought.

Permit me now, my young friends, whose improvement I have much at heart, and of whom my expectations are most sanguine, permit me to request your patient and candid attention, to what shall be addressed to you, I trust in the spirit of love, if not of power;

power; confult your own hearts, follow the dictates of your confciences, but be diffident of your own underftanding. Neither admit haftily, nor yield flowly and reluctantly. Affect not to know and to feel what you are either wholly ignorant of, know imperfectly, or feel only through the medium of prepoffeffion. The truth which you do know, and the power of which you really feel, neither be afraid nor afhamed modeftly to acknowledge and declare.

I will endeavour, in the fequel of this difcourfe, from the paffage which I have read, to remove fome difficulties which are defignedly thrown in the way of young minds, to prejudice them againft the gofpel.

It's minifters, they are told, make a trade of it; they have an intereft in its extenfion, as being fubfervient to the attainment of fame, or wealth, or power, or all the three. It is faid that the credit of the clerical order is their common aim, and their great bond of union. Our Evangelift was not a prieft, but a man of a liberal profeffion, and a profeffion in no age or country fufpected of a violent propenfity toward religion. He is Luke the beloved phyfician, in other words, a man of erudition, of obfervation, of refearch, of experience. What worldly intereft could he ferve, what reputation was he going to acquire, by writing the hiftory of the carpenter's fon, and of his motley retinue, compofed of publicans, fifhermen, fhepherds, and the other refufe of Galilee? Was he in the way to extend his practice, and increafe his gain, by rambling over the cities of Afia in the train of an apoftate pharifee, who lived on the produce of his labour in the occupation of a tent-maker? What fufpicion of felfifhnefs, of party-fpirit, of enthufiafm, can fix upon a man who devoted his time, his talents, to the inveftigation of facts which he felt to be important to himfelf, and deemed to be important to mankind, in the view of publifhing them to the world as an univerfal benefit? And in the fame fpirit, I would afk infidelity at this day, Whether the Chriftian miniftry be upon the whole a lucrative profeffion? A few fplendid beneficiaries excepted, who among us might not have done as well, or better, in the worldly fenfe of the word, in fome some one of the ten thousand channels which trade and commerce open to the exercise of avarice and ambition? Might not the same education, with the same talents, have raised us, with some of our fellow students, to distinction and affluence in medicine, at the bar, on the bench, in the senate? And does the Christian priesthood always draw together, like men embarked on the same bottom, and resolutely disposed to support each other to the last extremity? In what order of mankind do we find such diversity of opinion, such collision of interest, such contrariety of spirit and pursuit? The wonder is not, that Christianity should be a great, a popular, a flourishing cause, through the zeal, union and co-operation of its ministers; the miracle is, and it is by no means the weakest part of its external evidence, that Christianity should be a cause at all, considering the alienation, disunion, opposition of those who teach it; considering the estimation in which their persons and profession are generally held, and the vow of poverty which, voluntarily or involuntarily, the generality of them must make. When therefore you hear, young man, of the Christian priesthood as a well-compacted phalanx, engaged to maintain a cause feeble in itself, by harmony and mutual support, believe it not, for the reverse is the truth. It is the strength of the cause which sustains their feebleness, and counteracts their discord and mutual opposition. But when, on the other hand, you hear of their manifold infirmities, when you are told that they are " men of " like passions with yourselves," believe it, for it is most deplorably true. Nevertheless even in this admire the wisdom of the great Supreme, whose ordinance it is, that " we " should have this treasure in earthen vessels, " that the excellency of the power might be " of God, and not of us."

Again, it is insinuated, that Christianity was originally the fond persuasion merely of untutored and credulous minds, who admitted facts for their strangeness, doctrines for their novelty, and practices from an affectation of singularity, and the spirit of contradiction; and that it stole in upon the world, while the wise and prudent slumbered and slept. Quite the contrary. What was performed on one of the moſt public theatres of the globe, before multitudes of ſpectators of every poſſible deſcription, many undertook to record on the very ſpot, at the very moment, while the events were ſtill freſh, and where the facts were notorious. Before Luke ſat down to write, " many had taken in hand to ſet forth " in order a declaration of things" well known among their neighbours, and " moſt' " ſurely believed among them." Theſe ſeveral " declarations" could eaſily be compared, and their harmony or inconſiſtency inſtantly diſcovered, by every one who read or heard. The ſlighteſt deviation from truth could have been at once detected and contradicted. Beſides, theſe " declarations" were not a diſplay of novel and uncommon opinions, but a detail of ſimple facts. In detailing matters of opinion, the imagination of the writer may give a colouring not perfectly conformable to truth, his memory may be unfaithful, there may be a contrary bias on his underſtanding; but in recording matters of fact, the appeal is made immediately to the eye and the ear, and the moſt illiterate peaſant is in every reſpect as competent a judge as the moſt profound philoſopher.

losopher. Was Herod slumbering and sleeping when, alarmed at the idea of Christ's arrival, "he sent forth and slew all the children "that were in Bethlehem, and in all the "coasts thereof?" Were the scribes and pharisees asleep when they attended the footsteps of Jesus as spies, " watching him, whether " he would heal on the sabbath-day; that they " might find an accusation against him?" or when they laid wait " for him, seeking to " catch something out of his mouth," which they might turn to his disadvantage? or when they sent their disciples, with the Herodians " to entangle him in his talk?" Was Pontius Pilate asleep when he received an accusation against him, sat in judgment upon him, condemned him to the death of the cross? And were the ministers of justice asleep when they executed this dreadful sentence? No, the world was alive and awake to every transaction, and exerted all its power, cunning and malignity to quash Christianity in the bud. The gospel did not take advantage of carelessness and credulity, but had to fight its way in the face of vigilance, envy and hatred. And did our Evangelist execute the task which

he

he had undertaken in a superficial and slovenly manner? Let the work speak for itself. He goes to the fountain-head; weighs, compares his authorities; resorts to those "which from "the beginning were eye-witnesses, and mi- "nisters of the word:" he satisfies himself with nothing short of "a perfect understand- "ing of all things from the very first," that he might detail them in due order. Without affectation of eloquence, without pomp of expression, he unfolds matters of the highest moment with all the simplicity of a child, and having modestly introduced himself, in this short preface, immediately withdraws, and appears again no more; filled with the majesty of his subject, he loses sight of himself.

Again, the religion of Jesus has been represented as tolerably adapted, perhaps, to the herd of mankind, to the apprehension and use of persons of vulgar understandings, and in a low condition, but altogether unworthy of the regard of cultivated minds, in eminent stations: and young men of the higher order, in respect of talents, rank and refinement, have been misled by a conceit that it betrayed a want of intellect,

tellect, that it was derogatory from dignity, to think and believe with the multitude. As if there were a separate system of nature, and a different standard of truth, and a distinct code of morality, for the learned and the illiterate, for the noble and the ignoble, for the servant and his master. Here is one decorated with the most splendid ascription of human greatness, who has been instructed in the truths of the Christian religion, and who does not seem to be ashamed of it; else Luke would hardly have presumed to obtrude upon him another volume on the subject, and follow it up with another still, in continuation. The *most excellent* Theophilus, whether he inherited that high distinction from his ancestors, or had acquired it by merit; whether it were a personal title, or an appendage of office; whether it denoted mental or ministerial superiority, the most excellent Theophilus, I say, did not deem his excellency disgraced or diminished, by becoming a disciple in the school of the despised Galilean, by receiving farther and more full information, respecting " the things in which he had been instructed," that his doubts might be resolved, that his
mind

mind might settle on a sure foundation, and his soul be filled with "peace and joy in believing." We would not for a single moment suffer it to be imagined that religion, especially the religion of the gospel, can derive any lustre, authenticity, or importance from the quality, the genius, or the celebrity of those who profess it. No, it is of a nature to confer, not to borrow respectability. But when we find in every age of the Christian church, first-rate characters, in every estimable respect, embracing, maintaining, promoting it, and glorying in it, the conclusion cannot be considered as extremely arrogant, that it is not totally destitute of a foundation; that it is not so very irrational and absurd, as some of the strong spirits of the day would represent it. Without recurring to ages very remote, or leaving our own island, might it not be asked, Whether a faith adopted, prized, recommended, illustrated, enforced by an Isaac Newton, a Robert Boyle, a John Locke, a Joseph Addison, a Lord Littleton, not one of them a priest, did not present itself with something like evidence? and whether it would not become our apprenticed philosophers, before

fore they exchange the Bible for the Age of Reason, to give the Bible a fair hearing, and not reject it in the lump, on the authority of one who modestly pretends to blot it out at a dash, from memory, without having refreshed his recollection by turning it over for nineteen or twenty years.

Once more, the idea of arriving at certainty in matters of religion has been derided; and the evidence of the most authentic truths has been represented as amounting to a peradventure at most; and unexperienced minds have been discouraged from pursuing enquiry, from the supposed impossibility of arriving at discovery. Hence they become easily satisfied, and, because they cannot attain every thing, are without much difficulty persuaded to attempt nothing. Indeed this censure applies not to religion only, but to every object of pursuit which calls for exertion and perseverance. Unhappily, the argument, such as it is, addresses itself to a feeble part of human nature, a disposition to indolence, a love of ease. The young man thinks, Why should I take so much trouble in a career so unprofitable?

When

When I have done all, my progress is little or nothing. Why should I waste my time and labour in a hopeless attempt? Shall I dream of succeeding where so many have failed? This dastardly mode of reasoning has a direct, and a practical, tendency to fill the world with lukewarm, superficial, careless and unprofitable students, in science, in morals, in religion. The opposite principle ought to be strenuously inculcated on the minds of youth. They ought to be told, that to industry and perseverance nothing is hard, nothing impossible; that, as the dawning light gradually brightens into the perfect day, so bare possibility may rise into probability through its various gradations, till it amount to full and complete assurance. It was in the view of raising the perception, the belief, of his friend Theophilus up to absolute certainty, that St. Luke undertook to furnish him with unquestionable testimony concerning undoubted facts and events, the only kind of evidence of which the subject is susceptible. And knowing this great personage to be a reasonable being, he considers himself as having fulfilled his engagement, when he has produced his vouchers. The youngest

youngest person in this assembly now knows many things of which he was once entirely ignorant; knows some things much better than formerly he did; and has at length acquired full and absolute conviction on points which he once doubted or disbelieved.

These are the particulars, of which, from the text, I wish to have you admonished. The gospel is not a cunningly devised fable, the production of cunning, self-interested priests; neither did it creep into the world unobserved, and silently acquire force till it became too powerful to be resisted: It has in every age and nation made proselytes, genuine proselytes, of every rank and condition of mankind, and would stand firm in its native majestic dignity, whether rulers believed in it or not: Finally, the proofs of its divine authority, taken together, amount to absolute *certainty*, unless all historical and moral evidence is to be renounced as fallacious; and all knowledge is to be reduced merely to mathematical science, and the contracted sphere of every one's individual experience.

But

But that I may avail myself of every possible co-operation towards attaining the end which I have i view, I must earnestly implore the assistance of parents, and guardians, and all instructors of youth, in watching over the movements of opening minds, in guarding their hearts carefully against prejudice of every kind, even in favour of religion; in assisting them betimes to examine, and think, and judge for themselves. Let religion be presented to them, from infancy upward, in every mild, gentle and attractive form. Let it be impressed on their opening minds, that the only living and true God, the God and father of our Lord Jesus Christ, is love. Let the Scriptures, and the sabbath, and the public and private exercises of devotion appear to them, not as severe impositions, but as matters of privilege, and sources of delight. Uncommanded, unnecessary austerities and restraints defeat the end which they profess to aim at, and excite disgust at what is in itself lovely and desirable. To an over-rigid religious discipline in early life, I impute much of that libertinism and licentiousness which disgrace so many of our young men from the North,

the

the moment that they escape from the shackles of parental authority. They consider themselves as entitled to a compensation of liberty and pleasure, in youth, for the restriction and mortification to which their childhood was subjected, and, being their own pay-masters, they take it largely. Above all, let the moral principle be cultivated and strengthened from the beginning. Would you preserve your child from impiety, from infidelity, guard his heart against vice. Would you prevent his understanding from being perverted by erroneous and dangerous opinions, endeavour to keep his conscience pure, and his conduct irreproachable. We would not accuse even infidelity falsely, in alleging that it necessarily leads to vice. God forbid. It may be possible for an unbeliever to be a virtuous man. But we affirm without reserve, that the practice of vice naturally and necessarily leads to infidelity. When a man has quarrelled with his conscience, he must make up matters one way or other. He must either renounce his vices, and alter his conduct; or bring over his understanding to the side of his appetites, and seek refuge in unbelief from the persecution of his
own

### Lect. 5.  *Evidences of Christianity.*   159

own thoughts; and if appetite has acquired strength by indulgence, it is easy to see which way the balance will incline. Thus, as real religion and morality, so infidelity and vice, are inseparably embodied. Not that all who make a profession of religion are holy and just and good; or that all who doubt or disbelieve certain speculative opinions must of course be ill livers: but that good men must consider it as their interest that religion should be true, and the wicked make it their interest that it should be false; and we need not to be told how much the opinions of men are influenced by their interest, how readily they believe what they wish, and how slowly they admit what they fear to be true.

But you are well aware that no care on your part, no instruction, no precept will produce the desired effect, unless supported by example. Be therefore what you would have your young folks to be. Uniformity of conduct, gentleness of manners, placidity of temper, a steady but unostentatious piety, will have the force of ten thousand arguments, and beget conviction where dogmas fail. Having been

been enabled to act thus, you will be inspired with confidence toward God, that he will crown such labours of love with his blessing, that he will preserve your rising hopes from the " paths wherein destroyers go," make them well-informed and sound believers, wise, honest, good and useful men. If such pupils as these are brought to attend exercises of this kind, the work of the preacher will be easy and delightful; it will be a pleasure similar to that of dispensing to a numerous, wholesome, thriving family, wholesome food, and salutary admonition, to each one in his due measure, and at the proper season. May " the Lord give " us understanding in all things." Amen.

# LECT. VI.

#### John i. 18.

*No man hath seen God at any time: the only begotten Son, which is in the bosom of the Father, he hath declared him.*

MAN stands in an intimate relation to various orders of beings. Some are his inferiors, and subjected to his power and authority. Some are on a level with himself, but with endless shades of difference. Some rise above him on a scale of unknown, of unbounded excellence. He himself is on a progressively ascending or descending scale, of moral rectitude or depravity; and the termination of his mortal existence is hastening to decide in what direction his future and everlasting progress is to continue. Man early in life feels himself dependant, indebted, accountable. But on whom is he ultimately dependant, to whom is he chiefly indebted, and to whom is he finally responsible? The prosecution of this inquiry leads him step by step up to Deity; and he soon discovers that of all the relations in which he is placed, those in which he stands to God are by far the most interesting and important. He finds that there is a source of being and felicity whom he hath not seen, whom he knows very imperfectly, but of whom he wishes to know more, and more clearly, more satisfyingly. He finds himself under a weight of obligation which it is impossible for him ever to discharge, yet feels himself disposed to make some return. And he finds that he has contracted much guilt toward this beneficent Creator and Preserver, the consciousness of which fills him with many an uneasy apprehension, and suggests many an anxious inquiry. Thus a variety of emotions are excited in the human breast, according as the man considers himself in the light of a dependant, a debtor, or a criminal, such as a sense of submission, of gratitude, of fear, and of hope.

But though man possesses faculties, by the exercise of which he may acquire the knowledge

ledge of his relation to Deity, and is confcious of the powerful emotions which they excite within him, yet his unaffifted faculties are totally infufficient to inftruct him in the nature and the will of God, in the duties impofed upon him by the Author and Supporter of his being, and in what he has reafon to fear from his difpleafure, or to expect from his goodnefs. Left to himfelf, therefore, the firft of human beings is in a ftate of the moft deplorable ignorance and uncertainty, in matters of the higheft moment to him. His prefent exiftence is dark and comfortlefs, and a difmally oppreffive cloud hangs over futurity. Religion is juft as neceffary to man as food and clothing: with this difference, that while he is furnifhed with an inftinct capable of diftinguifhing between food and poifon, and with a fagacity capable of preparing and adapting his raiment to his circumftances, he poffeffes no inftinctive principle, no innate fagacity, to direct him in difcovering, diftinguifhing and applying the proper nourifhment, clothing, and ornament of his better part, the immortal mind. We accordingly find the acutenefs, ingenuity and good fenfe, of nations deftitute of a divine revelation, in things relating to the body and a prefent world, forming a complete, and a melancholy contraft, with their ftupidity and extravagance in religious opinions and practices. A fagacious, induftrious, obferving hufbandman had invented a better mode of cultivating the corn-plant, the olive, the vine, and had taught it to his neighbours; the next age exalts him into a god, and pays him divine honours. A beneficent and ufeful animal, by an eafy tranfition, is deified in its turn, and the idolatry imperceptibly defcends till it affumes a nutritious or a medicinal plant for its object. For the fame reafon, the fears of mankind being ever fully as powerful as their hopes or their gratitude, noxious, dangerous and deftructive plants, animals, and men have obtained religious homage and veneration; and malignant deities have difputed the prize with the benefactors of the human race.

We refort not to the favage uncivilized tribes for an illuftration of thefe remarks, but refer you to the hiftory of the moft enlightened nations of the heathen world, Phenicia, ancient

ancient Egypt, and Greece, and Rome; whose agricultorial, commercial, scientific, political, progress and improvement, astonish and delight the world to this day, while their theology, and religious ceremonies, only provoke derision, kindle indignation, or excite abhorrence. That the picture of civilized paganism, painted by the hand of the apostle Paul, in the first chapter of his epistle to the Romans, in strong colours indeed, is not however overcharged, we have the authority of their own writers, who unblushingly relate and describe what was unblushingly transacted. Their religion, so far from being the religion of nature, was, almost in every particular, a violation of nature, and a reproach to the human understanding. The question is not, Was the human mind capable of producing a more rational theology, and of prescribing a more reasonable service? but, Did it? and When, or Where? Was not the experiment awfully made? Had not the powers of the human mind full leisure and opportunity afforded them, to produce their noblest effort? Have they succeeded, or have they not? Infidelity, with all its boldnefs, is not prepared to anfwer in the affirmative.

Now the Chriftian, without apprehending the imputation of arrogance, prefumes to believe, and thinks he is able to prove, that Jefus of Nazareth has rendered this important fervice to mankind; that he has delivered the only true religion of nature; has alone unfolded the real character of Deity, has taught a worfhip worthy of man to prefent, and of God to accept; has enforced a law, the counterpart and obligation of which every one recognizes in his own bofom; has prefented an oblation acceptable to God, and falutary to the guilty creature; in a word, has bleffed the world with the very thing which it always did, and ever will need, a theology which the underftanding approves, to which the heart cleaves, and in which the troubled confcience finds certain repofe. God grant that, in fpeaking on fuch a fubject, we may not be permitted to " darken counfel by words with-
" out knowledge."

Permit

Permit me to repeat the proposition announced in the preceding Lecture, as the first link in the chain of internal evidence which we mean to produce, of the truth and divine original of the Christian religion: It is entirely conformable to all the ideas of Deity which we are enabled to form by the exercise of our own reason, on a serious contemplation of the great universe; in other words, it is the true and only religion of nature. " No " man hath seen God at any time: the only " begotten Son which is in the bosom of the " Father, he hath declared him."

I shall confine myself strictly to such views of God as are presented to us by Jesus Christ himself, in the course of his personal ministry. Our proofs will accordingly be entirely derived from the gospel history, and conveyed in the very words of the Saviour of mankind.

1. Then, the great leading idea of nature, which represents God under the endearing character of a *Father*, is also the great pervading idea of the Christian religion. Nations savage and civilized all agree in this.

It is at once an instinctive feeling of the human heart, and a conclusion of the intellect, derived from observation and experience. The simplest notion of paternity is that of a being who conferred existence upon us, and consequently was before us. After tracing up our original a step or two, we find ourselves brought close to the common Parent of the human race, whose " offspring we all are," and in whom " we live and move and have our " being." This relation combines all that is venerable in age, all that is respectable in authority, all that is dignified in wisdom, all that is amiable and attractive in beneficence, all that is irresistible and triumphant in compassion and tender mercy. Hence the aged, in general, are saluted by the honourable appellation of Father; hence it is bestowed on princes, and constitutes their noblest designation; hence the consolation which soothed the heart of Job under the pressure of calamity, " I was a Father to the poor;" hence the paternal delight which glows in the bosom of a benefactor toward the object of his goodwill, and the filial affection which overflows at the eyes of grateful sensibility. Christianity
whose

whose object it is to purify, to improve and to exalt all our feelings, all our faculties, accordingly displays, expands this relation through all its variety of influence and interest. Is Deity represented to us as a pattern for imitation? The great Teacher exhibits him not in the exercise of sovereignty, performing acts of power, or executing judgment; but in his character of Father, in which alone he is imitable, multiplying without end acts of kindness, showering down blessings even on the evil and the unthankful, and extending one act of grace after another, to the worst of criminals; not overcome of evil, but overcoming evil with good. " If ye love
" them which love you, what reward have
" ye? and if ye salute your brethren only,
" what do you more than others? But I say
" unto you, love your enemies, bless them
" that curse you, do good to them that hate
" you, and pray for them that despitefully
" use you and persecute you; that ye may
" be the children of your FATHER which is
" in heaven; for he maketh his sun to rise on
" the evil and on the good, and sendeth rain
" on the just and on the unjust."

What

What marks of a divine original are here? And here the fond expectations of nature, the fruit of experience, and the discoveries of revelation are one. If God were to vouchsafe to instruct men at all in religion, must it not be just such a religion as this, which presents views of himself so consonant to all that merits the name of Deity? Here he is clothed in all his majesty: " He maketh *his* sun to rise;" " He sendeth rain;" but his power is employed only in works of mercy. " His paths " drop fatness," in him the mildness and compassion of a Father blend with omnipotence and supreme authority. Every man has in his own breast a proof that this doctrine is from heaven, for he knows that he himself has been thus tenderly, thus indulgently treated. He recognizes in the God whom the Son declares in this gospel, the self-same being of whose bounty he is a partaker every day, who pities his infirmities, pardons his offences, forgets his ingratitude. Were man, on the other hand, to be permitted to form his own ideas of Deity, with an assurance that they should be realized, Who but this God could be a God to one of his character, and in his condition?

condition? Who *could* be the Father of mankind, the inftructor of the ignorant, the refuge of the miferable, the reftorer of the fallen, the portion of the wife and good, except the God and Father of our Lord Jefus Chrift? Nature, indeed, could hardly have raifed her expectations fo high; reafon durft not have drawn a conclufion fo bold; human imagination could not have formed a reprefentation of Deity fo lovely: but thus brought down to our perception, thus impreffed on the heart, thus recommended to the underftanding, thus difplayed to the imagination, who but muft be filled with peace and joy in believing, that the one living and true God, whom no man hath feen or can fee, is the very God with whom we have to do, and whom " the only begotten Son, which " is in the bofom of the Father, hath de-" clared." And yet this is the religion, merciful Father, this is the religion which one part of mankind affects to treat with contempt, which another hates and perfecutes, and which, alas, few underftand and prize according to its real worth and excellence.

2. But

2. But Jesus Christ has not only given us the justest, the most rational and the most satisfying *general* views of the Supreme Being, but has gone into a *particular* and *minute* detail of the ways of his providence, equally consonant to the appearances, and the dictates of nature, and to the conclusions of right reason. Nature and reason contemplate Deity not only as presiding over the higher orders of beings, in the superior departments of creation, but likewise as the vital principle which animates, supports and directs every class of creatures, nay, every individual of every class, whether inanimate, vegetable or animal. Nature and reason say God is light and heat in the sun, solidity in the rock, order in the revolution of the spheres, growth and fruitfulness in the plant, life and self-motion in the animal, as he is intelligence in the angel and in the man. And the despised Galilean, with an unaffected simplicity, at the same time with an energy peculiar to himself, exhibits a similar display of a constant, uniform and minute interposition of divine agency, through all the endless diversity of created nature. It is God who
clothes

clothes " the grafs of the field, which to day is, " and to morrow is caft into the oven." It is God who arrays each particular lily of the field in a beauty and luftre which eclipfe Solomon in all his glory. " Confider the " ravens: for they neither fow nor reap; " which neither have ftore-houfe nor barn, " and God feedeth them." " Are not two " fparrows fold for a farthing? and one of " them fhall not fall to the ground without " your father." And mark, how the doctrine of a particular providence, thus emphatically taught, addreffes itfelf to the neceffities, the defires, the hopes of man, a being fo much more glorious and important. It is pleafing to meditate on a common Father, who has of one blood formed all nations of men to inhabit upon the face of the whole earth, and whofe kingdom ruleth over all; but how much more pleafing to fay, " My " Lord and my God." " The very hairs of " my head are all numbered." I am " of " more value than many fparrows." " Am " I not much better than the fowls of the " air?" Shall He not much more feed and clothe me, faithlefs and unbelieving that I am?

am? Here again, then, the doctrine of the gospel is in perfect unison with the native emotions of the heart of man, and with the results of every one's hourly experience. And yet this is the religion which one part of mankind affects to treat with contempt, which another hates and persecutes, and which, alas, few understand and prize according to its real worth and excellence. But,

3. The voice of nature, of reason and of the religion of the blessed Jesus are one, in another respect, of high importance to human felicity. As man must have an author of his being, live under parental government, and subsist on immediate and particular parental supplies, so he must be provided with means and opportunities, and an object, for the disburthening of his heart, according to the various aspects of the divine providence. There are moments of bitterness which the heart must pass without a human partaker, and there are sources of joy with which an earthly stranger must not intermeddle. There are seasons and situations when nothing less than Deity can fill the void in the human soul,

Lect. 6.  *Evidences of Christianity.*   175

soul, when God himself alone can be the help meet for man. In other words, man has continually within himself a call to turn unto God, to retire from every creature, and to converse with a Father who heareth and seeth in secret. On this principle we ventured to affirm that religion is just as necessary to man as food and clothing. Unhappily for him, it is but too true, he frequently contrives to do without it, or with a very scanty portion; but his mind can no more subsist in a state of tranquillity and comfort while alienated from God, than the body can enjoy health and vigor without a regular supply of daily bread. He therefore who teaches men to pray, is one of the greatest benefactors of mankind, for he instructs them how to multiply, refine and exalt all their delights, and how to diminish, alleviate and remove all their woes. Jesus, the friend of the human race, has condescended to perform this gracious office. He knows what is in man, and what is good for man. He places the needy, the helpless, the guilty creature, or the joyful, the prosperous, the pardoned, the restored, in the bosom of his Creator. He opens all heaven to his view,

discloses

discloses to him the hidden treasures of eternity, and transforms this earth into a paradise, by unveiling the mansions of the blessed, who do the will of God, and rejoice continually before him. By teaching his disciples to say, "*Our* Father which art in heaven," he extinguishes all bitterness and wrath, he inspires and promotes every kind affection, he strengthens the bands of nature, and ennobles the various relations of human life. Every anxious worldly thought is repressed or relieved, when the heart has deposited all concern about the supply of the day with Him who " knows what things we have need of " before we ask them." How powerfully are thoughts and works of mercy impressed on the conscience, by remembering, in the presence of a much offended Father, how great our guilt is towards him, and that nevertheless we are encouraged to hope for mercy. How sweetly does the prayer correspond with the precept? " Forgive us " our trespasses as we forgive them that " trespass against us." " Be ye therefore mer" ciful, even as your Father in heaven is " merciful." What a guard is placed around

frail

frail exposed man, when the soul has poured out its apprehension of difficulty and danger, before him who controls all the powers of heaven, and earth, and hell; who can prevent all evil, or remove it, or turn it into good! How the mind expands, in contemplating the great and glorious name of this universal, all-gracious Parent, made known to all his children; adored, exalted, delighted in by them: and in surveying the progress of his everlasting, unchangeable kingdom of peace, and love and joy, commencing, increasing, flourishing on the earth, and hastening to be perfected, consummated in heaven! If such views of the nature, will and worship of the great Lord of all, be not approved of right reason, as they are clearly unfolded to us on the page of inspiration, Who shall instruct us to render a reasonable service? Or is the world prepared solemnly to renounce all devotional exercises and enjoyments? And is it, indeed, to be henceforward deemed a mark of superior understanding to deride piety, and to break off all commerce with the Father of spirits? No, " the only begotten Son who is in the bosom " of the Father, he hath declared him" to us, as the hearer of prayer, the God of all grace, the Father of mercies, the refuge of the miserable. He has declared to us how devotion blends with morality; how the life that now is, derives all its value, all its felicity, from the relation which it bears to that which is to come; how the worlds visible and invisible are subjected to one common head, who is carrying on one plan of eternal wisdom and goodness, of which the present and future happiness of the human race is one great, leading object. And such are the unspeakable benefits which the religion of Jesus Christ is conferring, at least disposed to confer, on the children of men; and yet this is the religion which one part of mankind affects to treat with contempt, which another hates and persecutes; and which, alas, few understand and prize according to its real worth and excellence.

4. But nature, conscience and Scripture concur in suggesting other ideas of Deity no less interesting to creatures such as we are. One God is our Father; his kingdom ruleth over all; He is the hearer of prayer, and

man

man occupies his higheſt ſtation, when proſtrated at the footſtool of the throne of grace: But this God is alſo a wiſe ruler and a righteous judge, and man is an undutiful, ungrateful child, a diſobedient and rebellious ſubject. Man is criminal and God is juſt. What proviſion can nature, can reaſon make, in ſuch a caſe? The miſerable effort of nature is to hide one's ſelf from the preſence of the Lord God amidſt the trees of the garden, and to conceal conſcious nakedneſs under a covering of fig leaves. The miſerable inquiry of unaſſiſted reaſon is, " Wherewith ſhall I come
" before the Lord, and bow myſelf before the
" Moſt High God? Shall I come before him
" with burnt-offerings, with calves of a year
" old? Will the Lord be pleaſed with thou-
" ſands of rams, or with ten thouſands of
" rivers of oil? Shall I give my firſt-born for
" my tranſgreſſion, the fruit of my body for
" the ſin of my ſoul?" Ah, this comes not up to the demands of the divine law, this ſatisfies not the human heart, this adminiſters no repoſe to the troubled conſcience. Deity rejects it with contempt and abhorrence: " I
" will not reprove thee for thy ſacrifices,
" or thy burnt-offerings to have been con-
" tinually

"tinually before me. I will take no bullock "out of thy houfe, nor he-goats out of "thy folds; for every beaft of the foreft is "mine, and the cattle upon a thoufand hills. "I know all the fowls of the mountains; "and the wild beafts of the field are mine. "If I were hungry I would not tell thee, "for the world is mine and the fulnefs thereof. "Will I eat the flefh of bulls, or drink the "blood of goats?" Here then all the powers of nature fail; here a difficulty prefents itfelf to reafon, which it is unable to folve; nothing remains but a fearful looking-for of judgment. "The foul that finneth fhall die." The fentence is juft, but, Is there no remedy? "Behold the Lamb of God, which taketh "away the fin of the world!" "The Son "of man is come to feek and to fave that "which was loft." "As Mofes lifted up "the ferpent in the wildernefs, even fo muft "the Son of man be lifted up; that who- "foever believeth in him, fhould not perifh, "but have eternal life." "I am the good "fhepherd; the good fhepherd giveth his "life for the fheep." "I give unto them "eternal life; and they fhall never perifh, "neither fhall any pluck them out of my
                                 "hand."

## Lect. 6. *Evidences of Christianity.*

"hand." "God so loved the world, that he gave his only begotten Son, that whosoever believeth in him should not perish, but have everlasting life." This is indeed a mystery of grace which no efforts of the human understanding could have discovered, a display of divine perfection which imagination itself durst not have portrayed, a method of salvation which "angels desire to look into," but are "unable to find out the Almighty unto perfection." This is a view of Deity which created nature could not have believed possible, till it was actually manifested. But now that it is manifested, how wonderfully, how delightfully, is it found to accord with the necessities of the guilty creature, with the general tenor of the divine government, with the trembling expectations of the heart of man, and with the fairest conclusions of human reason? Might not a miserable being look, for relief, to a God of mercy? Here it is to the full; a remedy that meets the disease at every point. Was it not meet that sin should be punished, the honour of the divine law vindicated, and the order of God's government maintained and supported? Behold, here, how awful justice is, sin how odious, the law

how

how refpectable, government how vigorous and impartial. Would not the criminal have had good caufe to acquiefce, and to rejoice, had it pleafed God to relax fomewhat of the feverity, or of the duration of his punifhment? How much more when he gracioufly remits it altogether? Do the princes of this world remunerate, and exalt to honour, the wretches whofe crimes they have pardoned? Is this a reafon why the great God fhould not? Shall we dare to arraign his wifdom, becaufe his ways are above our ways, and his thoughts above ours? Shall it be thought a thing incredible that God fhould be flow to anger, and of great kindnefs, becaufe man is ftern, implacable and unrelenting?

Man in his rude, dark, favage ftate, and man polifhed, intelligent, refined, has been, and is impreffed, with the idea of natural diftance from God, of the poffibility, but the difficulty, of reconciliation; he has entertained the idea of expiatory, propitiatory facrifice; of the fubftitution of victim in the place of victim, of the innocent fuffering for the guilty, of " the juft for the unjuft to bring " us unto God." Where could an idea fo
universal

universal have originated, but in the constitution and frame of the human mind? And is it to be rejected, merely because it is found to be the leading idea of the gospel? Are we to admit it where it appears in all its feebleness and absurdity, and spurn at it where alone it has a meaning, an object and an end? How strange! A man traduce the friend who has, unsolicited, become his security, and actually paid his debt? What! Admire the friendship of a Pylades and an Orestes, the one of whom was *ready* to lay down his life for the other? and no admiration expressed, no emotion felt, no tear of sympathy and contrition flow, when I hear of one who actually " dared to die," to die for me! What can have made the world so exceedingly mad against the name of Jesus? As a man, so inoffensive, so unassuming; as a sage, so meek and condescending; as a benefactor, so unostentatious and humble; as a sufferer, so patient and unresentful; as a God, so majestic yet so mild! What can have made the world so exceedingly mad against a religion, which encroaches on no one right or feeling of humanity, which abridges, condemns, restrains

no one particular of rational human comfort; which enjoins no one article of belief but what the heart wishes " and the conscience feels" to be true; which imposes no yoke of duty but what it is the interest of every man voluntarily to assume, and joyfully to wear, had the name of Christ never been mentioned on the earth ? What can have made the world so exceedingly mad against a religion, which aims at purifying, improving, exalting, perfecting human nature, by making man " partaker of a divine nature;" which tells him, what his own heart told him before, that in the great God, who made and sustains the universe, he has a Father in heaven ever able and ready to help; which instructs him that he who decks the lily, feeds the raven, supports the sparrow, the crane, the swallow on the wing, takes an interest far superior in himself; which gives him perpetual access to this greatest, wisest, best of beings, to rejoice in his liberality, to solicit the continuance of his bounty, to appeal to his compassion, to implore his forgiveness ? What, in a word, can have made the world so exceedingly mad against a religion, which shews to miserable, guilty man his debt discharged, his
iniquity

iniquity pardoned, the sentence of his condemnation "nailed to the cross;" which displays "heaven opened and Jesus standing at the right hand of God;" which exhibits death vanquished, disarmed; the fiery gulf extinguished; the great enemy loaded with everlasting chains; which discloses to our wondering eyes "new heavens, and a new earth wherein dwelleth righteousness;" which brings to light life and immortality? And yet this is the religion, with sorrow we repeat it, this is the religion which one part of mankind affects to treat with contempt; which another hates and persecutes, and which few understand and prize according to its real value and excellence.

If the representation given be any thing like the truth, then be assured, my young friend, that the person who attempts to put the religion of Jesus Christ, its doctrines, its morality, its positive institutions, in an odious or a ridiculous light to you, cannot possibly be your friend, any more than he who would teach you to laugh at the beauty and order of nature, to set your face against the decrees of eternal Providence, or to curse the wise and
necessary

necessary restraints of civil society. He who insinuates to you that Christianity is in any one respect inimical to your happiness, is telling you a solemn untruth; is wickedly endeavouring to pervert your understanding, and to harden your heart. If the principle of conscience be deadened within you, morality will not long survive it; for What hold has the world got of that man who has cast off all fear of God, or who has made a God for himself, except the restraints which the laws of society are obliged to employ against thieves and murderers? Let it be a maxim of prudence with you, both in matters of life and of religion, never to relinquish the ground you occupy, till you perceive another attainable, at least as good. Ask the man who would seduce you from the belief, love, and practice of "the things wherein you have been instructed," What he proposes should supply their place. He would decoy you from your Father's house, but has he provided for you a better home? What harm can it do you, what danger do you run, in living and dying a Christian? But is it equally wise and safe, to live and to die an infidel? If the religion of
the

the gospel be of God, then the Christian has every thing to hope and nothing to fear; while the unbeliever has every thing to fear and nothing to hope: or should it prove but a cunningly devised fable, that is suppofing the worst possible, the believer in Christ Jesus is a better and happier, and a more respectable man in this world; if there be an hereafter he cannot fall far below his unbelieving neighbour, and if there be none, he has gained much and lost nothing.

The next lecture which, if God permit, will be delivered this day three weeks, January the 14th, will be an attempt to prove that as the religion of Jesus Christ is entirely conformable to all the ideas of Deity which we are enabled to form by the exercise of our own reason, on a serious contemplation of the great universe; and accordingly the true and only religion of nature: so secondly, It is universally congenial to the constitution and frame of the human mind.

May the great parent of mankind, the God and Father of our Lord Jesus Christ, make

us

us all " perfect in every good work to do
" his will, working in us that which is well-
" pleasing in his sight, through Jesus Christ,
" to whom be glory for ever and ever.
" Amen."

# LECT. VII.

### Gen. xxii. 15—18.

*And the angel of the Lord called unto Abraham out of heaven the second time,*

*And said, By myself have I sworn, saith the Lord, for because thou hast done this thing, and hast not withheld thy Son, thine only Son:*

*That in blessing I will bless thee, and in multiplying I will multiply thy seed as the stars of the heaven, and as the sand which is upon the sea shore: and thy seed shall possess the gate of his enemies;*

*And in thy seed shall all the nations of the earth be blessed; because thou hast obeyed my voice.*

### Acts i. 7, 8.

*And he said unto them, It is not for you to know the times, or the seasons, which the Father hath put in his own power.*

But

*But ye shall receive power after that the Holy Ghost is come upon you: and ye shall be witnesses unto me both in Jerusalem, and in all Judea, and in Samaria, and unto the uttermost part of the earth.*

WE make frequent use in speech of the phrases, " every corner of the globe," " the whole world," " the whole universe," " universal nature," and the like. But we know not " what we say, nor whereof we " affirm." Grasping objects so vast, we remain in ignorance of those with which we are in close contact, and which are level to our capacity. He alone who made the worlds, understands the nature and extent, the uses and end, of his own work. While man is permitted to contemplate, and to enjoy, the beauty, harmony and beneficial influence of distant spheres, his activity and exertions are limited to his own. To climb to the summit of that mountain, or descend to the bottom of yonder valley; to dig a few inches into this cornfield, or a hundred fathoms into yonder copper-mine; to skim along the surface of the ocean, or to plunge a few feet under it; to ascertain

certain the qualities of this plant, or of that animal, by the indications of nature or the results of experience; thus far, and no farther, do the human powers extend. But man himself possesses a peculiar quality. Of the innumerable tribes which people this great globe, he alone is able to exist, and to enjoy life, in every latitude, and in every climate. To each particular region, particular species of plants and animals are adapted, in which they live, thrive, and attain perfection; but they cannot bear transplantation. Conveyed to a different situation, they become feeble and puny; they languish and die; or are preserved with so much trouble and expense in a sickly state, that curiosity or pride only would be disposed to make the experiment. But man is every where man. He can bear transplantation from the frozen horrors of the polar circles, to the burning heat of a vertical sun; and to be reconveyed to the torpid gloom of the icy zone from whence he came. With shades of character various as those of stature, features and complexion, the same characteristics of humanity are to be found, in the east and in the west, to the north and to the south.

The

The religion of Jesus Christ possesses a correspondent character of universality, and proves its original to be divine, from its complete adaptation to the nature and condition of man; not in this district or in that, living under this or the other form of civil government, in a lofty or a lowly estate; but man universally, Greek or barbarian, Roman or Scythian, bond or free. As Deity " hath made " of one blood all nations of men, for to dwell " on all the face of the earth," so he is presenting unto all nations of men a religion which addresses itself to the understanding, the heart, the conscience of every man, let his endowments, his rank in life, his worldly possessions, be what they may. If this shall be made to appear, from a simple elucidation of the nature and design of Christianity, as it appears on the face of Scripture, we shall have a powerful presumption at least, if not a proof, that the God of human nature, and " the God " and Father of our Lord Jesus Christ," is one and the same. This we are now to attempt, by shewing in a few particulars, that the religion of Jesus Christ is congenial to the constitution and frame of the human mind.

Now

Now there are three well-known universal characters of humanity, to which the gospel, and the gospel alone, most happily applies, ignorance, guilt, and subjection to bondage. In other words, all men stand in need of an instructor, of an intercessor, of a deliverer; and Jesus Christ undertakes, and fulfils, all these gracious offices to the human race.

I. Man is born, and continues long, in a state of ignorance. During the earlier periods of his existence, he is of all animals, at once the most interesting and important, and the feeblest, most helpless and most dependant. He must be clothed and fed by the hands of others. And when he comes to look about him, and to discern object from object, he discovers an instinct far inferior to that of many of the brute creation. He is slow of apprehension; and to tardiness of apprehension is generally added a certain degree of perversity of disposition. And, unhappily, those who are about him, and to whom he looks up for instruction, are themselves ignorant and perverse; unwisely severe, or unwisely indulgent, under the dominion of passion or of interest.

intereſt. Hence, the child, from the beginning, receives deceitful impreſſions of things, falſe, imperfect, perplexed information reſpecting the plaineſt and moſt important objects, which no future culture nor care is able to overcome. When time at length calls for the aid of regular nurture, To what attainments are the minds of youth directed? To accompliſhments rather ornamental than uſeful; to the power of naming the ſame objects in two, three or four different languages; to the art of pleaſing by modes of ſpeech and behaviour, to the means of thriving and ſhining in the world; too often, to things which pollute the imagination, miſlead the heart, and harden the conſcience. The very leading maxims of our education are erroneous and ſeductive. Under the plauſible epithets of *noble* emulation, *manly* ambition, *honeſt* pride, the worſt, the moſt deteſtable and deſtructive of human paſſions are generated in the youthful breaſt. The firſt leſſon which the promiſing, towardly boy receives f om his maſter, is: " Be the firſt of your form. Let no one " ſurpaſs you." And the fond parent's heart leaps for joy, to hear that the child underſtood

stood the lesson, and put it in practice; not considering to what all this leads; envy, jealousy, insolence, false shame, every evil work. The succesful candidate looks down with self-gratulation on his competitors; they regard him with hatred and aversion; conspiracies are formed to make his superiority sit uneasy upon him, and to undermine it; a flame is kindled, not with the celestial fire which exalts and refines, but with the infernal spirit of the wicked one, which devours and consumes. What is to result from this, when children wax into men, and the grand career opens to view? Consult the history of courts and cabinets, the history of the Alexanders and Cesars, the Scipios and Hannibals of ages past; the history of the statesmen and heroes of modern times, and it will be found, that the instructors of mankind, almost without exception, themselves misled by false ideas of glory, communicated them without reserve to the world, and the effect has been, and is, striving for the mastery has, in every age, converted the earth into a field of blood.

This some divines have called the state of nature; as if it could have been the intention of the Author of nature to people the globe with animals more ferocious than lions and wolves; for they devour not one another of their own fpecies. No, it rather belongs to the character of Deity to interpofe a remedy for fuch an unnatural ftate, and to bring men back to himfelf, by reconciling them among themfelves. And how was this to be effected? By a total inverfion of our maxims, of our fpirit and our plans; by making us unlearn what we had been taught, and to put ourfelves under the tuition of a new mafter, who fhould " fhew" to man " a more excellent way," and be himfelf the great example of what he recommended to others. This mafter, this grand defiderandum for the wifdom and happinefs of the human race, prefents himfelf to us in the perfon of Jefus of Nazareth; and for this bleffed purpofe the minifters of his religion are fent forth as witneffes for him, " to the uttermoft parts of the earth." The fpirit of the world had crept into his own little family: " There arofe a reafoning " among them, which of them fhould be " greateft." He mildly terminated the difpute, by placing a little child in the midft of them,

them, and by declaring that the way not only to rife in the kingdom of heaven, but even to obtain admiffion into it at all, was to reverfe their whole fyftem of fentiment and conduct, to renounce ambition, and to revert to the fimplicity, the docility of childhood. "Who-
" foever fhall humble himfelf as this little
" child, the fame is greateft in the kingdom
" of heaven." When I think of this, my fpirit is ftirred within me at the reflection, that on the eve of the nineteenth century, in Chriftian Britain, in her far-famed metropolis, it fhould be an amufement to grown men to urge on little children to do violence to their own nature, by beating, bruifing, tearing each other. The fame worldly fpirit actuated the wife of Zebedee, and her two afpiring fons, to folicit the two firft pofts of honour in his kingdom. He gently waved the demand, and, to prevent its producing difcord among the difciples, affured them all, that the way to rife in his kingdom was to defcend. " Who-
" foever will be great among you, let him be
" your minifter; and whofoever will be chief
" among you, let him be your fervant; even
" as the Son of man came not to be miniftered
" unto,

"unto, but to minister;" plainly intimating that usefulness is true greatness; that real dignity consists not in overtopping others, but in a voluntary humiliation of ourselves. Nor was this a vain parade of words, an ostentatious display of self-denial, a yoke imposed on the necks of others, which the imposer himself disdained to touch. The history and character of Jesus are comprized in two short sentences, "He went about doing good." "He was meek and lowly in heart."

Again, the spirit of the world, and the justice of the world, say, "An eye for an eye, "and a tooth for a tooth:" "thou shalt love "thy neighbour and hate thine enemy." This law is founded on the unnatural state of human society. Were the voice of the great Teacher understood and felt, no man's eye or tooth, no not a hair of his head, would suffer by the hand of violence; there would be no enemy to hate; the inhabitants of the world would be one vast united family, disposed to love, to cherish, and to assist one another. The spirit of the world saith, "Revenge is "sweet," "Raze it, raze it, even to the "foun-

" foundation thereof: happy shall he be that
" rewardeth thee as thou haft served us."
But what faith the Teacher sent from God?
" Love your enemies, bless them that curse
" you, do good to them that hate you, and
" pray for them which despitefully use you
" and persecute you." Whether of these two
spirits, it may be asked, is the better, the more
excellent, most congenial to the constitution
and frame of the human mind? The soul
must inwardly recoil from maxims and practices which prejudice and habit have rendered
current. It is truly mortifying to find two of
the most favoured of the whole college of the
Apostles, if we may give them that appellation, James and John, so dreadfully carried
away by the spirit of the world, so hasty in
their decisions, so ignorant of their master's
character, and of the design of his mission, as
to propose, in resentment of a slight piece of
disrespect, to call fire down from heaven to
consume a village of the Samaritans. His
meekness changes, for a moment, into severity:
" He turned, and rebuked them, and said, ye
" know not what manner of spirit ye are of,
" for the Son of man is not come to destroy

" mens lives, but to save them." It is truly deplorable to find the whole eleven, as we see in the context, so dreadfully absorbed of the spirit of this world, after all that they had seen, and known, of their master, after being eye-witnesses of his sufferings and of the glory that followed, still hankering after the dignities and emoluments of a temporal kingdom, and expressing an indecent curiosity about future events. With his native meekness, he represses the inquiry as improper and unprofitable, and by his answer instructs them, and instructs us, that, " It is not for man to " know the times or the seasons which the " Father hath put in his own power."

If, then, Jesus Christ has taught lessons of wisdom and morality suitable to all mankind, of every age and nation; if they are obvious to the capacity of every one possessed of common understanding, if they reconcile themselves, the moment that they are heard, to the radical principles of the human mind, if they have a manifest tendency to ameliorate the condition of the whole human race; and who can deny it? then, had he assumed no other character,

character, had he acted in no other capacity, the whole world of mankind is laid under infinite obligations to his wisdom and benevolence, and he stands confessed to every eye, except those of profligacy and prejudice, the dignified messenger and visible representative of the common Parent of the children of men. While, therefore, we think and speak respectfully of the jewish legislator, and of the venerable instructors of pagan antiquity, a Zoroaster, a Pythagoras, a Confucius, a Solon, a Lycurgus, a Socrates, a Plato, and a multitude that might be named, Can it be deemed a flight of enthusiasm, or condemned as a prejudice, if we venture to affirm, that the morality of the gospel is purer, more sublime, more efficient; that it is better adapted to the nature of man, and more productive of real happiness to him, than that of all those sages put together; and also that Providence has confirmed its superior excellency, by bestowing upon it a much wider range, and a much longer duration. But there is a

II. Second character which Jesus Christ sustains, of universal, and perpetual, application

and –

and ufe to the human race, that of Interceffor, or " Mediator between God and man." One of the earlieft perceptions of the human mind is confcious criminality. The child finds he has been acting amifs, the moment he begins to reflect at all. As he grows up, he feels his propenfity to what is forbidden grow ftronger and ftronger. He goes on to fulfil " the defires of the flefh and of the mind;" the breach becomes wider and wider between him, and the party whom he has offended, whether that party be a fellow-creature or the invifible God, againft whom all offence ultimately points. As his inward uneafinefs increafes, the wifh of remiffion and reconciliation increafes with it. Invention goes to work, and the means of peace without, in order to reftore tranquillity within, are imagined. Forming an idea of his Maker from what he knows of himfelf, a Deity fevere, fanguinary, vindictive, prefents himfelf to his affrighted imagination. And what wild extravagances has not this produced? Innumerable hecatombs have fhed their blood, and fmoked upon the altar of an implacable God. Thoufands of rams have yielded up their innocent

nocent lives, and ten thousands of rivulets of oil have flowed. Horrid human sacrifices have been presented: The parent has given his " first-born for his transgression, the fruit " of the body for the sin of the soul." The more that the feelings of nature have been violated, the more acceptable has the oblation appeared. Now, whatever horror and absurdity may be in all this, it is the indication of an universal sentiment. It is the feeble effort of a helpless, or of a guilty creature, to secure a friend, or to reconcile an enemy; and the generality of the practice is a direct proof of the generality of the feeling. Here again, then, Christianity comes in as the universal medicine, and introduces the trembling suppliant, not to the presence of an ever-thundering Jupiter, an earth-shaking Neptune, a blood-stained Mars, a far-darting Apollo, every one clothed in his peculiar terror, through the medium of a surly selfish priest, who divided the spoils of the votary with his worthless Deity; but to a " God" who " so loved the world " that he gave his only begotten Son, that " whosoever believeth in him should not perish " but have everlasting life," through the mediation

diation of a brother, a friend, " a friend that
" sticketh closer than a brother." What shall
we say? Even the God of Israel clothed him‑
self in terrible majesty. When he descended
to promulgate his law from Sinai, the " mount
" burned with fire," and a great people ap‑
proached, with fear and trembling, as near
as they durst, " unto blackness, and dark‑
" ness, and tempest; and the sound of a
" trumpet, and the voice of words, which
" voice they that heard intreated, that the
" word should not be spoken to them any
" more; and so terrible was the sight, that
" Moses said, I exceedingly fear and quake,"

It was reserved for the gospel of peace, to
announce to a guilty world, the one living and
true God, as the God of love; it was reserved for
the Author and Finisher of the Christian faith
to present the devout worshippers of Jehovah
at a throne of Grace, with these words of holy
confidence in their mouths, " Our Father
" which art in heaven." It was reserved
for John Baptist, the forerunner of Jesus, to
point out to mankind one victim, which should
supersede myriads, " the Lamb of God which
                                                            taketh

" taketh away the fin," not of an individual, a family, a tribe, a whole nation, but " which " taketh away the fin of the world." Here, and here only, the troubled confcience finds what it longed and looked for, a real atonement which reaches every cafe, of every wretched individual, of every age, " to the uttermoft " part of the earth." The fpirit of every other known religion difcovered partialities and prejudices, fenced itfelf round with walls and hedges, conferred exclufive privileges on all who were within the pale, and breathed deftruction to all who were without it. It is the glory of Chriftianity to have removed thofe ungracious fences, to have brought men nearer to one another, and the whole great family near unto God. The announciation of this bleffed era, of this fulnefs of time, by the mouth of angels is, " Glory to God in " the higheft, and on earth, peace, good will " to men," and good will among men. " Chrift fuffered for us, the juft for the un- " juft, that he might bring us unto God." Thus the bleffed Jefus executes, for man, two offices of the higheft importance to man. To ignorat, mifled, erring man, he points

out

out a path of duty simple, intelligible, practicable, of universal application, with this single index, in case of doubt or difficulty; "All things whatsoever ye would that men should do unto you, do ye also the same things unto them;" and to guilty man he proposes an universal propitiation, a purifying victim whose blood shed cleanseth from all sin; and to man, by nature and wicked works, far off, he presents an advocate with the Father, who "suffered, the just for the unjust, that he might bring us unto God."

At this stage of my subject, I feel it impossible to resist my inclination to translate, for the use of such of my hearers as may not have seen the original, or may not be acquainted with the language of it, a passage from a celebrated author, not generally supposed very partial to Christianity, and which some will therefore consider as the testimony of an enemy. John James Rousseau puts the following sentiments into the mouth of an intelligent village priest of Savoy, which he undoubtedly meant should pass for his own:

"I farther

" I farther acknowledge that the majesty
" of the Scriptures fills me with astonishment,
" the sanctity of the gospel speaks to my
" heart. Look into the books of the philo-
" sophers, with all their affected pomp;
" how mean they appear, when brought into
" comparison with this little volume! Is it
" possible that a book, at once so sublime, and
" so simple, should be the work of men? Is
" it possible that the person whose history it
" contains should himself be nothing more
" than a man? Where do we discover in him
" the tone of an enthusiast, or of an ambitious
" sectary? What gentleness and purity in his
" manners! What affecting grace in his in-
" structions! What elevation in his maxims!
" What profound wisdom in his discourses!
" What presence of mind, what acuteness, and
" what propriety in his replies! What com-
" mand over his passions! Where is the man,
" where is the sage, capable of acting, of
" suffering, and of dying without weakness,
" and without ostentation? When Plato draws
" the portrait of his imaginary just man;
" covered with all the reproach of criminality,
" and meriting all the rewards of virtue, he
" paints

" paints Jesus Christ stroke for stroke: the
" resemblance is so striking, that the fathers
" as one man felt it, and indeed it is im-
" possible to commit a mistake.  Under what
" prejudice, what blindness must that man
" labour who shall presume to state a com-
" parison between the son of Sophronisca
" (Socrates) and the son of Mary? To what
" a distance is the one removed from the
" other? Socrates dying, without pain, with-
" out disgrace, easily supports his character
" to the last; and unless that easy species of
" death, had reflected honour on his life, it
" might have been doubted whether Socrates,
" with all his superior powers, were any
" more than a sophist. He was the inventor,
" we are told, of morality. Others before
" him had reduced it into practice; all that
" he did was to tell what they had done, and
" to convert the examples which they had
" set, into so many precepts. Aristides had
" acted the part of a just man, before So-
" crates had given a definition of justice.
" Leonidas had devoted himself to death for
" his country, before Socrates had told us
" that the love of country is a moral duty.

" Sparta

"Sparta was a temperate city, before Socrates
"pronounced the eulogium of temperance;
"before he explained the nature of virtue,
"Greece had actually produced a multitude
"of virtuous men. But from what models
"among his countrymen did Jesus copy that
"exalted and pure morality, of which he
"himself alone furnished at once the lesson,
"and the example?" Here Rousseau refers to that part of the sermon on the mount which contains the parallel which Christ himself draws of the morality taught by Moses, and his own. Matt. v. 21, to the end; then thus proceeds. "From the bosom of the most
"furious fanatacism, the perfection of wis-
"dom caused its voice to be heard, and the
"simplicity of the most heroic virtues re-
"flected honour on the most abominable of
"all nations. The death of Socrates, calmly
"philosophizing amidst his friends, is the
"gentlest and most desirable which it is
"possible to imagine; that of Jesus, expiring
"in torment, insulted, mocked, execrated by
"a whole people, is the most horrible which
"fear itself can paint. Socrates, as he takes
"the empoisoned cup, blesses the man who
"puts

"puts it into his hand, and who melts into
"tears as he delivers it. Jesus, expiring in
"agonies from the idea of which nature re-
"coils, prays for his unrelenting murderers.
"Yes, if the life and death of Socrates be
"those of a sage, the life and death of Jesus
"are those of a God. Shall we be told that
"the history of the Gospel is an invention
"merely? No, no, my friend, nothing here
"has the air of fiction; and the facts tranf-
"mitted to us respecting Socrates, which no
"one pretends to deny, are less clearly attested,
"than those which relate to Jesus Christ.
"In truth, this is only putting aside the dif-
"ficulty, without doing it away. It would
"be more inconceivable that several men
"in concert should have fabricated the book
"in question, than it is, that one man should
"have furnished the subject of it. Never
"would Jewish authors have found out either
"that tone, or those morals; and the gospel
"possesses characters of truth so grand, so
"striking, so perfectly inimitable, that the
"inventor of it would be a more astonishing
"personage than the hero whom it displays."
Respecting the mysterious and incomprehen-
fible

sible articles of the Christian religion, the Savoyard vicar gives this sensible advice to his pupil, which I beg leave earnestly to recommend to the attention of my hearers of every description: "Young man, be always "modest and circumspect; respect in silence "what neither must be rejected, nor can be "comprehended, and humble thyself before "that great Being, to whom alone the truth "is known." I will not do Rousseau, with all his imperfections on his head, the injury, nor a modern railer against Christianity, whom I disdain to name, the honour, to contrast, comparison it cannot be, their spirit, their genius, their talents, their conduct. The one has purchased for himself a name which shall expire only with the world; the other, happily for the world, is already dead while he liveth.

3. The third universal character of human nature, to which the gospel most happily adapts itself, and by which it demonstrates it's divine original, is subjection to bondage. Jesus Christ is the great Deliverer of mankind, as he is the great Teacher and Intercessor. We speak not here of that civil bondage and oppression

pression, under which the greater part of the human race have groaned and travailed in pain together, from the beginning until now. This is truly deplorable; but Christ's " kingdom is not of this world." He came not to ascertain secular rights, but to confer everlasting privileges; He came not to raise up the throne of David which was fallen, nor to shake and overturn that of Cæsar which still stood; but to establish an universal empire of " righteousness, and peace, and joy in " the Holy Ghost," of which there shall be no end. He came to command, and to work deliverance, from a bondage to which the tyrant and his victim, the oppressor and the oppressed, the slave and his master, are equally subjected —" the bondage of corruption; the dominion " of the prince of the power of the air, the " spirit that worketh in the children of dis- " obedience." He came to deliver mankind from the power of death, through the fear of which men were all their life-time subject unto bondage.

1. Every man is in a state of subjection to the corruption of his own nature; he has
forged

forged fetters for himself, and habit makes them fit so easy, that at length he feels neither pain nor shame from his condition; and the generality of the case reconciles him entirely to his own. And what is the ignominy of those chains which gall the body, compared to the " fleshly lusts which war against the " soul?" This is the kind of deliverance which it was predicted He should accomplish, a prediction which He read aloud in the public synagogue and applied to himself, and indeed which it was the great end of his mission to fulfil. For to no purpose is ignorant man instructed, and criminal man pardoned, if he remain the slave of sin; to no purpose is the poison repelled, and its effect counteracted, if the patient desperately swallow repeated mortal doses. Now, corrupted man is that desperate suicide patient, armed with deadly poison, to destroy all that renders existence a blessing. The Jews vaunted their freedom as Abraham's seed, while they wilfully resisted the truth, and were devising the murder of an innocent person. Strange idea of liberty, for a man deliberately to shut his eyes that he may not see, and to gratify his own unruly passions, at

whatever

whatever expenfe to another, even that of life itfelf. "If ye continue in my word, ye fhall know the truth, and the truth fhall make you free. Whofoever committeth fin is the fervant," it ought to have been rendered "*the flave*, of fin. If the Son therefore fhall make you free, ye fhall be free indeed."

2. Man has another powerful tyrant with whom to contend, who takes advantage of his internal weaknefs and depravity, who leads men captive at his will, and, unhappily, at their own: who affumes the form of a friend, transforms himfelf into an angel of light to deceive the nations: who fhews men the kingdoms of this world and the glory of them, and promifes to beftow them on his deluded votaries: who propofes riches to the covetous, pleafures to the fenfual, honour and power to the ambitious, and men fall down and worfhip him, fome from hope, fome from fear. To deny the exiftence of fuch a being, is exprefsly to acknowledge his power, and to laugh the idea of his influence to fcorn, is to afford a proof of it's awful extent. The danger arifing from this quarter is, that no danger

danger appears. The great adversary finds it not to his purpose to retain his formidable character of a "roaring lion going about and seek-ing whom he may devour;" he has softened it down into his original character of serpent, saying, "ye shall not surely die, ye shall be as gods." To dissolve this fatal delusion, to destroy the works of the devil, to diminish, to shake, and at length totally to subvert his empire, to rescue the world of mankind from his yoke, was the great end for which the Son of God was manifested, and for this end he sent forth his witnesses to the uttermost parts of the earth, even "to open mens eyes, to turn them from darkness to light, and from the power of Satan unto God." And, wonderful mode of triumph! the seed of the woman in giving his heel to be bruised, crushed the serpent's head. Jesus, "by dying, destroyed him that hath the power of death, that is the devil:" which leads for a moment to contemplate the Saviour of the world, as conqueror of,

3. A third formidable adversary, but the last enemy which shall be destroyed, even death. It is the approach of this foe which clothes

clothes the other two in all their terror, which elicits remorse from the recollection of the past, and excites " a fearful looking for " of judgment," in the prospect of futurity. Even in the arms of dissolution, man feels himself immortal, but what is immortality without hope, immortality clouded with more than dismal apprehension? Prisoner of hope lift up thy head, the enemy though formidable, is not invincible. Jesus hath " abo-
" lished death, and brought life and im-
" mortality to light." " Being justified by
" faith" in Jesus " we have peace with God,
" we rejoice in hope of the glory of God; the
" day of our redemption draweth nigh."
Hear the voice of the Son of God and live:
" I give unto them eternal life; and they
" shall never perish, neither shall any pluck
" them out of my hand: my Father which
" gave them me is greater than all; and
" none is able to pluck them out of my
" Father's hand"—" I am the resurrection,
" and the life; he that believeth in me,
" though he were dead, yet shall he live:
" and whosoever liveth and believeth in me,
" shall never die."

And

And thus Jesus of Nazareth approves himself the best friend of the human race, in all the respects in which ignorant, guilty, miserable man stands in need of a friend. Thus the gospel proves it's divine original; proves that it is of him who made man, who knows what is in man, and what is good for man, from it's universal, and complete, adaptation to the constitution and frame of the human mind; it illumines what is dark, and strengthens what is weak; it brings peace to the troubled conscience, and subdues the power of indwelling corruption; it confers " the glorious " liberty of the Sons of God, and makes " feeble helpless man more than a conqueror;" it bruises Satan under his feet, and plucks the sting out of death.

But " we see not yet all things put under" Messiah the Prince. We have still to deplore the awful extent of the empire of ignorance and error—the wilful ignorance of one part of mankind, and the mysteriously-permitted ignorance of another. We have still to lament over the multitudes who never heard of " re-" demption through the blood of Christ," and

over

over the ſtill more wretched multitudes who madly trample it under their feet, as an unholy thing. We have ſtill to mourn over the voluntary ſlaves of ſin and ſatan, and the unhappy victims of the ſecond death. But let us not be difcouraged. The cauſe of " the " truth as it is in Jeſus" has ſurmounted many difficulties, has vanquiſhed many opponents, has levelled many ſtrong holds. Had this counſel, and this work been of men, long before now it would have come to nought; but, being of God, it has not been overthrown, it cannot be overthrown. From the paſt we can reaſon to the future. The Scriptures have been fulfilled, are fulfilling, and not " one " jot or one tittle ſhall in any wiſe paſs—till " all be fulfilled." In the ſeed promiſed to Abraham, " ſhall all the nations of the earth " be bleſſed:" but " it is not for us to know " the times or the ſeaſons, which the Father " hath put in his own power." But when we pray to our Father in heaven, we have encouragement to ſay: " Thy kingdom come; " Thy will be done in earth, as it is heaven." " —His name ſhall endure for ever; his name " ſhall be continued as long as the ſun: and " men

" men shall be blessed in him; all nations
" shall call him blessed. Blessed be the Lord
" God, the God of Israel, who only doth
" wondrous things: and blessed be his glo-
" rious name for ever; and let the whole
" earth be filled with his glory." Amen, and
amen.

# LECT. VIII.

### Luke XXIII. 39—43.

*And one of the malefactors, which were hanged, railed on him, saying, If thou be Christ save thyself and us.*

*But the other answering rebuked him, saying, Dost not thou fear God, seeing thou art in the same condemnation?*

*And we indeed justly; for we receive the due reward of our deeds: but this man hath done nothing amiss.*

*And he said unto Jesus, Lord, remember me when thou comest into thy kingdom.*

*And Jesus said unto him, Verily I say unto thee, To-day shalt thou be with me in Paradise.*

WITH innumerable marks of resemblance, which completely ascertain that all nations of men are formed of one blood, there are marks of discrimination equally

equally decisive, which demonstrate that every man is a singular individual, possessed of something peculiar to himself, moving in a sphere which is exclusively his own, and destined to fill a station, and to fulfil a purpose, for which he, and he only, is qualified. But this all-important individual has not only striking characteristics which clearly distinguish him from every other, but is himself, likewise, in a state of perpetual fluctuation and change. He is the same rational, conscious, responsible being, that he was from the beginning; but both the physical and the moral agent has undergone, and is constantly undergoing, an endless variety of transformation of relative state; of intellectual, of moral character; of corresponding tranquillity or disquiet. Newton was once ignorant, Samson came into the world a feeble infant, David's heart smote him for having touched Saul's skirt, yet permitted him to accomplish the death of Uriah; there was a period when Hazael shrunk from the thought of blood, and a period when he calmly digested the murder of his too confident royal master; the two thieves, in the text, who had brought upon

upon themselves the dreadful punishment of the cross, entered on their career harmless, perhaps amiable, little children.

At every period, and in every state, of his existence, man needs a monitor, a guide, a guardian, a comforter, a supporter. There are seasons and situations in which every internal resource fails, and every stream of consolation from without is dried up: when the man, thrown back upon himself, feels only exhausted powers, depressed spirits, perplexed thoughts, tormenting apprehensions; or, cast upon the wide world, finds only unavailing sympathy, or cold neglect, perhaps bitter reproach, and insult more cruel than death; or, plunged into futurity, floating on the surface of a boundless ocean, discerns no object through the darkness which covers it, or objects which only overwhelm with astonishment, or which rouse despair. In other words, there are seasons and situations in which religion, and religion alone, can raise and support the spirit, comfort the heart, and illuminate the prospect. And when we say religion, we mean Christianity; for what else deserves the name; what else is adapted to the effect? We have attempted

tempted a proof, in the two preceding Lectures: That the religion of Jesus Christ is entirely conformable to all the ideas of Deity which we are enabled to form by the exercise of our own reason, from a serious contemplation of the great universe; that is to say, it is the true and only religion of nature: and that it is universally congenial to the constitution and frame of the human mind: We are, from the induction of a few particular facts, now about to endeavour to prove, thirdly, that the religion of the gospel is most happily adapted to the feelings, the necessities, and the expectations of the human heart, at every successive stage, and in every possible condition of human existence, and that this too furnishes a strong presumption, if not a demonstration, of it's divine original.

I am well aware it may be said, that these are mere distinctions without a difference; that we have been fancifully parcelling out the human mind into a variety of qualities and operations which cannot in nature be separated or distinguished; as if three or more several applications could be made, on the
same

same subject, to the same individual, in a variety of respects; as if the being which discerns, which resolves, and which feels, were not one and the same. The anatomy of the mind, and of the body, is widely different. The parts of the external frame run indeed into each other; strengthen, support, nourish each other, but they remain for ever separate and distinct. The eye with its powers, faculties and results is never confounded, even by the vulgar, with those of the ear, the palate, or the hand. It is not so with those of the mind. Its powers are inseparable, indistinguishable. They mutually exchange names, assume each other's forms, execute each other's functions; they lead and are led by turns; or rather they constitute one active, determining principle, which it is impossible to define, but of whose existence and energy every reflecting man is conscious. It is, however, in most cases, with the mind as it is in the body; every extraordinary force in any one particular faculty is rarely, if ever, found associated with equal or similar force in all the other faculties. From an uncommon acuteness of vision, or of hearing, or of taste, or of the

other bodily senses, I should suspect a dulness or a deficiency, in those which are not the leading, or master, sense. In like manner, from a mind all eye, all intellect, we are led to expect cautious resolves, and cold exertions. A resolute disposition waits not for the calm deductions of sober reason, and frequently disregards the contingent, and even the probable or inevitable, consequences which may fall heavy on the heart; and, under the impulse of vehement affection or aversion, or any other domineering passion, the man feels the force of no argument that does not coincide with the present impulse, and he fluctuates from resolve to resolve, according as the tide sets in this way or that. In the present imperfect state of humanity, where, alas! shall we find an unclouded understanding dictating the decisions of the will, and these carried into effect with all the heart and with all the soul? But this leads us to the very point at which we are aiming. Take man in whatever light, under whatever character, you will, as an intelligent, as a self-determining, as a sensible and feeling being, or all at once, and in one, the gospel of Christ rises to him, descends
with

with him, purſues him through all his wanderings, ſtands by him when every thing elſe fails and forſakes him; it teaches his beſt reaſon how to reaſon, it gently conſtrains him to chuſe the good and to refuſe the evil, and, by ſhedding abroad the love of God in the heart, makes the hardeſt road of duty a way of pleaſantneſs, and a path of peace.

The penitent fellow-ſufferer of our bleſſed Lord exhibits man placed in very peculiar circumſtances, and it may be conſidered as an extreme caſe. Before, therefore, that we attend more particularly to it, let us look into a few others, which more frequently occur; and obſerve how Chriſtianity meets them at all points, thereby proving itſelf to be of Him who knows all men, and who needed not that any ſhould teſtify of man, for he knew what was in man. Obſerve

1, How ſweetly, how ſuitably, the goſpel applies itſelf to the condition and character of harmleſs childhood, of ingenuous, intelligent, and as yet uncontaminated youth. Behold Jeſus himſelf, in all the affecting intereſt of infancy in a state of poverty and depression, but marked out by signs in heaven, and signs on earth, to a rank which eclipses the state of Kings. Behold him in all the lovelinefs of intelligent, modest, unassuming youth, retiring from the temple, where his understanding and answers had astonished every listening ear, and had captivated all hearts, descending with his mother and Joseph into the obscurity and reproach of a village of Galilee, becoming " subject to them;" and, in this humble retreat, " increasing in wisdom and stature, and " in favour with God and man." What a pattern to propose to our children! What an engine to work on the opening mind, on the tender susceptible heart! Behold him in the maturity of wisdom, in all the majesty of goodness, in all the plenitude of power and authority, descending to the level of little children, speaking kindly of them, and to them, receiving them into his arms, pronouncing his benediction upon them, declaring them the heirs of the kingdom of heaven, the charge of angels, the darling care of his heavenly Father. Hear the good Shepherd recommending attention to them as to the

lambs

lambs of his flock, carrying them in his bosom, laying down his life for them. What a hold is here laid on the youthful affections! "The "most dignified of all beings loves me, che- "rishes me, will suffer no one to do me "wrong. He condescends to admonish, to "instruct, to bless me. He has opened all "heaven to my view, he laid down his life "for my sake, he is gone to prepare a place "for me. My Lord and my God! thou art "drawing me with cords of love, I give my- "self up entirely to thee. I am young, ig- "norant, inexperienced; be thy wisdom my "guide through life. I am a fallen, guilty "creature, forgive me, restore me, strengthen "me. I am liable to disease and death, but "thou art able to heal every malady, both of "the body, and of the mind; and when I "leave this world and die, I shall go unto "thee, which is far better."

2. Take the opposite extreme of human life, and observe how admirably adapted the religion of Jesus is to the condition and character of age. Every thing in the man has changed. The bodily organs are all debilitated,

Q 3  blunted,

blunted, decayed; the mental faculties are impaired, deranged, destroyed; the result of a long life's experience is "vanity of vanities, "all is vanity." The reduced, the forlorn, the joyless creature, the poor remains of what he was, is become a burthen to himself, and to all around him. But this dark state is illumined, this depression is relieved, and the sinking heart finds support and consolation from the "exceeding great and precious "promises" of "life and immortality brought "to light by the gospel;" from the assurance that the day cometh when "all who are in "their graves shall hear the voice of the Son "of God and shall come forth;" from the animating, the unbounded prospect of "new "heavens and a new earth wherein dwelleth "righteousness;" from the delightful confidence that to be "absent from the body is "to be present with the Lord." Thus were the last days of Simeon cheered and comforted. He was waiting for the consolation of Israel, and he waited not in vain. He lived to see "the Lord's Christ," to embrace him, to rejoice in him; and every other object becomes uninteresting and insipid; "Lord, now lettest
"thou

"thou thy servant depart in peace, according to thy word, for mine eyes have seen thy salvation." Hence the face of Stephen derived a lustre not his own, and shone like the face of an angel; he "saw heaven opened, and Jesus standing on the right hand of God." Hence Paul, the aged, was made to "rejoice with joy unspeakable and full of glory," in the prospect of being made a sacrifice in the cause of his master, and in the brighter prospect of the glory that should follow: " I am now ready to be offered, and the time of my departure is at hand. I have fought a good fight, I have finished my course, I have kept the faith. Henceforth there is laid up for me a crown of righteousness, which the Lord the righteous judge shall give me at that day.—For the which cause also I suffer these things; nevertheless I am not ashamed: for I know whom I have believed, and am persuaded that he is able to keep that which I have committed unto him against that day." Thus, once more, the solitude and languor of his exile to the isle of Patmos, "for the word of God, and for the testimony of
"Jesus

of "Jesus Christ," and the weight of accumulated years, were alleviated to the beloved disciple, by the sublime communications of the Lord's day, by the visions of the Almighty, by the foretastes of the glory to be revealed, by the gracious words which flowed from the lips of his glorified master: "Fear not; I am the first and the last, I am he that liveth and was dead; and behold I am alive for evermore. Amen, and have the keys of hell and of death." These are not the dark peradventures, the trembling uncertainties, the fond *ifs*, the timid conjectures, the half-formed conclusions of virtuous and enlightened paganism; of a Cyrus, a Cato, a Cicero, groping in the dark; rather hoping in immortality than daring to believe it; but the solid conviction of believers in Christ Jesus, "who know their ground, and were "ready always to give an answer to every "man that asked a reason of the hope which "was in them." There is a

3. Third well-known condition and character of human life, with its corresponding feelings and affections, to which the gospel peculiarly adapts

adapts its instructions, its support, its consolation; and which Christ himself displays as furnishing the leading proof of his divine mission: " to the *poor* the gospel is preached." There is a great class of mankind of whom the world makes no account, whom it despises and tramples upon, but who are of high estimation in the sight of God. The poor in spirit invite insult and oppression from the proud and the aspiring; instead of attracting kindness, challenging encouragement, and ensuring protection: but Jesus Christ pronounces them blessed, because " theirs is the kingdom " of heaven." The poor in condition are treated as the offscouring of the earth; and, being the great majority of mankind, it seems as if the many were destined to become the victims of the few. But Christianity replaces mankind in an order more natural, and more equitable. That he might be a suitable instructor and example to the world, Jesus Christ assumed not a high station, nor great affluence, in which he could have had few disciples, and still fewer imitators; but, in an humble condition, He exemplified the corresponding temper and dispositions, meekness and humility, that

he

he might be a teacher of all, a pattern to all. Some of the moſt ſignal of his miracles were, accordingly, performed for the relief of the ſons and daughters of poverty. Starving, fainting multitudes received from his hand a ſeaſonable and ample ſupply. They had the accumulated ſatisfaction of participating of the repaſt which nature craved, and of beholding their proviſion multiply in the hand of the diſtributor.

But the goſpel hiſtory, copying always from real life, exhibits poverty not as a ſimple evil, but blended, as it generally is, with ſome additional circumſtance of depreſſion and diſtreſs; that it may exhibit, at the ſame time, it's own native tendency to reach, and to remedy, the evil to it's utmoſt poſſible extent. Bartimeus was not only reduced to the ſad neceſſity of begging his bread by the way-ſide, but, deprived of eye ſight, was at the direction and diſpoſal of thoſe who ſaw, and they were ungenerous and unkind; they endeavoured to quaſh his ſuit, and to ſtifle the voice of his appeal. Happily for him, though blind, he had a tongue to cry for mercy, and Jeſus the

Son

Son of David had an ear of compassion, which was never deaf to the call of misery. The mind's eye had already discerned the great prophet " who should come into the world," and the first object which met the restored bodily organ was the great Restorer of fallen humanity in person. " Immediately he re-
" ceived his sight, and followed Jesus in the
" way." Poverty and blindness are, alas! a frequent association: no wonder then that it presented itself oftner than once in the progress of Him " who went about doing good." Bartimeus solicited and obtained relief, but the eye of Jesus prevented the tongue of the man blind from his birth, and his pity outran the complaint of distress, and the arm of power operated an unimplored cure. In this case, the illumination of the bodily eye seems to have preceded, and to have produced, the dispersion of moral and intellectual obscurity. The man distinguished not the Son of God, in the person of him who had anointed his eyes. His natural good-sense discerned indeed a prophet, and a worshipper, a man, of God; but it required another exertion of the power and grace of the Redeemer to exalt the conviction

conviction of natural reason into a principle of living faith on the Messiah. " Jesus said " unto him, Doft thou believe on the Son of " God ? He answered and said, Who is he, " Lord, that I might believe on him? and " Jesus said unto him, Thou haft both seen " him, and it is he who talketh with thee. " And he said, Lord I believe. And he wor- " shipped him."

Behold the beggar Lazarus " laid at the " rich man's gate, full of sores," perishing for hunger; " desiring," but desiring in vain, " to be fed with the crumbs which fell from " the table" of unfeeling wealth, and thoughtless profusion; the pangs of famine sharpened to him by the sight and hearing of riotous waste. Can there be a lower depth of human wretchedness?—a body all ulcer, the keeneft cravings of nature unsupplied, the bitterness of dying neglected, unpitied. See that longing, languishing, desponding look was his laft; with that lengthened groan fled " the spirit " unto God who gave it." Mark how the consolations of religion interpose. Behold the angels of God, ministring spirits sent forth to

minifter

Lect. 8.   *Evidences of Christianity.*   237

minister to the heirs of salvation, depositing their charge in the bosom of the Father of the faithful. The man who had in his life-time received evil things, who had submitted patiently to the will of God, and cleaved to the prospects of immortality, is now comforted, he remembers his misery no more, he enjoys eternal rest.

Once more, look at the " man lame from " his mother's womb;" incapable of self-motion, of earning subsistence, except by supplicating tones and looks, borne of others to the place of alms day by day, to solicit a precarious pittance from persons almost as poor as himself. With eyes fixed on the disciples of the carpenter's Son, he expects to receive something to procure him a morsel of bread. What must have been his astonishment and delight, on hearing " the name of Jesus of " Nazareth" pronounced; and to feel his feet and ankle-bones receiving strength! " He leap-
" ing up stood, and walked, and entered with
" them into the temple, walking, and leaping,
" and praising God." And " the poor shall
" never cease out of the land;" " The poor

we

" we have always with us." And are they alone of this description, think you, who subsist on charity, who earn a hard and scanty fare with the sweat of their brow, who rise up early, and sit up late, and eat the bread of sorrows? Ah how many are there, whose own heart alone knoweth its bitterness? who are constrained to conceal the shame of poverty under the vail of composed looks and a fair appearance; who want and pine in secret, that they may seem to abound in the public eye? How many have the mortification of seeing all their projects fail, all their painful labours, all their honest industry prove fruitless, all their worldly hopes perish? What must become of such, did not Christianity repress each murmuring thought? did not the " man of sorrows and acquainted with grief" reconcile the mind to a mean condition, and a hard lot, by representing his own? " the foxes " have holes, and the birds of the air have " nests, but the Son of Man hath not where " to lay his head;" did not a dawn of hope arise, of " treasures in heaven, where neither " moth nor rust doth corrupt, and where " thieves do not break through nor steal."

This

This is the Christian's joy and crown of rejoicing; this is the mystery which the world cannot unfold; this is the miracle which the Spirit of the living God alone can operate: "As unknown, and yet well-known; as dying, and behold we live; as chastened, and not killed; as sorrowful, yet alway rejoicing; as poor, yet making many rich; as having nothing, and yet possessing all things." Where, but in the school of Christ, will a man learn, in whatsoever "state he is, therewith to be content; how to be abased, and how to abound;" where else shall he be instructed, "both to be full, and to be hungry, both to abound and to suffer need?" Where else shall he behold the precept, and the pattern, in perfect harmony?

4. Let us now look for a moment into the opposite condition and character of human life, affluence and its concomitants, influence, and power, and splendor, with the sentiments which they usually inspire; and let us observe how Jesus Christ, in the gospel, adapts his admonitions to this external state of man, and

to

to the spirit which it excites. Persons of a poor and low estate, frequently express an affected contempt of riches, and disguise real envy of the wealthy and prosperous, under the mask of pitying and despising them. But no man's person, and no condition of humanity, are in themselves despicable or hateful; for all is the work of an infinitely wise Providence. When the blessed Jesus, therefore, speaks of riches, or addresses his advice to the affluent, it is never with acrimony, contempt, or unkindness, but in the spirit of meekness, of compassion, of regret. If he points out the danger of a worldly spirit, if he condemns it, he is warning men to be on their guard against it, that they may learn to combat, and to subdue it. See yonder ruler addressing himself to Jesus Christ. Riches and power have not corrupted him. Though a ruler, and a man of large possessions, he is neither insolent nor assuming; he is modest and well-bred; he has lived a virtuous life, he is concerned about the salvation of his soul. His character and deportment are so unexceptionably amiable, that " Jesus beholding him, " loved him." Alas, his condition was a
snare

snare to him. He had yet to learn the true use of wealth. He understood, admitted, practised the *letter* of the law; but the *spirit* of it he felt not, even, " Thou shalt love thy " neighbour as thyself." It had never entered into his thoughts that the poor man could be his neighbour, or could have a claim upon his estate. He would do any thing to inherit eternal life, except making the sacrifice of his silver and gold. We are left however with a glimmering of hope, that his case, though dangerous, might not be desperate, that the sorrow which he expressed, might be after a godly sort, and " work re-
" pentance unto salvation not to be re-
" pented of."

With a wisdom truly divine, which traces the human heart through all its intricacies, Christ discerned the master-spring which puts, and keeps, the little world of man in motion, and He bends the whole force of his doctrine to oppose and counteract it. One brother lays hold of the whole inheritance of his father, and hardens his bowels against his own mother's son. The disappointed brother,

considering the wisdom and authority of Jesus, as favourable to his claim of a portion of the heritage, would gladly have employed him as an umpire. Jesus saw the spirit of the application, and repelled it. He came not to adjust secular interests. He saw the same spirit working in both brothers, and took occasion from it to caution mankind against that " evil concupiscence which is idolatry," and the root of all evil. " Take heed, and be-
" ware of covetousness; for a man's life
" consisteth not in the abundance of the
" things which he possesseth." The character which he delineates, to give weight to his remonstrance, and to confirm his doctrine, is that of a poor, sordid wretch, who represents a great multitude, overwhelmed by abundance, deferring enjoyment from year to year, till what was already too much, should become superfluously more; a man bent only on useless accumulation, and sinking all thoughts of a life to come, in making a provision for this world, which he was incapable of tasting: a case of folly so egregious, were it not so common, as to merit even in this world the treatment of lunacy. Affecting
view

view of a man, who " layeth up treasure for " himself, and is not rich towards God!" In the history of the rich man at whose gate Lazarus was laid, Christ pursues the effects of a worldly spirit to its native and certain, though remote consequences. He is not accused of having acquired fortune by unjustifiable methods, nor of employing it as an engine of cruelty and oppression. Neither is he charged with burying one talent after another in the ground, without daring to use it. But there are more ways than one of abusing the things of this world. He is swallowed up of " the lust of the flesh, and " the lust of the eyes, and the pride of life." " Clothed in purple and fine linen, and faring " sumptuously every day," he has become callous to the demands of suffering humanity; absorbed in self, it is nothing to him what wretches feel; " to-morrow shall be as this day, and much more abundant;" and the delusion goes on, till the thoughtless, unhappy wretch is overtaken by death and judgment.

But the gospel history has transmitted to us, together with these, an instance of the just and generous use of substance, and of the power of true religion to new mould the heart of even a rich and worldly-minded man. It is that of Zaccheus, the chief of the publicans; against whom it is plainly insinuated, and indeed admitted by himself, that he had accumulated property by means highly unwarrantable. The presence and purity of Christ overawed him into a sense of justice, and compelled him to make ample restitution: " Lord, " if I have taken any thing from any man, " by false accusation, I restore him fourfold." Then, and not till then, there was room for works of mercy, and the humbled, softened extortioner joyfully divides the remainder of his fortune with the poor. Then " salvation " came to his house," and thus " the Son of " man came to seek and to save that which " was lost."

Having thus adduced common and well-known conditions of human life, childhood and age, poverty and wealth, through a variety of gradations, as illustrative of the power and grace of the gospel, in ameliorating the state and character of man, and thereby demonstrative

monstrative of its divine original, we conclude with leading your attention, in the

Fifth and last place, to that singular and affecting instance of human misery, and of divine mercy, which is the subject of the history read at the opening of this discourse; for to adduce every instance to our purpose were the work not of a Lecture, but of a whole life.—We have here a man in a state of dreadful extremity, such as even this valley of tears exhibits not every day. A man floating on the confines of two worlds, in all the agony of bodily torture, pursued with all the remorse of an accusing conscience, telling him that he suffered justly, that he was receiving the due reward of his deeds; a man alarmed with the overwhelming apprehensions of instant judgment, and a miserable eternity. The hand of the executioner is lifted up to strike the blow which is to extinguish hope for ever, and, terminating bodily pain for a season, to let loose upon the soul the worm that dieth not. Awful interval, but not given up to the blackness of absolute despair! All is not lost, for the sinking eye can yet supplicate, and the faltering lips pronounce a requeſt. "Lord "remember me when thou comeſt into thy "kingdom!" Who is this that calls Jeſus Lord, now that he is deſpiſed and rejected of all men; now that his diſciples have forſaken him and fled; now when they that ſee him laugh him to ſcorn; now that his ſtrength is dried up like a potſherd; and his tongue cleaveth to his jaws, and he is ſinking into the duſt of death? Who is he that aſcribeth to him a kingdom, at this hour and power of darkneſs, when earth has renounced him, and the rays of heaven are intercepted, and hell triumphs? Who is he that prays to one who has reſigned the power of ſaving himſelf? O man, great is thy faith! Againſt hope thou believeſt in hope; and thy hope ſhall not make thee aſhamed. And who is He that from yonder triumphant ignominy diſpoſes of heavenly thrones, who opens and ſhuts at his pleaſure the everlaſting doors of the inviſible world, who plucks the trembling creature as a brand out of the burning, and tranſports the priſoner of hope into the paradiſe of God? He on whom help is laid, the Lord mighty to ſave, even to the uttermoſt, them that come

unto

unto God through him, seeing he ever liveth to make intercession for them. Thus, then, from the sweetest, mildest, meekest condition of human life, to the most dreadful extreme of depravation, and criminality, and distress, the gospel becomes " all things to all men ;"—the instructor of babes, the consolation and joy of old age, the provision of poverty, the monitor of riches, the refuge of the miserable.

Put thyself, therefore, young man, under the tuition of this divine Instructor. Look to him, and learn of him to be meek, and patient, and submissive. This amiable period of your existence is passing away. The blossom begins to fall from the tree. Every thing has its season, and is beautiful in its season. The bud passes into the flower, and the flower into fruit, which gradually swells and colours into maturity. But if the bud be blighted, the spring will have no beauty, the summer no promise, autumn no fulness, winter no provision. An hour lost or misspent in the morning, makes a hurried, confused day, and an unpleasant, a remorseful evening. Do not unwisely increase the labour and difficulty of next year, by loading it with the indolence, the folly, or the vice of that which is now spending itself. Behold Jesus, at the age of twelve years, "about his Father's business;" " in the temple, sitting in the midst of the " doctors, both hearing and asking them " questions;" so that " all who heard him " were astonished at his understanding and " answers." Learn of him to listen and to inquire. Behold him going down with his parents to Nazareth, and becoming " subject " unto them;" and go and do likewise, and like him thou shalt " increase in wisdom and " stature, and in favour with God and man."

What shall be done for thee, my aged friend? now that " the evil days are coming on, and " the years drawing nigh, when thou shalt " say, I have no pleasure in them;" now that " the sun, and the light, and the moon, and " the stars are waxing dim; and the clouds " return after the rain;" now that " the " keepers of the house" begin to " tremble," and " the strong man to be bowed down, and " the grinders to cease, because they are few, " and those that look out of the windows
" are

"are darkened;" now that "fears are in
"the way, and the almond tree flourishes, and
"the grashopper becomes a burden, and de-
"fire fails." All these things are in the
order and course of nature, and are not to be
regretted as a real evil: Satiated of life, thou
art ready to say with Job; "I lothe it, I
"would not live alway; my days are vanity:"
and with the apostle of the Gentiles, "having
"a desire to depart and to be with Christ;
"which is far better." Now thou knowest
the "sureness of that foundation which God
"hath laid in Zion;" the excellency of that
"hope which maketh not ashamed;" the un-
decaying vigor of that faith which "still
"shall bring forth fruit in old age:" which
is ever "fat and flourishing." That which
was the ornament of youth, and the guide of
life, will prove a support to the sinking spirit,
and a crown of glory encircling the hoary
head. Hold "the beginning of thy con-
"fidence stedfast to the end." Like Simeon,
with Jesus and his gospel in thy embrace,
thou canst smile in the face of death; thou
canst look up in holy triumph, and say: "Lord;
"now lettest thou thy servant depart in
"peace,

"peace, according to thy word: for mine "eyes have feen thy falvation:" and with Paul the aged; "I know whom I have believed, and am perfuaded that he is able to keep that which I have committed unto him againſt that day." I muſt not reverſe this portrait. The heart ſinks at the idea of old age deſtitute of the confolations of religion, deferted of God, defcending into the grave without hope. "Seek the Lord while he "may be found; call upon him while he is "near."

To you, all ye ſons and daughters of want, the goſpel of the bleſſed Jeſus recommends itſelf with peculiar propriety. "To the poor "the goſpel is preached." This was given as one of the diſtinctive characters of the Meſſiah; as a proof that Chriſt was he "who "ſhould come," and that no other was to be waited for. Behold the Author and Finiſher of your faith ſuffering hunger and thirſt, as ye ſometimes do. Behold him "deſpiſed "and rejected of men;" without "a place "where to lay his head;" his wants ſupplied by the ſympathy and gratitude of pious women,

### Lect. 8. *Evidences of Christianity.* 251

women, who "ministred unto him of their "substance." Behold the carpenter's son, the companion of fishermen, conversing with the simple, feeding with the poor, walking from place to place on foot, in every form of humiliation; and cease from pride, cease from discontent. Be reconciled to the hardships of a necessitous, laborious, obscure condition of life. Be "poor in spirit," be patient, be diligent, be resigned to the will of God. "The world is not your friend, nor the "world's law;" feeling the powers of a world to come, "lay up for yourselves trea- "sures in heaven, where neither moth nor "rust doth corrupt, and no thief breaketh "through to steal." "Fear not *little* flock, "it is your Father's good pleasure to give "you the kingdom."

Let not the "rich of this world" be "high- "minded, but fear." Let them not "trust "in uncertain riches, but in the living God, "who giveth them all things richly to en- "joy." "Take heed and beware of covet- "ousness, for a man's life consisteth not in "the abundance of the things which he pof-
"sesseth."

" feffeth." Meditate feriously on the danger to which your fituation is expofed. "How hardly fhall they that have riches enter into the kingdom of God!" Think on the temptations arifing out of ample means to indulge "the luft of the flefh, and the luft of the eyes, and the pride of life." In proportion to your danger be your vigilance, your jealoufy over yourfelves, your diffidence in your own wifdom and ftrength. "Sell that thou haft and give to the poor, and thou fhalt have treafure in heaven," and go and follow Jefus.

Let the miferable of every defcription look to the compaffionate friend of the wretched and forlorn. For this end is he "exalted a Prince and a Saviour." "The Lord hath fent him to bind up the broken-hearted, to proclaim liberty to the captives, and the opening of the prifon to them that are bound:"—" to appoint unto them that mourn in Zion, to give unto them, beauty for afhes, the oil of joy for mourning, the garment of praife for the fpirit of heavinefs." Son, daughter, of woe, "arife, he calleth "thee."

Lect. 8. *Evidences of Christianity.*

"thee." "Look to me and be saved." "Come unto me, all ye that labour, and are heavy laden, and I will give you rest." "Fear not; for I have redeemed thee, I have called thee by thy name, thou art mine: when thou passest through the waters I will be with thee; and through the rivers, they shall not overflow thee; when thou walkest through the fire, thou shalt not be burnt; neither shall the flame kindle upon thee." The expiring thief cried for mercy, and obtained it. With a broken and contrite heart he prayed, "Lord remember me," and he was heard, and accompanied his Saviour from the agony of the cross to the paradise of God. It is "he that liveth, and was dead; and behold," saith he, "I am alive for evermore. Amen; and have the keys of hell and of death."—"Blessed and holy is he that hath part in the first resurrection; on such the second death hath no power, but they shall be priests of God, and of Christ:" to whom be glory for ever and ever. Amen.

LECT.

# LECT. IX.

### JOHN XVI. 33.

*These things I have spoken unto you, that in me ye might have peace. In the world ye shall have tribulation: but be of good cheer; I have overcome the world.*

EVERY instant of a thinking man's life may be considered as a point of prospect, or a point of reflection. We are either reviewing the past, or diving into futurity. We are like travellers, who avail themselves of every little eminence on the road, to measure with their eye the track which they have been pursuing, and the space which is still extended before them. The present moment continually disappears at the moment; just as the spot on which we stand to view a landscape, itself disappears, though it be the centre and focus of all that we behold. It was an object of importance before we reached it, and it

will

will recover its importance when we come to look back upon it. Our prospects necessarily take a colour from our retrospects. It is natural for us to expect, in some future attainment or deliverance, a compensation for the disappointments and disasters which we have endured; and, from the goodness of an indulgent Providence, we hope for the continuation, progress and improvement of the blessings which we have enjoyed. " Man never " is, but always *to be* blest:" he never lives and enjoys, but is continually busied in making preparation to live and to enjoy. Whatever he possesses, there is still a farther possession attainable; whatever he may suffer, hope looks forward to a period of repose and recompense. But fear likewise mingles in the cup of human life, and embitters it. The present good may be lost, it may be marred, it may be impoisoned by some baleful infusion. The present pressure may increase till it become intolerable; and this sorrow is, it may be, but the beginning of sorrows. The visible world vanishes, and the world of spirits rises to view; time expires, and eternity resumes it's awful empire. Man in old age,

age, in decay, even in death, feels the principle of immortality strong within him; and, according to the prospect before him, it is a source of the purest delight, or of the most oppressive sorrow. The first great concern, then, of a reasonable being, is the improvement and amelioration of his present condition, in a consistency with the felicity of a future and eternal duration. That weighty concern, the Father of our spirits has graciously taken into his own hands, and, viewing his creature man as intimately connected with both worlds, has provided, and disclosed, the means of certain happiness for him, in the life which now is, and in that which is to come. Man himself was wholly unequal to this. Man left to himself becomes a mere creature of this world, and, swallowed up of the things of time, becomes insensible to the powers of the world to come; or, under the influence of an ill-informed principle of religion, makes it a duty to sacrifice the present life entirely to the prospects of immortality. The religion of Jesus Christ, if we had the wisdom to be regulated by it, firmly establishes the one, without shaking the foundation of the other.

S      It

It strengthens the bands of human society, rivets the obligation of relative duty, sanctions and sanctifies innocent and lawful earthly enjoyments, rectifies the disorders, and controls the effects of human passions, administers consolation under, and finds a way to escape from, all the miseries which flesh is heir to. But at the same time, we are not permitted for a moment to forget, that all these things are transient, that they are a preparation for, and a progress toward, a higher, a holier, a happier, and a more permanent existence, brought to light by the Gospel. To unfold the native influence of Christianity on our present state and condition, as a farther proof of its divine original, is to be the attempt of this lecture.

The life of man is not merely a current flowing incessantly downward, with uniform speed, in a channel throughout of the same depth and wideness, but a stream undergoing every instant, sudden and unexpected variations; now, precipitated over the rock, and anon, slumbering through the plain; here, confined within barriers which hardly afford a passage, and there, spreading into an ocean; to-day, to-day, swollen above it's banks by the torrent from the mountain, to-morrow, drunk up by the fervent heat of a vertical sun. He must have lived a very short time in the world, or life must have flowed in a very even tenor indeed, or he must be a person little given to observation, who is not conscious of something more than the mere lapse of time, of the transition from one measurement of human life to another. Who among us is so young as not to have felt, and so forgetful as not to recollect, the sad transition from health to sickness, from ease to pain, from joy to sorrow? Were there not seasons and situations in which we needed a counsellor, a comforter, a supporter; when we looked for them, but found them not? Are there not cases which baffle all created skill, to cure, or even to mitigate? Dare we hope to be in future exempted from the common lot of humanity, or can we believe that the arrows of the Almighty are exhausted; or is it possible to presume on our own internal resources against the evil day? If not, O let us listen to the words of life, flowing from the lips of Him who spake as never man spake: " Come unto me, all ye " that labour and are heavy laden, and I will " give

"give you rest." "These things I have spoken unto you, that in me ye might have peace. In the world ye shall have tribulation: but be of good cheer, I have overcome the world."

In these words Jesus fairly proposes to his disciples, what he both could and would bestow upon them; all the blessings included in the comprehensive term *peace*; and He points out where it resided, " in me ye shall have peace." With equal candor He declares what they were not to expect from their relation to him; not worldly case, honour, power, riches; but the reverse of these, worldly distress and tribulation. He administers strong consolation under the worst that could befal them; it was temporary, and therefore tolerable; it could reach the body, without affecting the composure and tranquility of the soul; " be of good cheer." And finally, he shews the possibility of a triumph over the world, whatever form it might assume, in an instance with which they were intimately acquainted; " I have overcome the world." A brief recapitulation of these particulars, will contain all that we mean to advance on the subject.

1st. Jesus

1st. Jesus Christ candidly proposes to his followers, what he both can and will bestow upon them; all the blessings included in the comprehensive term *peace*: thus and thus, says he, have I spoken, " that ye might have " peace." The original state of the world was perfect harmony. " God saw every thing " that he had made, and behold it was very " good." All was order in external nature; the earth in rich profusion yielded her increase; the animal tribes, at peace among themselves, yielded an united and a joyful submission to their common lord. His sway over them was exercised with lenity and affection. Man, rejoicing in conscious existence, superiority, felicity, referred all to the God who made him; and Deity rejoiced in all his works. The creation of " an help " meet for man" extended the empire of peace, and the spirit of love. The entrance of sin into the world, disturbed this blessed harmony, rendered guilty man a terror to himself, tore asunder the bands of affection, transmitted the spirit of discord into the brute creation, generated elementary strife, " drove out the man, placed cherubims, and
" a flaming

"a flaming fword, which turned every way, "to keep the way of the tree of life." Ah, we now know too well what peace is, from its fierce oppofite; from the pangs of an accufing confcience, and the threatenings of a violated law; from domeftic difcord, and national animofity; from the confufed noife of the warrior, and garments rolled in blood; from the many-formed evils which wretched mortals endure, and from a fearful looking for of judgment to come. Is it a light thing, then, to hear of " peace on earth and good will to men?" What heart is fo hard, what fpirit fo bold as to refolve on everlafting war? What, remain an eternal prey to the ftings and fcorpions of a hell in the breaft? What, carry the hatred, and difcord, and wrath of this miferable life, into a never-ending ftate of being! What, lie for ever under the juft difpleafure of a holy and righteous God! The foul recoils from an idea fo horrible, it cleaves to the glad tidings of great joy, it opens to receive the great Peace-maker, it beholds paradife reftored, the way of the tree of life laid open, the fpirit of love revived, all heaven poured into the bofom. Is it nothing to a

guilty

guilty creature to be assured that his sins are forgiven, that he is reconciled unto God, that he is passed from death unto life? Is it nothing for him to feel corruption every day dying within him, and the image of Christ gradually forming in his heart? Is it nothing to be " filled with peace and joy in believing," and to " rejoice in hope of the glory of God?" O, what do we not owe to him whose words procure, inspire, a peace which passeth all understanding! " Blessed be the peace-
" maker; He is the Son of God."

Is there one among us who has known the bitterness of alienation, of estrangement, from a parent, from a brother, from a friend who was as his own soul; and who, through the mediation of wisdom and goodness, has been made to taste the delight of reconciliation, of renovated sentiments and habits of tenderness; let him declare the obligation conferred by the friend of mankind, who, by the sacrifice of himself, has purchased our peace; who " suffered for sins, the just for the unjust,"
" that he might bring us to God." What are the things which Christ has spoken, to confer

confer this holy compofure, this unutterable peace? Look into the context, "The Spirit "of Truth will come, and will guide you "into all truth; he will fhew you things "to come: your forrow fhall be turned into "joy: I will fee you again, and your heart "fhall rejoice, and your joy no man taketh "from you: whatfoever ye fhall afk the "Father in my name, he will give it you: "afk and ye fhall receive, that your joy may "be full: The Father himfelf loveth you, "becaufe ye have loved me, and have be- "lieved that I came out from God."

2dly. He points out where this peace refides, where it is laid up: "that *in me* ye might "have peace." He who made peace is alfo the confervator of it. Reftored friendfhip is of a delicate texture. It calls for vigilance and circumfpection. A relapfe into cold-nefs and difaffection might prove irrecoverable. The hand which united the broken cord muft keep it knit together. Man, frail man, muft not be entrufted with the management of his own moft valuable poffeffion, he cannot be the guardian of his own peace. It is

is the hand of a Mediator; it is laid up
" with Chrift in God." When the believer
looks into himfelf, he finds no ground of
confidence; he fees much to diftrefs, and to
difcourage him; he fees " a law in the mem-
" bers, warring againft the law of the mind,
" and bringing him into captivity to the law
" of fin which is in the members." This
difturbs inward peace, this produces a conflict which rends the fpirit, and produces
this defponding exclamation: " O wretched
" man that I am! who fhall deliver me from
" the body of this death?" But the words
of Jefus reftore the balance of the foul, and
ftill the complaint: " In me ye fhall have
" peace." That corruption fhall not prevail;
" My grace is fufficient for thee: for my
" ftrength is made perfect in weaknefs."
" Thofe, Holy Father, that thou gaveft me,
" I have kept, and none of them is loft. I
" give unto them eternal life; and they fhall
" never perifh, neither fhall any pluck them
" out of my hand. My Father which gave
" them me is greater than all: and none is able
" to pluck them out of my Father's hand."
" Abide," therefore, " in me, and I in you.

As

" As the branch cannot bear fruit of itself,
" except it abide in the vine; no more can
" ye, except ye abide in me: for without me
" ye can do nothing." Christ having thus proposed unreservedly what he was able and ready to bestow, on his disciples, peace with God, peace of conscience, peace among themselves, and, as far as in them lay, peace with all men, with equal candor declares,

3dly. What they were not to expect from their relation to him; not the respect, the applause, the enjoyments of the world, but it's resentment and hatred: "In the world ye shall have tribulation." This comes directly to the point which we have in view. When we look into life, we find all men breaking out into occasional fits of complaint against the world, and alleging with the prophet, in the moment of spleen, that they do well to be angry. They had created an ideal world to themselves; and not finding that creation realized in experience, instead of accusing their own rashness and presumption, they complain of the order and justice of Providence. Their path was ever to be smooth, their plans prosperous;

prosperous; "the stars in their courses" were to fight for them. They had not taken into the account, changes, and war, and death. Expectation raised too high, on the one hand, and an injudicious security on the other, mar the relish of earthly comforts, and aggravate the unavoidable miseries of human life. Like spoiled children we peevishly reject ten thousand blessings which are within our reach, because a single one is denied us. Reason discerns the folly of this, but reason is a feeble principle when counteracted by ardent passions, and by powerful interests. In truth, sudden transitions, unless " the heart is estab- " lished by grace," produce humiliating effects on the human mind. Unexpected success renders mere man vain, insolent, self-sufficient. Under the pressure of unforeseen calamity, he becomes melancholy and dejected, and gives all up for lost. In both cases the the world is all in all, and immortal interests are swallowed up of the feelings and pursuit of the moment. What man needs, therefore, is a regulating, active, commanding principle, which will not change with the wind, which will not follow the impulses of the

moon;

moon; which will accompany him into the bright regions of prosperity, admonish him, guide him, guard him, and open to his view a brighter region, which shall eclipse all " the " kingdoms of this world and the glory of " them;" and which will descend with him into the depths of adversity, to soothe, to cheer, to comfort him; and which, even in death, will not forsake him. And it is this which recommends the gospel of Jesus Christ to the approbation and choice of every one, who would get through life creditably, usefully, happily; and who knows and feels that he has an interest in worlds beyond the grave.

Had the object of the Christian Leader been to obtain for himself a name among the great of the earth, to form a numerous and powerful party, would he have denounced the cross to his followers, would he have imposed the yoke of mortification and self-denial, would he have threatened them with " tribulation" in the world? But far be from the Saviour of mankind such mean, such unworthy views. He came to instruct men, to redeem them, to bless them; to shew them,
in

in his own person, how the cross might be borne, how the world might be overcome. He knew that the friendship of the world is enmity against God, and he prepared his disciples for a voluntary renunciation of that friendship, that they might be at peace with God. Will it be alleged that the case is now altered; that the spirit of the world is softened down, that the enmity has ceased? Ah no! the follower of Jesus must still be admonished to be cautious, to be vigilant, to beware of men; to be jealous over himself with a holy jealousy. " Love not the world, neither the " things that are in the world. If any man " love the world, the love of the Father is " not in him; for all that is in the world, " the lust of the flesh, and the lust of the " eyes, and the pride of life, is not of the " Father, but is of the world."

The poor and afflicted part of mankind are apt to imagine that poverty and its concomitant distresses constitute the whole of worldly tribulation, and the only species of it. They often envy those who are much greater objects of compassion than themselves. They have

have no conception of the splendid misery of greatness; of the torments of disappointed ambition, of mortified pride; of the deceitfulness, the solicitude, the insufficiency, the uncertainty of riches. They reflect not, as they ought with gratitude, that while the miseries of their hard lot are carrying them beyond the world, leading them to God, rendering the support and consolations of religion, and the prospects of immortality sweet unto them, the vanities and pleasures of life are deadening the worldly mind to all serious impressions, and sinking the immortal being into the mere animal. But it is the glory of Christianity to adapt itself equally, and with effect, to all conditions, and to every change of condition. Like its great Author, itself without " vari- " ableness or shadow of turning," there is not a vicissitude to which our mortal existence is exposed, to which it is not ready to apply a counsel, a caution, a cordial, a promise. God in his providence is pleased to try that man with uncommon worldly success. From indigence and obscurity he has risen into celebrity and affluence; whatever he doth prospers, his character is fair, his conscience clear,

clear, his conduct irreproachable; all men speak well of him. Ah, he is "set in slippery "places;" if religion do not hold him up, he will stumble and fall. His own heart will mislead him, a fawning flattering world will ensnare him; he is in danger of forgetting himself, and of forgetting God. Where is his security? What shall carry him through the conflict? the salutary admonitions, the edifying example, of the real friend of men. These earthly treasures perish with the using: the moth may devour them, the rust may corrupt them, thieves may break through and steal them away. " Lay up for yourselves " treasures in heaven:" " Seek first the king- " dom of God and his righteousness." " Be " not high-minded, but fear." " Learn of " me, for I am meek and lowly in heart, and " ye shall find rest to your souls."

Is the opposite, and more common trial, the allotment of providence to thee, my friend? Hast thou experienced the sad exchange of sickness for health; of obloquy and reproach for friendship and flattery; of scarcity for abundance? Be of good cheer. Thou hast
not

not loſt the teſtimony of a good conſcience, thou haſt not made ſhipwreck of thy faith. The maſter whom thou ſerveſt "was deſpiſed "and rejected of men, a man of ſorrows and "acquainted with grief." He endured hunger and thirſt; he had not where to lay his head; he was taken from "priſon and from "judgment; he was cut off from the land of "the living." "In the world ye ſhall have "tribulation." But bleſſed are ye "when "men ſhall revile you, and perſecute you, "and ſhall ſay all manner of evil againſt you, "falſly, for my ſake. Rejoice and be exceeding glad, for great is your reward in "heaven." "Bleſſed are they that mourn, "for they ſhall be comforted." "Be not "afraid of them that kill the body, and "after that have no more that they can do." "Even the very hairs of your head are all "numbered:" "Fear not, therefore: I ap- "point unto you a kingdom, as my Father "hath appointed unto me, that ye may eat "and drink at my table in my kingdom." At theſe words, the drooping ſpirit revives, and the countenance brightens up. The world is reduced to its proper compaſs, loſes its weight,

weight, loses its terror, loses its empire. "The sufferings of this present time are not worthy to be compared with the glory which shall be revealed in us." "For our light affliction, which is but for a moment, worketh for us a far more exceeding and eternal weight of glory; while we look, not at the things which are seen, but at the things which are not seen: for the things which are seen are temporal, but the things which are not seen are eternal."

4. But is this merely a fine spun theory? the invention of a man at his ease, and calculated for men at their ease; but which evaporates into thin air, when the fiery trial comes? No, he who administers the consolation, who announces the coming storm, who can direct and temper its fury, has given the example of patient suffering, of persevering and succesful conflict, of final and complete triumph. "I have overcome the world." He cannot be said to overcome the world who shuns it, who withdraws from it; but he who lives in it, and yet lives above it. Victory over the world consists not in hating, traducing,

ing, avoiding mankind, much less in unnecessarily provoking their resentment and unkindness, in order to have matter of accusation against them; but in mingling with them and shewing kindness to them; in opposing the spirit of meekness to violence; in condemning corrupt maxims and licentious practices, not by affected austerity, and the harshness of reproof, but by simplicity of manners, a steady and uniform dissent, and a holy abstinence from all "appearance of evil." There are cases indeed which, with frail, fallible man, the truest courage is to fly, for in frail, fallible man, the prince of this world when he cometh, will ever find some vulnerable part of which to take advantage, and "we are not ignorant of his devices;" but the Captain of our salvation, in advancing to the combat, had nothing on which the adversary could fix. Temptation from every quarter, and of every kind, was resisted and overcome. The cravings of hunger, the thirst of glory, the love of fame, were all suppressed in him, whose meat and drink it was to do the will of his heavenly Father, and to finish his work. Who overcomes the world? He who may be a king, a king, and will not; he who has the treasures of the earth, and of the sea, at his command, yet satisfies himself with drawing the penny of the day from a fish's mouth; he who can mix with publicans and sinners, and receive no contamination: he who perseveres in welldoing, though treated with insult and ingratitude; he who, possessed of power to avenge himself, exercises only the superiority of beneficence; he who is " not overcome of evil, " but who overcomes evil with good." Thus it was, blessed Jesus, that it pleased thee to conquer, and thus thou hast taught us to conquer also. Thus didst thou approve thyself the Son of God; not by condemning, and destroying the world, but by resisting its power, exposing its illusion, subduing its influence. Impart to us of thy wisdom and strength, that we also may overcome, and sit down with thee in thy throne. " This is the victory that " overcometh the world, even our faith." " Who is he that overcometh the world, but " he that believeth that Jesus is the Son of " God ?"

Wouldeſt thou, then, O man, provide thyſelf with an infallible guide, a ſure ſupport, and an invincible guard, amidſt all the changing ſcenes of this tranſitory life, "look to "Jeſus the author and finiſher of thy faith;" go in his ſtrength, imbibe his ſpirit, repoſe confidence in his grace. He interceded for you while he was yet on earth, and in heaven he maketh continual interceſſion for you. "Now I am no more in the world, but theſe " are in the world, and I come to thee. Holy " Father, keep through thine own name thoſe " whom thou haſt given me, that they may be " one as we are. Theſe things I ſpeak in the " world, that they might have my joy fulfilled " in themſelves; I have given them thy " word, and the world hath hated them, be- " cauſe they are not of the world, even as I " am not of the world. I pray not that thou " ſhouldeſt take them out of the world, but " that thou ſhouldeſt keep them from the " evil. Sanctify them through thy truth: " thy word is truth. As thou haſt ſent me " into the world, even ſo have I alſo ſent " them into the world. Neither pray I for " theſe alone, but for them alſo which ſhall

believe

"believe on me through their word: that they all may be one, as thou, Father, art in me, and I in thee; that they also may be one in us: that the world may believe that thou haft fent me." This is the fure foundation which God hath laid; this the bond which unites all the members of that body, whereof Chrift is the head; which unites the primitive difciples with all who have believed, or fhall believe, through their word, to the end of the world; which unites the church militant on earth, with the church triumphant in heaven. Thus "Godlinefs is profitable unto all things, having promife of the life which now is, and of that which is to come." Thus every condition of life is regulated, improved, fanctified: Health and vigor are directed to ufeful exertion for the glory of God and the good of man, and the bed of languifhing is fmoothed and cheered: affluence and fuccefs are fecured from vanity, finful indulgence, and forgetfulnefs of God; and poverty, difappointment and diftrefs are preferved from finking into defpair. Thus the interefts of time and of eternity, fo oppofite in themfelves, are made perfectly confiftent, and

ftrengthen

strengthen and support each other. And thus an obscure carpenter's son of Nazareth in Galilee, the instructor of a little handful of fishermen, who understood neither themselves nor their master, has actually done more toward ameliorating the character and condition of the human race, than all the sages, legislators, and sovereigns that ever existed: he has diffused a light over human life unknown before; he has given a universality to the moral principle which was before cramped by personal, political regards; and has, by giving due weight to every worthy temporal interest; established those of eternity on their native unshaken basis. We " speak as unto " wise men, judge ye what we say."

The next Lecture, with the permission of Providence, will be an attempt to prove, That the religion of the gospel is the strongest and sweetest cement of human society; and therefore an object of serious attention to every one who wishes to maintain domestic peace, who wishes to see his country prosper, who would see the human race happy, who considers transient objects as part of the plan of Providence,

Providence, and who, while he is in the world, ufes it without abufing it, knowing that all thefe things fhall be diffolved; and who is looking for "another country, that is "an heavenly, a city which hath foundations, "whofe builder and maker is God." It will give me pleafure to meet you, for this purpofe, this day fortnight, the 25th of the prefent month. May God accompany with his rich and powerful bleffing all the means of inftruction and of improvement, and to the Father, to the Son, and the Holy Spirit, the one living and true God, be afcribed the kingdom, and the power, and the glory, for ever. Amen.

# LECT. X.

MATT. VI. 10—12.

*Thy kingdom come; thy will be done in earth, as it is in heaven;*
*Give us this day our daily bread;*
*And forgive us our debts as we forgive our debtors.*

"GODLINESS is profitable unto all things, having promise of the life that now is, and of that which is to come." Supposing Christianity to have made no discovery of a future existence; supposing life and immortality not to have been brought to light by the gospel; what unspeakable obligations is the world laid under to it, for the present comfort which it administers, for the light which it diffuses, and the security which it bestows? Unhappily we are but too much under the influence of temporal views and motives,

motives, and too much difposed to facrifice, to thefe, unbounded profpects, and immortal interefts; but we are not permitted by the law of our nature, nor by the fpirit of religion, to be infenfible to the obligations, nor indifferent to the occurrences, of our prefent ftate. In no one refpect does the religion of Jefus Chrift more approve its divine original, than in its gracious tendency to promote the felicity, and to preferve the order of human fociety. It is, indeed, deeply to be lamented, that this firft of bleffings to mankind has been perverted and abufed to the vileft and moft inhuman purpofes; but who can affirm, with a fhadow of truth, that any fpecies or degree, I will not fay of atrocity, of cruelty, but of coldnefs or unkindnefs, is authorized, or countenanced by the gofpel? Who, on the contrary, can deny, that the Author and Finifher of the Chriftian faith, in his doctrine, in his conduct, by his miracles, has ftrengthened the bands of nature, impreffed the obligations of focial duty, and that in fo far as the power of his religion is felt, underftood, and in activity, the ftate of the world is proportionably ameliorated, and earth fo far refembles heaven?

The

The bufinefs of the prefent Lecture, then, will be an attempt to prove, That the religion of the gofpel is the fweeteft and moft powerful cement of human fociety, and therefore an object of the moft ferious concern to every one who wifhes to maintain domeftic peace, to enjoy national profperity, and to contribute to the improvement and felicity of mankind.

Though every man be a feparate creation of God; a world within himfelf, placed in a peculiar fphere, and fubjected to an individual refponfibility; yet every man is, at the fame time, more intimately or more remotely connected with intelligent beings of various orders, from whom he derives, and to whom he communicates, exiftence, information, joy, forrow; in whofe deftiny his own is involved; from whom he cannot detach himfelf even in thought, through the whole extent of his duration. This mutual relation, and its corresponding affections, are the work of the Father of Spirits, for the wifeft and moft gracious of purpofes. According as they are cultivated or infringed, man rifes into the angel, or degenerates into the demon. The

focial

social principle has got deeply rooted in our hearts, long before we are conscious of it: it " grows with our growth, and strengthens " with our strength;" it accompanies us through life, and even in death forsakes us not. It collects the intelligence, the exertions of the savage tribes; and it constitutes the glory and the felicity of polished life. But with all this, the world has often been reduced to a desert; cruel prejudices, clashing interests, ungovernable passions have encroached on the social instinct, enfeebled it, destroyed it. Streams of blood have flowed from age to age. At the close of the eighteenth century, learned, civilized, Christian Europe, alas, is as ferocious and implacable, as in the rudest ages of our rude pagan ancestors. Where lies the blame? The religion which we profess breathes " peace on earth, and good will " among men." But we are not under the power of that religion. The spirit of Christianity enters not into, directs not, controls not the counsels of the princes, and of the nations, which avail themselves of its venerable name. Hence wars and fightings, and every evil work. Hence in subordinate associations,

ciations, faction, cabal, intrigue; men hating one another, envying one another, supplanting one another; hence, in private families, discord, jealousy, strife; "a man at variance "against his father, and the daughter against "her mother, and the daughter-in-law against "her mother-in-law, and a man's foes they "of his own houshold." But the religion, which has been loaded with the reproach of such enormities, unequivocally disavows and condemns them. Let us look into it, mark its native tendency, imbibe its spirit, and learn to "be kindly affectioned one towards another, "with brotherly love forgiving one another."

The source of all public union, is conjugal and filial affection. Here we are to look for the nursery of virtue, the foundation of social strength and importance, the glory of states and kingdoms. If the fountain be poisoned, the stream, through every ramification, must be corrupt. And what has Christianity not done to purify this fountain, to give solidity to this foundation? It has restored the institution of marriage to its primitive simplicity, equity and obligation. The legislator of the
Jews

Jews laid down, it is true, the original law of God and nature, with clearness and precision, but the character of the wayward people whom he governed, rendered a strict interpretation and observance of that law difficult, and induced him to relax in certain particular cases: but the Christian law-giver, who came indeed to make atonement for transgression and to reconcile the guilty, abates not in a single iota the authority of the law; with the purity and dignity becoming his high character, he re-establishes the ordinance of heaven, which will not, cannot bend to humor the passions and the interests of changing mortals. The letter of the law went no farther than to restrain men from the grosser acts of violation; but the spirit of the law, according to its divine interpreter, places a guard over the eyes, over the thoughts, over the heart, and secures domestic peace and honour on the immoveable basis of religion.

Is it without design that the great Teacher sent from God so frequently represents Deity to us, under the endearing character of Father? O no, this relation first exalts us to heaven; and

and then sends every man to his own home; to his own bosom. The parent is admonished of the wisdom needful to direct his conduct in managing the important trust committed unto him. He is admonished of the tenderness, the compassion, the patience, the forbearance, the forgiveness, which uninstructed, feeble, helpless, perverse children stand in need of. He learns to be merciful, as his Father in heaven is merciful. The child, drawn with the bands of a man, with cords of love, beholds in the superior intelligence, in the care, the affection, the vigilance of an earthly parent, an emanation from the pure fountain of all good; a sense of dependance, of obligation is produced; the heart overflows with gratitude. All parties are reciprocally endeared to each other: they are twice blest, blest in what they give, and in what they receive. The will of God is "done on earth, "as it is done in heaven."

With what heavenly wisdom does our divine master mould the relative duties of life into a devotional form, and thereby gives them life, energy, elevation? While we pronounce, from
one

one mouth, the solemn address, "*Our* Fa-
"ther," all bitterness and wrath die within
us; a common relation and interest are clearly
discerned, and powerfully felt; the spirit of
love glows in every breast. Dare we utter
the petition read at the opening of this discourse, "Thy will be done," with a consciousness of habitually neglecting or resisting
the known will of God; with a disposition to
disturb the peace of society; with the dreadful imputation of kindling a hell upon earth?
No, a sense of the divine presence overawes the
mind; our spirit and practice must not contradict our prayers. What we earnestly implore at a throne of grace, it will be our
earnest endeavour to obtain and realize. Was
it without meaning and design that Jesus gave
the world a glimpse of himself, at the age of
twelve years, in the maturity of wisdom
blended with the simplicity of the child: and
that after filling with astonishment " at his
" understanding and answers," all who heard
him, he meekly and modestly retired from
the temple with his parents, and " went
" down with them, and came to Nazareth,
" and was subject to them ?" What a mild
lesson

lesson to tender ingenuous youth, of that subordination without which no society can subsist, of the respect due to parental feelings, to parental authority; of the submission, resignation and restraint which the condition of human life imposes on our early inexperienced years? Was it without design that, in the course of his public ministry, little children obtained such a share of his attention, drew down his benediction, were proposed by him as a pattern to the aged; that he made this emphatical declaration concerning them: "I say unto you, that in heaven their angels do always behold the face of my Father which is in heaven:" "take heed that ye despise not one of them." "It is not the will of your Father which is in heaven that one of these little ones should perish." What a check to the projects of pride, avarice and ambition, which directs so often the parental heart, in making provision for children; what a reproof of inattention to their spiritual interests; what a stimulus to lay up for them treasures in heaven?

How many inſtances ſtand on this record, of the condeſcending intereſt which the friend of mankind took in the conſervation, or reſtoration, of domeſtic comfort and happineſs? Witneſs the miraculous cure of the centurion's ſervant, of Peter's mother-in-law, of the woman of Canaan's daughter, of the poor man's lunatic ſon: Witneſs his habits of intimacy with the affectionate family of Lazarus and his ſiſters, and the glory which he manifeſted at the marriage of Cana in Galilee. Witneſs the reſurrection of the widow's ſon of Nain, of the ruler Jairus's daughter, of Lazarus after he had been in the grave four days. Above all, witneſs that affecting diſplay of friendſhip and of filial duty and affection, in the midſt of dying agony: "When "Jeſus ſaw his mother, and the diſciple "ſtanding by whom he loved, he ſaith unto "his mother, Woman, behold thy Son. Then "ſaith he to the diſciple, behold thy mother; "And, from that hour, that diſciple took her "unto his own home." But this ſympathy with domeſtic feeling was totally exempted from a participation in the prejudices and partialities of parental weakneſs, or in the complaints of peevifhnefs. The mother of Zebedee's children met with a repulfe when fhe prefumed to folicit undue diftinction for her two fons; and Martha received little encouragement to repeat an accufation of her fifter's unkindnefs.

When the whole is taken together, is it poffible to deny, that there is here a felf-evident tendency to improve fociety at its very fource, that in fo far as the little communities, which are the conftituent parts of the great family of the human race, enter into thefe views, are actuated by this fpirit, and continue united by this bond, the ftate of the world at large is amended. And when this becomes univerfal, oh that the period might in mercy be haftened! The petition which Chrift has taught his difciples to put up, will be crowned with an anfwer of peace. Thus the direct object of Chriftianity is to confirm, and to ftrengthen obligations which are interwoven in the conftitution and frame of our nature, which the heart joyfully recognizes, and which the confcience approves. What a bleffed object, to fupport the conjugal union by the fanctions of religion, the exercifes of devotion, the profpects of immortality! What is it to keep alive the facred fire of paternal and filial affection, by conftant fupplies from the altar of God; and to eftablifh the great law of love among brethren on the bafis of Chriftian charity, that " love of Chrift which paffeth know- " ledge!" It is unneceffary to rife to a higher fcale of human life, and to embrace a wider range of fociety; for if the component parts be found and uniform, they will readily coalefce and adhere: if the fame fpirit pervades the whole, there will be no difference but that of greater and lefs. Every family will be an epitome of its village or city; every city of its province, each province, of the empire, and all the kingdoms of the world will then be one great " kingdom of our God and of his " Chrift, and he fhall reign for ever and " ever."

But, in this ftate of imperfection, it needs muft be that offences come. The ftate of fociety muft be difturbed; the felfifh, the proud, the implacable fpirit of this world will arife, and Chriftianity muft have to deplore, that

its

its precepts, however reasonable, its genius, however mild, its defigns, however gracious and beneficent, are borne down by a torrent of angry or interested paffions. But even in this unhappy cafe the gofpel gives not all up for loft. It makes provifion for the worft that can happen. As the object of the firft prayer which we have been meditating, is the prefervation and extenfion of focial joy, fo that of the other is the reftoration of it when loft, " Forgive us our trefpaffes as we forgive " them who trefpafs againft us." Mark, as we go along, the petition " give us this " day our daily bread," which expreffes the anxiety of the individual about perfonal fubfiftence, blends even that with focial affections. Even daily bread has no fweetnefs if eaten in folitude; it is for another, whom he loves as his own foul, that man implores the bleffing of food. There is more than one concerned in afking it, more than one in receiving, more than one in giving God thanks. And fee, with what knowledge of the human heart, it is placed between a prayer which would make earth refemble heaven, and one which would

would bring heaven back to earth, if unhappily it had withdrawn.

When offence has taken place, there is in human nature a dreadful propensity to perpetuate and extend it. The mind broods over it, and it finds its way to the tongue; a stranger intermeddles with it. The breach is widened, the spark becomes a conflagration, very friends are separated. Whence is all this? The religion of Jesus Christ was not resorted to, his authority was not felt. Reconciliation hung on one quavering note, and the tongue was too proud to give it utterance. In some codes of morality, revenge has been exalted to the rank of virtue, and in the most ancient and most respectable of heathen poems, the unrelenting resentment of a highminded individual is the prominent and favourite feature of the piece. But this has no place, no not for a moment, in the Christian system. The heart, the eye, the tongue, the hand, of the disciple of Jesus, all, all are bound up; and the offence is done away, not by the savage running down his prey, and drinking the blood of his victim, but by the
sacrifice

sacrifice of his own gall, by a victory over his own spirit. Next to a state of undisturbed harmony, of uninterrupted love, the most desirable surely is the sweetness of reconciliation, the re-union of souls which ought not to have been separated. The state of human nature not admitting of the first, the gospel has done all that could be done, in procuring for us the second. Alienated from God by nature and wicked works, we are reconciled by the blood of his Son. Hateful and hating one another, we are brought within the bond of the same covenant, and are no more strangers and foreigners to each other, but fellow citizens of the saints, and of the houshold of God.

Reconciliation is the felicity peculiar to man. Angels never left their first estate, never knew the misery of distance and displeasure, cannot taste the delight of being brought nigh, of being restored to favour. Demons are implacable, irrecoverable, " re- " served in everlasting chains under dark- " ness." Man, though cast down, is not destroyed. From this source his happiness flows, " Being justified by faith we have peace with " God,

"God, and rejoice in hope of the glory of
" God." This is the leading idea of the
whole gospel difpenfation; " God in Chrift
" reconciling the chief of finners unto him-
" felf, not imputing unto men their tref-
" paffes." Under its facred influence, behold
men finking all the animofity of the carnal
mind toward each other, in " bowels of
" mercies, kindnefs, humblenefs of mind,
" meeknefs, long-fuffering;" " forbearing
" and forgiving, even as Chrift forgave."
And here, as in the former inftance, our bleffed
Lord moulds the precept into a prayer. In-
ftead of inforcing obedience by argument, or
of terrifying into compliance by multiplying
threatenings againft the refentful, the unmer-
ciful, he proftrates us together, as miferable
offenders, in the prefence of God, and makes
the relenting of our own minds, the melting
of our own hearts towards others, the ftandard
of our fupplication to God, and the meafure
of our expectation from him. "Forgive us
" our debts as we forgive our debtors."
What a folemn appeal! It forms an effential
part of the devotional fervice of our national
church: It is frequently employed by all de-
nomi-

nominations of profeſſing Chriſtians. How well ought it to be weighed! Who would not ſhudder at the thought of ſuch a prayer uttered by the lips of an auſtere, revengeful, inflexible character? Such an one indirectly imprecates vengeance on his own head. What ſhall become of him, if he is dealt with as he deals by others? " He ſhall have judgment with-
" out mercy who hath ſhewed no mercy."
But the word, the example, the ſpirit of Chriſt ſubdue every high thought, bring back men to one another, and bring them together unto God. I will no longer limit my beneficence to a narrow ſtandard; " How often
" ſhall my brother offend againſt me, and I
" forgive him, until ſeven times?" I will not take my fellow-ſervant by the throat, for a debt of a few pence, ſaying, " pay me that
" thou oweſt," while I am ſupplicating to be releaſed from a debt of ten thouſand talents which I am utterly unable to pay. I will remember the words of Jeſus: " I ſay not
" unto thee until ſeven times; but until
" ſeventy times ſeven."

In thefe two ways the fpirit, and the precepts, and the practice of Chriftianity, manifeftly tend to fupport human fociety; by preventing difcord, by rendering ftill more amiable and dear to each other, thofe who already are fo; by making the ordinary duties of life not a heavy yoke impofed, but a voluntary, a reafonable, a pleafant, a religious fervice; by drawing down the temper and difpofitions of heaven, to infpire and regulate the intercourfe and purfuits of men upon earth: And where, unhappily, love has been interrupted, by haftening to re-eftablifh it, in the exercife of patience, in the fpirit of meeknefs, in the bowels of kindnefs and tender mercy: in this affurance, that the nobleft triumph which a man can obtain, is one over himfelf; that he who is taught in the fchool of Chrift to fubdue his own fpirit is invincible, as a prince he has power with God and with man, and fhall prevail.

All that has been faid refpecting the influence exercifed by Chriftianity on domeftic union, might be extended, circle after circle, to every religious, every civil community.

Let

Let each of us endeavour to feel, and to act under, the obligation annexed to our own peculiar fphere. Let inclination here co-operate with the appointments of Providence, the regulations of well-ordered fociety, and the plaineft dictates of religion. Your reward even in this world is fure. For if the fpirit of Chrift Jefus carries you ufefully and fuccefsfully through thefe labours of love, you have fecured a heaven upon earth; or fhould you have the affliction to fail, fhould you have to ftruggle with the overwhelming reflection that your " houfe is not fo with " God," you fhall have the teftimony of confcience bearing you witnefs that you made it your endeavour to " keep the unity of " the fpirit in the bond of peace," and " the " peace of God which paffeth all underftand- " ing fhall keep your heart and mind through " Jefus Chrift."

The next Lecture, to be delivered, if God permit, this day fortnight, March 11th, will be an attempt to fhew, That the gofpel of Chrift is the only fatisfactory interpretation of the great myftery of Providence.

From

From what has now been said, ingenuous youth will be inftructed, that it is a very high privilege to addrefs their heavenly Father in prayer; and to cherifh and fupport kind affections, toward all with whom they are connected, by the fpirit of piety and devotion. They will difcern that the exercifes of religion have a happy influence on the duties, and the enjoyments of individual, and of focial life. They will become fenfible that in proportion as the obligations of Chriftianity are underftood and felt, their relative fituation will be improved. They will become more amiable in the eyes of others, and be more difpofed to love, ferve and oblige thofe with whom Providence has united them. In other words, they will fee it to be their higheft intereft here, as well as hereafter, to have their temper and conduct regulated by the gofpel of Jefus Chrift.

Wherever Chriftianity exerts its genial power, the focial principle is ftrengthened and purified. The family in which it refides becomes a Bethel, "the houfe of God, the "gate of heaven." The conjugal tie waxes ftronger and ftronger, from the profpect of immor-

immortality, from the approach of that state wherein both parties shall be "as the angels "of God in heaven." The paternal and filial duties and affections are regulated and refined. Authority is exercised without severity, and submitted to without murmuring. The servant and his master acknowledge, love, and serve one master, even Christ. Should offence come, and discord arise, the spirit of the blessed Jesus withdraws the fuel, and the fire goes out. A kingdom under this influence, would be one great family, a band of brothers, " dwelling together in unity," among themselves, and invincible from without: the fabled age of gold would be restored, and the paradisiacal state would commence. " Great " voices" shall at length be heard " in heaven, " saying, The kingdoms of this world are " become the kingdoms of our Lord, and of " his Christ, and he shall reign for ever and " ever." " Amen. Even so, come, Lord " Jesus."

# LECT. XI.

---

### JOHN I. 1—5.

*In the beginning was the Word, and the Word was with God, and the Word was God.*
*The same was in the beginning with God.*
*All things were made by Him; and without Him was not any thing made that was made.*
*In Him was life; and the life was the light of men.*
*And the light shineth in darkness; and the darkness comprehended it not.*

### REV. I. 17.

*I am the first and the last.*

### ROM. XV. 13.

*Now the God of hope fill you with all joy and peace in believing, that ye may abound in hope through the power of the Holy Ghost.*

THOUGH

THOUGH we derive all our knowledge from objects which affect our senses, those are the most interesting objects which do not fall under the cognizance of sense. The being whom I call my friend is surely something more than a figure of such a form and stature, endowed with the power of uttering articulate sounds, and of assuming placid and agreeable looks. These are indeed the means whereby he makes himself known to me, but the real object of my affection is not what I see, and hear, and touch; it is the vivifying, immaterial principle, communicating itself to a similar principle in me: and this communication can be kept up though the diameter of the globe interpose, nay though the spirit may have escaped from the clay tabernacle. The sounds which reach my ear are merely a tremulous motion excited in the air, but they awaken my soul to rapture, and the recollection of them renews the rapture a thousand and a thousandth times. The characters traced on that bit of paper are mute and lifeless, but I discern in them the spirit of life of the man whom I love; I can read his heart

heart in what the tongue dictated, or the fingers drew. "There is a spirit in man; the inspiration of the Almighty giveth him understanding." And as man has the power of communicating himself to man, with the rapidity of lightning, so the Father of spirits, in a thousand ineffable ways, can make himself known to the spirits whom he hath made. "The invisible things of him from the creation of the world are clearly seen, being understood by the things which actually exist, even his eternal power and Godhead." As I am sure of the existence of my friend, and of his moral and intellectual endowments, the moment I hear him speak, or observe the glance of his eye, or read his letter, I am equally assured of the existence and perfections of the invisible God, by looking around me, or when I open this volume, and when I commune with my own heart.

But infinity attaches to every thing that relates to Deity. It is the perfection of human friendship to be free from all mystery, from all concealment, to have every thing in com-

mon; and the parties being limited beings, full communication is easily practicable. But the communications of Deity must of necessity be at once luminous and obscure, plain and mysterious. Human friendship needs no mediator, no interpreter; it is marred, sometimes destroyed, by interference. But there can be no friendship between God and man except through a mediator. Thus alone it can be formed at first, and thus alone it can be maintained and supported. And such a Mediator, from the very nature of the thing, must possess the character of both parties. As "children are partakers of flesh and blood, "he also himself likewise took part of the "same. He took not on him the nature of "angels, but he took on him the seed of "Abraham"—being, at the same time, "the "brightness of God's glory, and the express "image of his person," "being made so much "better than the angels, as he hath by inhe-"ritance obtained a more excellent name than "they." By this union of nature he is completely qualified to "be a merciful and faith-"ful high-priest, in things pertaining to "God, to make reconciliation for the sins
"of

" of the people." It was not neceſſary that there ſhould be a divinely commiſſioned interpreter of nature, for nature preſents uniform appearances, ſeen and underſtood of all men. The works of creation were perfected at once, and continue to be what they were from the beginning; but every ſucceeding inſtant exhibits a new providential arrangement, which the human underſtanding is unable to fathom or explain; but which it is of high importance for man to underſtand. In condeſcenſion to human weakneſs, ignorance, and wretchedneſs, it pleaſed God to raiſe up a ſucceſſion of public inſtructors, to call men to attend to the ways of Providence, and to unfold its myſteries; to record events paſt, and to announce what Deity was about to do. "At ſundry times, "and in divers manners, God ſpake in time "paſt unto the fathers by the prophets;" who beſides local and temporary objects, united in holding up to the world one great, univerſal, unchanging object, to which all referred, and by which all was explained. He "hath in theſe laſt days ſpoken unto us by "his Son, whom he hath appointed heir of "all things, by whom alſo he made the "worlds." Thus a uniformity of deſign is manifested and maintained, and, amidst all the fluctuating, inefficient purposes and attempts of men, one grand purpose of "Him who worketh "all things after the counsel of his own will," has been undeviatingly going forward, and is advancing toward perfection. The gospel is the solution of all the difficulties which the course of providence presents: "No man hath "seen God at any time; the only begotten "Son, which is in the bosom of the Father, "he hath declared him."

3. The Son of God is the great interpreter of the Eternal Mind in his character of Creator of the universe. The world is but of yesterday. It could not have produced itself. It cannot be the effect of chance. How came it thus? "In the beginning was the Word, "and the Word was with God, and the Word "was God. All things were made by Him; "and without Him was not any thing made "that was made." This intimates that a plan was from eternity formed, of which the fabrick that we behold is the execution; and it proves that he who is emphatically called "the Word," was the sole and supreme agent in this great work. When we view a beautiful

tiful and useful piece of mechanism, when we read an ingenious and instructive book, we become acquainted with the author, we see his mind in his performance, we admire and love him; we become wise through his wisdom, and strong in his strength. Such is the medium expanded between us and an unseen Jehovah. Thus the great teacher has brought Deity down to our perception. This is the stupendous machine which he has constructed, this the wonderful volume he has written. All these tell us what God is; the almighty, all-wise, all-gracious first cause, and last end, of every thing that exists; thus " the only begotten Son, which is in the bosom " of the Father, hath declared him" to us. Creation was not completed till man was formed, and man was destined to be the brightest image of God here below. Man alone of terrestrial beings is conscious of his own existence, he alone is capable of knowing the hand which formed him. He discerns Deity not only in a creation without him, and round about him, but in his own person, in every particle of his body, and especially in the powers of his soul. Man was crowned with glory and honour, because in due time the

Son of God was to become man, that he might redeem his creature man. " In him " is life, and the life is the light of men ; " He is the true light which lighteth every " man that cometh into the world."

2. History is the record of the divine conduct, and without christianity it were utterly inexplicable. When we consider historical events as the result of human counsels, we are perplexed and confounded. We see nothing but clashing interests, half-formed designs, impotent and perishing efforts. We behold empires formed and falling to pieces as if by accident; a huge discordant chaos, not a beautiful and regular structure. But viewed as the operation of infinite wisdom, a new light is diffused over the face of the mighty deep, the discordant particles unite, and a heap of dry bones start up into a mighty army. We see men without knowing each other, and without concert, actually co-operating; and, under the controling influence of heaven, accomplishing purposes not their own, frequently the very opposite of what they had formed. In the sacred history alone we have

a cona continued series of facts the most valuable, and the most universally interesting, and they all relate to the same commanding object which was proposed to man from the beginning, which has been kept constantly in view, and has lost nothing of its weight or lustre by length of duration. What that object was, and is, you need not to be told. The world was created and is supported to serve as a theatre for displaying the work of redemption; and new heavens and a new earth shall arise to unfold its everlasting glories.

They little understand the true nature and character of Christianity, who consider it as unknown to the world till the times of Augustus Cesar. Jesus Christ says of himself, "before Abraham was I am," and his testimony is confirmed by every iota of the Mosaic history, and of the Jewish economy. The apostle of the Gentiles refers us to three very distant periods of the Old Testament church for a proof of the Messiah's pre-existence, and of his universal character as the Saviour of mankind, whether Jews or Gentiles. "Now I say, that Jesus Christ was a "minister

"minister of the circumcision for the truth
"of God, to confirm the promises made unto
"the Fathers: and that the Gentiles might
"glorify God for his mercy; as it is written,
"For this cause I will confess to thee among
"the Gentiles, and sing unto thy name: And
"again he saith, Rejoice ye Gentiles with his
"people: and again, Praise the Lord, all ye
"Gentiles, and laud him all ye people: and
"again Esaias faith, There shall be a root of
"Jesse, and he that shall rise to reign over
"the Gentiles, in him shall the Gentiles
"trust." The passages here quoted from
Moses, from the Psalmist, from Isaiah,
clearly prove that, at three very different periods of the Jewish church, the leading design
of Providence was expressly announced, and
that full and explicit intimation was given
of an approaching great deliverance, not to
the Jews only, but to the Gentiles also; and it
cannot admit of a doubt, that the deliverance
to which they refer, is that which Jesus Christ
effected by his incarnation, life, death, and resurrection. Here, then, the gospel sheds a
cheering light on the mystery of Providence,
and on the history of mankind, in the concurring

curring and exprefs declarations which He, " at fundry times and in divers manners," made to the world, refpecting the perfon and work of the Redeemer. In farther illuftration of this branch of my fubject, I fhall take the liberty of tranfcribing what I have advanced, to the fame effect, on another occafion.

Not to infift on that firft and general prediction, concerning the " feed of the woman," who was to be " the bruifer of the ferpent's " head," let us advance to the period when God began to reduce into a particular form, and fyftem his purpofe of good will to men; that is, when Abraham, at the age of feventy-five years, was called of God from his kindred and habitation; was feparated not only from his idolatrous neighbours, but from his own neareft relations; was fent into a ftate of perpetual banifhment, childlefs, and beyond all hope or probability of progeny; and yet, under all thefe difadvantages, was conftituted and declared the heir of the promife, the progenitor of that illuftrious Saviour, in whom at length, " all the families of the earth fhould " be bleffed."

From

From that moment, we fee a fence planted around the Patriarch and his family, which the violence of hoftile furrounding ftates was not able to break through, nor the revolutions of neighbouring kingdoms to pluck up, nor the waftes of all-devouring time to impair, till the defigns of heaven were accomplifhed.

In all the fubfequent events which affected this family and their defcendants—their various conditions and places of refidence—the declarations made to them—the obfervances enjoined them—the changes of their government, from its eftablifhment to its annihilation.—all kept in view the object prefented to their venerable anceftors—the MESSIAH, or SHILOH, to whom " the gathering of the " people fhould be." That men, living fo remote from each other in point of time, and under fuch various afpects of Providence, fhould be led to confider one and the fame object as poffeffing a fupereminent excellency and importance, and, however differing in other refpects, to find them in perfect union here, is not to be accounted for on the ufual principles of human nature, nor from the ordinary

dinary current of human affairs; and therefore can proceed only from the Lord of hosts, who is " wonderful in counsel, and excellent " in working."

If it be asked, Wherein consists the credibility of that record, which conveys the knowledge of these things to us? It may be answered, That this very harmony and consistency will be admitted as no inconclusive argument, by the candid and unprejudiced. To those who believe a superintending Providence, in the administration of the affairs of this world, the truth and importance of these sacred Oracles will be at once demonstrated, from the care which that Providence has evidently exercised over them, in guarding them not only from external danger, but also from internal corruption. To what remote antiquity must we recur for the origin of the earliest of these sacred Books? Through what a long extended line, must we pursue their progress, till they were completed? From how many accidents have they been preserved? How many generations of men have they outlived? How many revolutions
of

of the world have they withstood, and escaped? The persons who were divinely inspired to compose them, are long since departed. The men, and the nations, who often attempted to destroy them, have many ages ago been cut off from the face of the earth. That nation which was once the guardian and repository of them, is now dispersed and scattered abroad, and exhibits a striking and lasting monument, in its character and punishment, of the eternal, immutable truth of the Revelation of God to their forefathers. The languages, in which the Scriptures were originally written, are gone into disuse, except among the learned few. Nevertheless the word of JEHOVAH is an open treasure to every kindred, and people, and tongue. The wit of man has been employed against it, and it maintains its ground. The malice and power of men have attempted to crush it, and yet it remains in full vigor. The weakness of superstition, and the madness of enthusiasm have aimed at perverting it, but it still runs pure. The fury of successively contending parties, has tortured and wrested it to their several purposes, but, when their violence is extinguished and forgotten, it preserves

ſerves an awful, ſteady, and unpliant dignity. And the experience of the paſt, leaves us no room to doubt of its future ſtability and progreſs.

I ſhall add but one conſideration more, under this part of the ſubject. The credibility of the Holy Scriptures of the Old Teſtament, as conſtituting a proof of the Goſpel, will be put beyond a doubt, if we conſider through what hands they have been tranſmitted to us. Can the Jews, the inveterate enemies of Chriſtianity, the murderers of the Lord of glory, be ſuſpected of a deſign of contributing toward the chief ſupport of the Chriſtian faith? Surely no!—But yet they have done it. Without ſeeing the end which God had in view, they carefully preſerved the inſpired books; they had them numbered to a line, nay to a ſingle letter, to prevent all addition or diminution; and they have thereby, unknown to themſelves, furniſhed the world with the cleareſt evidence of what they would willingly cruſh and deſtroy; and, to this day, they exhibit their own condemnation as the ground of their hope.

If

If it be asked, farther, Why the knowledge, and possession, of the Scriptures, a matter of universal concern, were so long limited to a peculiar spot, and to a peculiar people? It may be answered, That in the very act of calling Abraham and his family, to the high honour of being the guardians of the divine Revelation, and the ancestors of our Saviour according to the flesh, an express intimation was given, that such distinction was not for their sake merely, but for the general good; that, at length, ALL Nations might be blessed in One who should descend from that particular family, and in consequence of promises and predictions which were, for a season, to be deposited with them, in behalf of the world at large. And the history, not only of that people, but of the surrounding and succeeding nations and empires, satisfyingly proves, how wisely, and how well, an end so benevolent was answered, by means, at first sight, so improbable.

That people " to whom pertained the adop-
" tion, and the glory, and the covenants, and
" the giving of the law, and the service of
" God,

"God, and the promises: Whose are the fathers, and of whom, as concerning the flesh, Christ came," were, for many ages, doomed to an unsettled, wandering state. They travelled from country to country. They were apparently suspended of Providence, as a spectacle before the eyes of all the nations whither they went, to warn them of the folly and wickedness of idolatry, and to call them to the living and true God.

The venerable patriarchs themselves were early employed in this service. Abraham was sent to Egypt, and afterward sojourned among the Philistines. Isaac also lived all his life long in the midst of Idolaters: and Jacob was appointed to sojourn many years among the Assyrians, for the purpose of conveying thither the knowledge and the worship of the one Supreme. And when it pleased God, at length, to establish their posterity in a country of their own, the spot which He chose was the very centre of the great and extensive empires which then divided the known world. These empires, unknown to each other, were, one after another, extending their conquests and

and their boundaries, while the preparation of the Gospel of peace, was haftening to its maturity in the hands of a few Hebrew shepherds; till, at length, the promifed, the appointed, the expected, the feafonable hour, "the fulnefs of time" came, the Prince of peace appeared.

I fhall mention fome ftriking circumftances in the ftate of the world, at that period, tending to evince the fpecial care which the divine Providence exercifed over it, and to exhibit the evidence of Chriftianity which flows from it. While the arms of Greece, under Alexander the Great, as he is commonly ftyled, were reducing to fubjection the eaftern world, and adding the vaft empires of Affyria and Perfia to the Grecian; Rome was, in the weft, by violent, and rapid ftrides, haftening to univerfal dominion in Europe. And the fierce difputes which enfued upon the death of Alexander, which armed his fucceffors one againft another, and difmembered the large and unwieldy fabric of his kingdom, paved the way for the Roman ftandard, till it advanced from conqueft to conqueft, to plant

itfelf

itself in remotest Asia. And thus, immediately previous to the Christian era, half the globe had become subject to one power, and was combined in one mighty system of government, beyond comparison greater than the world ever saw before or since. To increase our wonder, in order to facilitate the introduction and diffusion, of the Gospel, the commotions of the nations suddenly subsided, the bloody portal of Janus was shut, and all was hushed into universal peace: and that, at a time when science shone in all her splendor, and when philosophy was seated upon the throne. Here, then, was a field wider than ever opened at any other time, in which truth was to expatiate, and a test was applied to it, which nothing but the truth could stand. And thus, He who *shakes the Heaven and the Earth, the Sea and the dry land, shook and settled all nations*, when the *desire of all nations* was to *come*. And hence, we are instructed, that the truth of God was bounded for a time, to prepare the way for its more unlimited extent afterwards; it was laid up in Judea, that thence, as from a centre, its light might diffuse itself over the whole Roman empire.

And all this is of God, who alone " knoweth " the end from the beginning, faying, My " counfel fhall ftand, and I will fulfil all my " pleafure." For the eftablifhment of your faith, Chriftians, Alexander fought and conquered; Socrates and Plato taught; Auguftus made peace, and commanded the world to be taxed; Ifaiah and Daniel prophefied.

Such are the grounds of your faith and hope in Chrift, arifing from the hiftory and ftate of the world previous to, and at the time of, his appearance. We now advance to that period itfelf; and fhall confider, How far the perfon whom we call Lord and Mafter, anfwered the expectation formed of him, and fulfilled the predictions fpoken concerning his perfon, character and office; and fhall examine the proofs which he perfonally exhibited of his being the Meffiah.

It is an acknowledged principle of natural Religion, That, from the known wifdom and mercy of God, his creatures in diftrefs have reafon to expect relief; but, the time and manner of granting fuch relief, they muft not

take

take upon themselves to determine, but leave it to that Wisdom which is the ground of their hope. Previous, then, to an intimation from Heaven, Who could have said, by whom, and in what manner, He was to work deliverance for his miserable and guilty creatures? Such an intimation He was graciously pleased early to give, as the encouragement of our hope; and now, that the great work of redemption is finished, we can discover a fitness and propriety in the means employed, and a light is thrown on the mystery of Providence, though we durst not presume to say what these ought to have been, until they were discovered to us.

The person who came upon the merciful errand of salvation, was God's own eternal Son, humbled to our level, made a partaker of our meanness and misery, but totally free from our guilt. In such a deliverer, then, we behold One, who, we have reason to believe, would enter thoroughly into our case, from the near relation which he bare to us, and who, at the same time, could suffer no impediment nor interruption in his benevolent work,

work, from any neceſſary attention to his own private intereſt; One, placed in a ſtation where he could ſet us a perfect example of all holineſs, and poſſeſſing a nature wherein he could, by death, make a full atonement for ſin; and, at the ſame time, in virtue of a ſuperior nature, give value to that atonement, remove the curſe which was in full force againſt his guilty brethren, whom he came to ſave, and, through death, open to them the way which leads to eternal life. Then, and never till then, was fully underſtood the meaning of thoſe bloody ſacrifices which were, from time to time, offered up to appeaſe divine juſtice; and of that, and ſuch like expreſſions, " without ſhedding of blood there " is no remiſſion of ſin." And here we alſo diſcover the reaſon why Chriſt is in Scripture denominated " the Lamb *ſlain*, from the " foundation of the world."

But again, the arrival of Jeſus Chriſt did not take the world by ſurprize. The ſending of his Son into our world, was no new and ſudden intention of the everlaſting Father, in the four-thouſandth year from the creation;
but

but it was a deliberate purpose, formed before all worlds, and declared to man, the instant his condition required a Saviour. That declaration was repeated, and was rendered clearer and fuller, as time rolled on, till it became so pointed and particular, as to leave candid minds, who were informed of it, no room to hesitate concerning the application, when the object of the heavenly Revelation actually appeared.

To adduce only one or two out of that cloud of witnesses, which prove Jesus Christ to be He, of whom God spake to the Fathers by his servants the prophets, let me refer you to Israel's dying bed, and dying words, in the blessing which he pronounced upon Judah his fourth son: " The sceptre shall not depart " from Judah; nor a law-giver from between " his feet, until Shiloh come: and unto him " shall the gathering of the people be:" These words were spoken as long *before* Christ's day, as it is from it down to the present period. Jacob's whole family consisted then of no more than seventy souls, and these driven, by famine, for subsistence into a strange

strange land; and that land soon proved a house of bondage to them. Six hundred years, and more, elapse, before a king is known at all in Israel; and when one is at length chosen, not the tribe of Judah but of Benjamin furnishes the sovereign. When that tribe was, after so long a delay, called at length to the regal dignity, the youngest son of a younger family is placed on the throne. In the third generation, the throne is shaken to the very foundation, and a violent revolution strips the crown of Judah of ten tribes, and erects a formidable rival kingdom. But this very revolution, instead of weakening or destroying the destined succession, serves only to illustrate and to ascertain it. In process of time, a hostile invasion plucks up the kingdom by the roots; and both prince and people are carried captive into an enemy's country. But yet, in the very wreck of empire, in the almost necessary dissolution which a seventy years captivity must produce, the existence of the state is preserved, and the royal line is maintained unbroken; and Judah is again miraculously established in his own land; till, at last, the kingdom changes a

temporal

temporal for a spiritual head, in the person of the blessed Jesus. And, after so long a period, the sceptre at length departs from Judah, when the Jews themselves give up the right of judging, to a foreign power, and acknowledge they have no King but Cesar;—thus proving the truth of God, in the appointment of Him whom they were zealous to deny.

The noted prediction of Moses, "a pro-
"phet shall the Lord your God raise up unto
"you of your brethren, like unto me; him
"ye shall hear in all things, whatsoever he
"shall say unto you," which is recorded in Deuteronomy xviii. 15. and applied by the Apostle to Jesus Christ, Acts iii. 22: The minute description of the material and particular circumstances of Christ's death, as delivered by David in the 22d Psalm; of his death and burial, by Isaiah in the 53d Chapter of his prophecy—and of the precise time, and end, of his sufferings, defined by Daniel toward the end of chapter 9th. of his book, constitute so many distinct and separate proofs, in their exact correspondence with the events which took place, in the land of Judea, under

the administration of Pontius Pilate, that no one but our divine Master could be the object of these prophetical enunciations; and, united, they form such a weight of evidence, as nothing but inveterate and determined prejudice is able to withstand.

But our blessed Lord did not remain merely passive, in furnishing us with evidence whereon to build our faith. That we might place all confidence in him, as a Saviour, he claimed a divine original—he called himself the Son of God. And how was this claim supported? He did the works of God. He exercised an unlimited authority over the whole world of nature; over things visible and invisible. The prince of the power of the air fled at his command. The boisterous elements heard and obeyed his word. Disease, and death, and the grave, fulfilled his pleasure. To his penetrating eye the darkest recesses of the human heart stood unveiled, and hell itself could find no covering. To adduce proofs were superfluous to those who are accustomed to read the Gospel. And these things were not done in a corner, nor performed before persons who
were

were difpofed to believe. The difplays of this divine power were neither few nor doubtful, but were exhibited in the face of the fun, before multitudes of fpectators, and of thofe not a few who were mortified and provoked with what they faw; who were under every difpofition to detect and expofe an impofture, had it exifted, and who were not deftitute of ability, or opportunity, for making every inquiry neceffary to this purpofe.

It will be faid, That the evidence arifing from miracles is good only to thofe, who were eye and ear witneffes of them. This would be to reduce hiftorical evidence within a very narrow compafs. In what a deplorable ftate of ignorance and uncertainty would the human mind be involved, were nothing to be confidered as true and certain, but what falls under the cognizance of our own fenfes? In other cafes, and Why not here? we reft, and act, on the evidence of credible witneffes who have undoubted accefs to right information. Concerning the exiftence, the character, the life and death of Socrates, nobody pretends to entertain a doubt. The fame may be faid
concern-

concerning the other fages, philofophers, moralifts, and heroes of antiquity. And yet, I will appeal to the candor of the impartial Deift himfelf, whether the evidence, of which we are in poffeffion, concerning Jefus of Nazareth, be not much more clear, full, direct, and unfufpicious, than that which refpects any other name exifting previous to, contemporary with, or even coming after, our Divine Mafter, down to the age which immediately precedes our own. Indeed the happy revolution which wrought the temporal deliverance of thefe kingdoms, an hundred and ten years ago, is an event not more clearly authenticated to me, than the deceafe which Chrift accomplifhed at Jerufalem, for the falvation of a loft world, when Tiberius Cefar was Emperor of Rome, and Pontius Pilate governor of Judea. Unlefs, therefore, the ages paft are to be reduced to an univerfal blank, unlefs dark oblivion is to draw her fable mantle over all preceding events, with her rude hand demolifhing every venerable monument, with her malignant pencil blotting out each precious record; unlefs human knowledge is to be confined to the little circle in which every man expatiates,

expatiates, to the few fleeting years which he spends upon earth, and to the slender, unimportant facts, which fall under his own observation,—and Who can bear to think of assenting to this? the truth, and the importance, of the Gospel, rest upon a rock, against which the folly, the madness, the desperate wickedness of man—against which *the gates of hell,* shall never prevail.

Thus we find Christianity diffusing light over the history of all ages and nations, and explaining many particulars of the divine conduct, which would otherwise have remained mysterious and unaccountable. And thus deeply do we stand indebted to the great Interpreter of the counsels of the eternal Mind, by whom God " made the worlds," " whom " he hath appointed heir of all things," unto whom " all power is given, in heaven " and in earth." How can we discharge our debt of gratitude to him, but by walking in his light, by searching the Scriptures, by pondering the ways of Providence? Let us compare natural things with spiritual, and spiritual things with spiritual; and " the spirit
" himself

"himself will help our infirmities." God has been pleased to establish an intimate relation between the careful and diligent use of appointed means, and the interposition and agency of his sovereign grace. To the humble and persevering inquirer what is difficult becomes easy, what is obscure becomes clear; before him " every valley shall be exalted, " and every mountain and hill shall be made " low: and the crooked shall be made straight, " and the rough places plain." The day cometh when all that is now " hard to be " understood" in the word of God; all that is now inexplicable in the dispensations of Providence, shall be unfolded. What the wise and righteous Governor of the world doeth, in many cases we know not now, but we shall know hereafter. " We know in part, and we " prophesy in part : but when that which is " perfect is come, then that which is in part " shall be done away." Then " we all with " open face, beholding as in a glass the glory " of the Lord, shall be changed into the same " image, from glory to glory, even as by " the spirit of the Lord."

Thy

Thy own lot, my friend, is, it may be, an enigma; thou "walkeſt in darkneſs, and "haſt no light;" thou haſt been led through intricate and myſterious paths; haſt many a time been reduced to think, and to ſay; "All "theſe things are againſt me:" art now tempted to ſay, I muſt ſink under this trial: "The Lord hath forſaken me, and my Lord "hath forgotten me." Look to the Saviour, and be "lightened." "Truſt in the name "of the Lord, and ſtay upon thy God." The enigma ſhall be reſolved, and thou ſhalt be made to ſee, and to confeſs to the glory of God, that all was working together for thy good. Be patient, be reſigned, and "hope "to the end;" and the "hope" of the Chriſ‐ tian "maketh not aſhamed."

LECT.

# LECT. XII.

### John xi. 23—26.

*Jesus saith unto Martha, Thy brother shall rise again.*

*Martha saith unto him, I know that he shall rise again in the resurrection at the last day.*

*Jesus saith unto her, I am the resurrection and the life; he that believeth in me, though he were dead, yet shall he live:*

*And whosoever liveth, and believeth in me, shall never die: Believest thou this?*

WHEN a beloved object is removed from us by death, we resign it slowly and reluctantly. The voice which has for many years vibrated delightfully on our ear, we are unwilling to believe is for ever silenced; we hang over the tremulous lips for a while, expecting when they shall move again, and utter the sounds which used to kindle the soul

to

to rapture. I have feen my friend afleep. The animated orbs, which told me quick as thought what he felt and underftood, underwent an eclipfe. I faw on his countenance the image of death, but rejoiced in the temporary fufpenfion, becaufe I knew it was going to reftore invigorated animation and intelligence. But that was the fleep of death. Thefe eyes are to open no more. I muft " bury my dead " out of my fight." Here nature leaves me to mourn; and philofophy offers a cold confolation which my heart rejects. Perfuaded at length that I have loft what I loved, I purchafe with Abraham a poffeffion of a burying place; I erect with Jacob a pillar over my Rachael's grave; I infcribe with David on the monumental urn facred to the memory of my Jonathan, " Lovely and pleafant in life, " and in death undivided." But ftill I am not at reft. Was that bleffing beftowed upon me only to be taken away? Was my cup thus fweetened only to render this infufion more bitter? What is left but that my gray hairs defcend with forrow to the grave?—Till " life " and immortality were brought to light by " the gofpel," this was the fad eftimate of

human

human exiftence; and a little cavity in the earth, or the afhes remaining from a funeral pile, fettle the account between the parent and the child, between the hufband and his wife, between a man and his brother. But now the dark valley is illuminated: the king of terrors is difarmed; my brother, my friend, my child is not dead, but fleepeth. " Let us alfo go and die with him." It is the glory of Chriftianity, after having inftructed, regulated, fweetened the life that now is, to difclofe a continuation of being which knows no period.

Many have, without the aid of revelation, agitated the queftion refpecting the foul's immortality; but the body never came into confideration. It was given up as for ever loft; and one half of that nation to whom the lively oracles of God were committed, openly denied the exiftence of angels and fpirits, and, confequently, the refurrection of the dead. But now we are emboldened to demand, as Paul did of king Agrippa, " Why fhould it " be thought a thing incredible with you " that God fhould raife the dead?" Why

Z  fhould

should it be thought a thing incredible that He who, through a process of vegetation, rears the stately oak out of the putrid acorn, and, through progressive animation, transforms the incrusted worm into the gaudy butterfly, and the feeble, unthinking infant into the vigorous, intelligent man, should, for purposes still more noble, awake the slumbering dust to "new-" "ness of life," and "change the vile body" "that it may be fashioned like unto Christ's" "glorious body?"

This is the "mystery which was hid from" "ages and generations," which the learned and polite Athenians laughed to scorn, which the resurrection of the Lord Jesus has unfolded, and to which the believer in Jesus cleaves as "all his salvation and all his desire." This, therefore, fills up the measure of God's goodness to the children of men, and recommends the gospel to all who deplore the ravages of time and death, and "who rejoice in hope of" "the glory of God."

But what is the evidence which Christianity furnishes of the immortality of the soul, and

of

of the resurrection of the body? We endeavoured in a former lecture to shew that the religion of Jesus is most happily adapted to the feelings, the necessities, and the expectations of the human heart, at every successive stage of our existence. It is eminently so in the case before us. There is a well-known propensity in man exciting a wish to repose, when dead, with those whom he loved in life. Even savage tribes venerate the sepulchres of their ancestors, and look with desire to them as their own. Jacob cannot die in peace till he has obtained assurance that he shall lie with his fathers, and be buried in their burying-place. Joseph exacts a similar security from his survivors, and expires giving " commandment concerning his bones," as if there were society in the grave. Mary, we find in the context, indulged a mournful pleasure in resorting to the grave of her departed brother, and in weeping over it; and Jesus mingles his tears with hers, sanctioning by this example of sympathy, the expression of a decent and moderated sorrow, which he was going to turn into joy. When, therefore, we behold Jesus visiting the house of mourn-

ing, weeping over the tomb of a friend, confoling the afflicted, the heart opens to the reception of a religion which meets its feelings, soothes them, relieves them; and which proves itself to be divine, by being thus accommodated to the nature of man. If it be natural to care for the body, how it is to be fed and clothed in life, and where, and with whom it is to be laid in death; if it be pleasant to meet with tenderness and sympathy, under the loss of what we loved as our own souls; then under what obligations are we laid to that " friend who sticketh closer than a brother," who not only makes the present support of our bodies his care, but has unveiled their future state of immortality; who not only vouchsafes to accompany the mourner to the tomb of departed worth, but to display the salvation of God in quickening the dead? The doctrine, and the proofs of immortality, are so interwoven with the texture of the gospel, that an attempt to separate them would be an attempt to destroy; and the difficulty attending the exhibition of them arises not from scantiness and inaptitude of materials, but from an abundance and luminousness
  which

which put selection to a stand. To preserve order in thought, and to assist recollection, we shall arrange what is further to be advanced on the subject, under the three following heads. 1. Explicit declarations of Jesus Christ respecting his own power over death. 2. Actual exertions of that power over others. 3. His own resurrection from the dead.

1. Jesus Christ made frequent and explicit declarations of his power over death. This was a pretension never advanced before by any prophet, public teacher, or leader of a party. Such men were indeed abundantly liberal in promises of the riches, honours and pleasures of this life, but who ever proposed as a recompence to his followers, a prolongation of being to perpetuity, exemption or deliverance from death; or who ever presumed to threaten his adversary with endless punishment, with an immortality of woe? " As the Father
" raiseth up the dead, and quickeneth them,
" even so the Son quickeneth whom he will."
" He that heareth my word, and believeth
" on him that sent me, hath everlasting life;
" he

" he is paſſed from death to life;" " the hour
" is coming, and now is, when the dead
" ſhall hear the voice of the Son of God, and
" they that hear ſhall live. For as the
" Father hath life in himſelf, ſo hath he
" given to the Son to have life in himſelf;
" the hour is coming in the which all that
" are in the graves ſhall hear his voice, and
" ſhall come forth, they that have done good,
" unto the reſurrection of life; and they that
" have done evil, unto the reſurrection of
" damnation. Every one which ſeeth the
" Son, and believeth on him, ſhall have ever-
" laſting life: and I will raiſe him up at the
" laſt day. This is the Father's will which
" hath ſent me, that of all which he hath
" given me, I ſhould loſe nothing, but ſhould
" raiſe it up at the laſt day." And in the
verſes read at the opening of the lecture,
" Thy brother ſhall riſe again; I am the re-
" ſurrection and the life; he that believeth in
" me, though he were dead, yet ſhall he live:
" and whoſoever liveth and believeth in me
" ſhall never die, believeſt thou this?"

Of his empire over death, as it affected his
own perſon, the declarations are clear, manifold
and

and unequivocal, "I lay down my life, that
" I might take it again. No man taketh it
" from me, but I lay it down of myself. I
" have power to lay it down, and I have
" power to take it again." Among other
proofs of his divine miſſion, this was to be
the moſt illuſtrious, and he foretels it before it
came to paſs, " Deſtroy this temple,"
ſpeaking of the temple of his body, " and in
three days I will raiſe it up." Now though
ſome of the Jews affected to miſunderſtand
his meaning, and others wilfully miſrepre-
ſented it, it is certain that the chief prieſts and
phariſees underſtood him well, and took their
meaſures accordingly, for after his burial they
" went to Pilate, ſaying Sir, we remember that
" that deceiver ſaid, while he was yet alive,
" After three days I will riſe again. Com-
" mand therefore that the ſepulchre be made
" ſure until the third day, leſt his diſciples
" come by night and ſteal him away, and
" ſay unto the people he is riſen from the
" dead. So the laſt error ſhall be worſe
" than the firſt." His death and reſurrection
were frequently the ſubject of converſation
with his diſciples, but they ſhrunk from it,

they believed him not. "Jefus began to fhew unto them how he muft go unto Jerufalem, and fuffer many things of the elders, and chief priefts, and fcribes, and be killed, and be raifed again the third day. Then Peter took him, and began to rebuke him, faying, be it far from thee Lord; this fhall not be unto thee." At another time, while they abode in Galilee, Jefus faid unto them, The Son of Man fhall be betrayed into the hands of men, and they fhall kill him, and the third day he fhall be raifed again: and they were exceeding forry." The fame great event occupied the thoughts, and conftituted the theme, of Mofes and Elias on the mount of transfiguration, who " appeared in glory, and fpake of his deceafe which he fhould accomplifh at Jerufalem." And as they came down from the mountain " he charged them that they fhould tell no man what things they had feen, till the Son of Man were rifen from the dead; and they kept that faying within themfelves, queftioning one with another what the rifing from the dead fhould mean." But was there no intimation of a refurrection previous to the appearance

pearance of Jesus Christ in the flesh? Yes, but it was not understood nor believed till the great Teacher came to open up the Scriptures. The Sadducees triumphed in the thought of putting a case which should reduce the doctrine of the resurrection to an absurdity, but they only furnished Him with an opportunity of exposing their ignorance and error, in " not knowing the Scriptures and the power " of God," and of deducing from Scripture a proof of what they meant to overturn. " As touching the resurrection of the dead, " Have ye not read that which was spoken " unto you by God, saying, I am the God of " Abraham, and the God of Isaac, and the " God of Jacob. God is not the God of the " dead, but of the living, for all live unto " him." As the period approached, the notices of his death, and of " the glory that " should follow," became more and more pointed and distinct. " And Jesus, going up " to Jerusalem, took the twelve disciples apart " in the way, and said unto them, Behold we " go up to Jerusalem; and the Son of Man " shall be betrayed unto the chief priests, and " unto the scribes, and they shall condemn
" him

"him to death, and shall deliver him to the Gentiles to mock, and to scourge, and to crucify him; and the third day he shall rise again." Here he declares his power not only over death, but over the concomitant circumstances of it; as afterwards, in the very agonies of death, he asserted and exercised a power of conferring immortality, and of disposing of seats in the paradise of God, in the case of the penitent thief. But we proceed in the

2. Second place to shew how these declarations were supported; for had such extraordinary powers been claimed, without being exerted, who would have believed their existence? but, confirmed as they are by a multitude of facts, operated in the presence of clouds of witnesses, who shall dare to call them in question? We shall first adduce the actual exertions of the power of Jesus Christ over death in others. They shew us the state of death in four several gradations, manifesting successively the empire of the Redeemer over death in every state.

The

The first is the case of the ruler of the synagogue's daughter, a maid of about twelve years of age. Her father had left her in extremity, and went to supplicate Jesus in her behalf. While they are on the way to the house, she expires. There was hope, while life remained, that the interposition of Christ's miraculous power might effect a cure; but, with life, hope is extinguished; to restore the dead is considered as exceeding even his power, and a messenger is dispatched to announce the change which had taken place, and to prevent his taking unnecessary trouble. The case is given up as lost: the mournful offices of death have commenced when Jesus arrives. So convinced were all present that the spirit had left the body, that they rejected the idea of *sleep*, as an insult to their understanding. What must have been their astonishment; to behold her whom they had seen expire, whom they had laid out as dead, at a word revive, arise, walk, receive nourishment, recover not only life, but perfect soundness, from a mortal disease, in a moment? Of this the witnesses were neither few nor inconsiderable, nor of doubtful character. No wonder that

that " the fame thereof went abroad into all " that land," and that it fhould have been tranfmitted to us as a ground of hope, and a fource of joy.

The fecond inftance is that of the widow's fon of Nain, who was farther advanced in life, for in the hiftory he is denominated " a " man," and he had continued a longer time under the dominion of death, they were carrying him out to burial. The widowed mother of an only fon would not be precipitate in performing thefe melancholy rites; the proofs of death muft have been fadly fatisfactory before fhe proceeded to pay this laft debt of parental tendernefs. It was fo ordered of Providence, that Jefus came attended on this occafion with *many* of his difciples, and *much* people. The funeral proceffion from the city was likewife numerous. Of what fact is it eafier to attain abfolute certainty than that the figns of death are apparent? Here Jefus is moved, not by prayer, but by compaffion; he interpofes unfolicited, and as if he had been calling one out of a gentle flumber, fays to the dead, " Young man, arife." The word is is armed with a quickening power, "he that was dead sat up, and began to speak." Neither was this done in a corner, neither could it be hid. "There came a fear on all, "and they glorified God, saying, that a great "prophet is risen up among us, and that God "hath visited his people; and this rumor of "him went forth throughout all Judea, and "throughout all the region round about." To this display of almighty power, among other proofs of his divine mission, Jesus himself refers John Baptist, when he sent his disciples with this inquiry, "Art thou He that "should come, or do we look for another?" "Tell John what things ye have seen and "heard; how that the blind see, the lame "walk, the lepers are cleansed, the deaf hear, "*the dead are raised*, to the poor the gospel "is preached:" and what proof of Deity can possibly exceed this?

The third exemplification of Christ's empire over death, is the resurrection of Lazarus, in the passage more immediately before us. Here every thing is minute and impressive. Jesus had lived in habits of peculiar friendship

with

with this man and his family. They were probably nearly of an age. Here then was a man dying in maturity of life, the well-known inhabitant of a populous village, not two miles distant from the metropolis of the country. The disease, whatever it might be that shortened life, was left to its course, and the offices of sympathy and friendship had been apparently neglected. But this seeming neglect has a wise and gracious design. The difficulty was not to prevent the disciples, through credulity, from imposing on others, but to produce conviction in themselves, of truths the most indubitable. Lazarus is left to die, and is miraculously restored to life, that they who were to be witnesses to others, might know the certainty of the things which they were to teach; that they themselves might be cured of unbelief. The sisters of Lazarus had learned from Christ, the doctrine of the resurrection at the last day, but seem not to have been acquainted with the two instances of anticipated resurrection just now mentioned; else it would have served as a plea, and as a foundation of hope, in their own case. They both agree in expressing regret at

Christ's

Christ's absence, and reflect on it as the cause why their brother died. Martha, indeed, rather hints than declares an expectation that Jesus would interpose in their behalf, but she immediately retracts it, and gives up the point, from the consideration that the body had been already four days in the grave. The many Jews who came to comfort the mourners, were of various characters and dispositions, as the event demonstrated, for some of them believed, and some of them went with a malevolent intention to the pharisees, and told them what things Jesus had done. What mountains, then, were in this case to be removed? Behold a grown man dead, and buried already four days: see men slow of heart to believe in the power and grace of their Master, disposed rather to die with their departed friend, than to entertain a hope of his revival: see two afflicted women, slowly resigning themselves to the will of Providence, and ceasing from all hope: see a multitude of partial, prejudiced spectators, with a mass of stone upon their hearts, much more ponderous than that which lay upon the grave of Lazarus. Behold the friend of mankind melted

melted into tears, as he surveys the ravages of sin and death, approving himself a man, before he assumes and exercises the mighty power of God. That power is directed and limited to its proper object. What human force can perform, it is called upon to perform. The all-powerful voice which cried aloud, " Lazarus come forth," could likewise have removed the stone, and loosed the prisoner when quickened; but human hands are sufficient for such purposes, and are accordingly employed. When we have done our part, and not till then, are we warranted to expect the interposition of a divine agency.

The fourth display of the Redeemer's power over death, is exhibited as an effect of his own resignation of life. " When he had
" cried again with a loud voice, he yielded
" up the ghost; and behold the vail of the
" temple was rent in twain, from the top to
" the bottom; and the earth did quake, and
" the rocks rent; and the graves were
" opened, and many bodies of saints which
" slept arose, and came out of the graves after
" his resurrection, and went into the holy
" city,

Lect. 12.  *Evidences of Christianity.*

" city, and appeared unto many." Here we have the liberation of a great multitude, who had long been subject to the king of terrors, and probably had seen corruption; and the effect was produced not, as in the former instances, by an act of power, but out of seeming weakness. This weakness of death, however, is omnipotence itself. These sleeping saints feel its quickening power, these dry bones begin to stir, and to come together bone to its bone, and, preceded by him who is the " first fruits " of them that sleep," assume a new and more glorious form, fashioned like to Christ's glorious body. Then was fulfilled the word which he spake, " The hour is coming, and " now is, when the dead shall hear the voice " of the Son of God, and they that hear shall " live." Thus, " at sundry times, and in " divers manners," Jesus Christ exercised sovereignty over death, in the case of others. But in the

III. Third place, his own resurrection constitutes the grand display of his triumph over death, and him that hath the power of death: and it is in the wisdom of God transmitted to

us,

us, with a clearnefs and fulnefs of evidence that ftops the mouth of infidelity. The certainty of Chrift's death has never, that I know of, been called in queftion. The body hung lifelefs on the tree, before the eyes of a great multitude, fome of them deeply interefted in the bloody cataftrophe, and all deeply affected when the fcene clofed. The foldiers, men inured to the fight, and practifed in the works of death, came to relieve agonizing nature by a finifhing ftroke, but " when they " faw that he was dead already, they brake " not his legs, but one of them with a fpear " pierced his fide, and forthwith came there " out blood and water;" a farther proof that he was actually dead. Neither could Jofeph of Arimathea, nor Nicodemus, be poffibly miftaken in this point, who wound the body in linen clothes, with fpices, after the manner of the Jews, and thus depofited it in the fepulchre.

There is another circumftance worthy of attention, ftrikingly marked by one of the Evangelifts. The body of Jefus was depofited in " a new fepulchre, wherein was never man " yet

"yet laid." Whether, therefore, a resurrection actually took place, or an imposture had been committed, the glory or the infamy could attach but to one person. It was Jesus of Nazareth who, to the conviction of a cloud of witnesses, hung dead upon the cross; it was Jesus of Nazareth who, to the conviction of a cloud of witnesses, was consigned to a new tomb hewn out of a rock; it was he, and no other, who could be the object of attention, on this momentous occasion, to friends or to enemies. The former were either to enjoy the triumph of detecting a deception, while the others were to be covered with shame; or the disciples were to partake of the triumph of their risen and exalted Master, while his enemies should be confounded. Let us see in what manner both parties conducted themselves. The persecutors of Jesus Christ, while he yet lived, and after his death, did every thing that could be done to prevent or to expose imposture. In the wisdom of God they were permitted the full exercise of their sagacity, power and malevolence, and the solicitude which they expressed completely betrays the apprehensions that haunted them. They had but to remain quiet, and permit the pretensions

of "that deceiver" to demonstrate their own folly. They had but to sit still and smile at the fond credulity, zeal and attachment of the two counsellors, Nicodemus and Joseph of Arimathea. Whence comes this jealousy of twelve obscure, unconnected Galileans, one of whom had sold his master into their own hands, another had publicly denied him, and all of whom had forsaken him and fled? What, alarmed at the address or courage of a few females, whom every form of death is apt to intimidate! Ah, their own fears of the resurrection are much more powerful than the hopes of the disciples, or they never had made such an application as this to the Roman Governor: " Sir, we remember that that de-
" ceiver said, while he was yet alive, After
" three days I will rise again. Command
" therefore that the sepulchre be made sure
" until the third day, left his disciples come
" by night, and steal him away, and say unto
" the people, He is risen from the dead. So
" the last error shall be worse than the first."
Pilate grants them full permission to employ every precaution that they could devise for their security, and they availed themselves of it to the uttermost. " They went and made
" the

" the sepulchre sure, sealing the stone, and
" setting a watch."

The incredulity, the dejection of the followers of Christ; their want of concert, of co-operation, form a complete contrast to all this. They are concerned only about their personal safety. They believed not the repeated declarations of their Master. They have given up the cause as lost. The women went early on the third day merely to *look at* the sepulchre, and some of them provided with " sweet spices" that they might anoint the dead body of their friend, but without a ray of hope, that they were to pay him living honours. Two of the disciples went down that same day from Jerusalem to Emmaus, under a full conviction, that their expectations were groundless. To the risen Saviour himself, who joined them on the way, but whom in his present form they knew not, they sadly detail the story of Christ's sufferings, and of their own despair. Their eyes being at length opened, they return in haste to Jerusalem to announce to the eleven what they had seen and heard, but " neither believed they them."

"Afterward he appeared" personally "unto the eleven, as they sat at meat, and upbraided them with their unbelief, and hardness of heart, because they believed not them which had seen him after he was risen." One of them was absent at this interview, and he resolutely rejects the joint testimony of all his colleagues, witnessing the fact: Armed at all points in the mail of incredulity he declares; "Except I shall see in his hands the print of the nails, and put my finger into the print of the nails, and thrust my hand into his side, I will not believe." What marks of collusion, then, are here? Are these men qualified either to undertake a bold enterprize, or to weave an imposture? Were persons so simple, so timid, so disunited, fit for storming a post guarded by a band of Roman soldiers; or for contriving a tale which should pass upon the world, at a period so inquisitive, so enlightened, and in a spot, where all the sagacity, learning and power were engaged on the other side? Of all believers the infidel surely is the most credulous.

While

While such was the spirit, the views, the occupations of the opponents, and of the adherents, of the Lord Jesus, He was in supreme majesty fulfilling his own purpose and grace, in his own way, in defiance of the hostility of the one, and independent of all aid, from the other. Where is the body of him, who was crucified, and which was deposited in the tomb? Let "the chief priests and "pharisees" exhibit it, if they can, in a state of death, after the third day, and for ever stop the mouth of silly women and credulous mechanics. Ah, they have been "kicking "against the pricks," they have been contending with omnipotence, they have presumed to oppose human cunning to heavenly wisdom. What security is a cavern hewn out of a rock, a door of stone, a seal, and a watch, against the convulsion of "a great "earthquake," the might of an "angel of "the Lord," nay the almighty power of the Lord of angels?

But the appearances of Jesus Christ, "shew- "himself alive after his passion," were neither few nor doubtful. By "many infallible "proofs"

"proofs" he demonstrated the certainty of his resurrection from the dead, " being seen" of many witnesses " forty days," and " speak-"ing of the things pertaining to the king-"dom of God." Let the Apostle of the Gentiles sum up the evidence for us. It stands on the sacred page: 1 Cor. xv. 3—8. " For " I delivered unto you first of all, that which " I also received, how that Christ died for " our sins, according to the Scriptures; and " that he was buried, and that he rose again " the third day, according to the Scriptures: " And that he was seen of Cephas, then of " the twelve: After that he was seen of " above five hundred brethren at once: of " whom the greater part remain unto this " present, but some are fallen asleep. After " that he was seen of James; then of all the " apostles. And last of all he was seen of " me also, as of one born out of due time." This is the testimony of one who once was a declared and furious enemy of the Christian faith, and who did all he could to destroy it; but who both in his opposition to it, and in his support of it, acted on principle.

Is

Is it nothing, my friends—I was going to make my appeal to the enemies of Christianity—Is it nothing, that the truth of the resurrection of the Lord Jesus has been admitted by the not least enlightened part of mankind, and has maintained its ground, during a period of eighteen centuries. Is the extensively happy moral influence which it has been exercising during that period, upon the temper and conduct of them who believe it, to be accounted nothing? Is it nothing that so many myriads of human beings, through so many ages, have been cheered and comforted; have been stimulated to the performance of painful duty, have patiently supported painful suffering, have met the king of terrors with composure, with joy, animated with those prospects of immortality which the resurrection of Christ has disclosed to the enraptured eye? Is it nothing to see " Rachel, weeping for " her children, and refusing to be comforted " because they are not" by an infusion of this precious cordial revived and strengthened? See, she rises from the ground, wipes away her tears, and is no more sad, because " they " are" with Christ, who " will raise them
" up

" up at the laſt day." Is it nothing, when I am called to " bury my dead out of my ſight," the ſon whom I loved, whom I inſtructed, whom I ſaw increaſed in ſtature, and in favour with God and man, all that parental partiality can picture; and whom I ſaw pale, and emaciated, and panting, and expiring—is it nothing to contemplate him " entering into peace, reſt-" ing" with the redeemed " in their beds, " walking in his uprightneſs," while the fleſh reſts in hope? Is it nothing, under the preſſure of affliction, the preſſure of years, the decays of nature, the gradual and certain approaches of death, to be able to look up and ſay, " I know that my Redeemer liveth," He orders my lot, he ſuſtains my drooping head? Bleſſed Jeſus, " Thou wilt ſhew me " the path of life: in thy preſence is fulneſs " of joy, at thy right hand there are pleaſures " for evermore." Who is there in this aſſembly, that will not go home this evening with an impreſſion more faint or more profound on his heart, in favour of moral excellence, with kinder affections, with a warmer diſpoſition to what is good, with a more perfect reſignation to the will of God, in proportion

portion as the truth of this great leading doctrine of the gospel has laid hold of his mind? May we all "be filled with peace and joy in "believing" it; and "rejoice with joy un- "speakable and full of glory; receiving the "end of our faith, even the salvation of our "souls."

The doctrine of the resurrection of Jesus being established, and, blessed be God, it is "built upon a rock, and the gates of hell "shall not prevail against it," then

1. Every other particular of the Gospel dispensation is confirmed; every article of doctrine, however sublime and mysterious, is rendered credible, is ascertained; and every other fact standing in connection with it is firmly supported. This is the key-stone of the arch, on which every other bears, which unites all to itself, and cements the several parts into one solid, harmonious whole. Take this away, and all is disjointed, enfeebled, falls to pieces. When, therefore, I meet in Scripture "things hard to be understood," this shall resolve my doubts, and check my presumption:

presumption: "The Lord is risen; He is "risen indeed." When I am "in heaviness "through manifold temptations," when hope languishes, and faith is ready to fail, I will cast myself on this "foundation of God" which "standeth sure:" Jesus died, and rose again. For

2. The resurrection of Christ inspires the purest and most exalted delight to the soul of man, as constituting a proof of its immortality, of a state of existence beyond the grave. The mind is relieved from the depressing, the dreadful idea of annihilation. The Saviour passed from the cross to Paradise, carrying triumphantly with him the companion of his sufferings, while their bodies hung lifeless on the tree. And the resurrection sensibly demonstrated that death is not the extinction of being, but the transition from one state to another; that He who exerted this divine power, has the absolute disposal of man in every possible mode of existence. But the self same event opens a prospect the most melancholy and overwhelming to every unregenerated, unbelieving soul of man. Immortality

tality opens upon him in all its endless, hopeless misery; a " worm that dieth not; a fire that never shall be quenched,"—" Everlasting " destruction from the presence of the Lord, " and from the glory of his power." May Jesus deliver us all from the wrath which is to come.

3. The resurrection of Christ is the foundation of a doctrine peculiar to Christianity— the resurrection of the body. This was an idea so new to the learned Athenians, and, in their apprehension, so absurd, that " when " they heard" Paul preaching in Mars-hill, " the resurrection of the dead, some mocked." However the mind might have pursued its own future existence into invisible worlds, the future existence of the body was given up, or rather never thought of, by the learned and the unlearned, by the polished Greek and the rude Barbarian. The experience and history of mankind had furnished no ground whereon to rear such a fabric. The doctrine, as we hinted above, was indeed laid up in a sacred oracle delivered by Moses, but it was unknown to, or not understood by, the generality

even

even of the people to whom that oracle was committed, much more was it unknown to the reſt of the world. It was referved to the great Teacher to bring it to light, and to put the unbelieving Sadducees to ſilence, by referring them to what God ſaid by the mouth of their great prophet, at the burning buſh, concerning their venerable anceſtors, Abraham, and Iſaac, and Jacob, who, dead to the world, all lived to God, in the whole of their human exiſtence, in their body as well as in their ſpirit. And what but the belief of this made dying Jacob give it in charge to his ſons, to bury him with his Fathers? What but this faith could induce Joſeph to " give com- " mandment concerning his bones?" But, Chriſtians, the truth of the doctrine reſts not merely on an ancient declaration in the writings of Moſes, but on a fact of unqueſtionable authenticity, in the New Teſtament. That the dead are to be raiſed is a truth demonſtrated, for Chriſt roſe from the dead. And " if the ſpirit of him that raiſed up " Jeſus from the dead dwell in you; He " that raiſed up Chriſt from the dead ſhall " alſo quicken your mortal bodies, by his
" ſpirit

"spirit that dwelleth in you." "Since by man came death, by man came also the resurrection of the dead. For, as in Adam all die, even so in Christ shall all be made alive. But every man in his own order: Christ the first fruits, afterward they that are Christ's at his coming."

4. This suggests another interesting consequence of our Lord's resurrection, constituting another doctrine peculiar to Christianity; "Unto them that look for him shall he appear, the second time, without sin unto salvation." To this grand consummation the eyes of the Christian world are directed: "He hath appointed a day, in the which he will judge the world in righteousness, by that man whom he hath ordained; whereof he hath given assurance unto all men, in that he hath raised him from the dead." The end of this glorious manifestation is the most solemn and interesting: "The Lord Jesus shall be revealed from heaven with his mighty angels, in flaming fire, taking vengeance on them that know not God, and that obey not the gospel

"pel of Jesus Christ; who shall be punished
"with everlasting destruction from the pre-
"sence of the Lord, and from the glory of
"his power; when he shall come to be glo-
"rified in his saints, and to be admired in
"all them that believe, in that day." Thus
great events past, look forward to great events
yet to come, and exercise a commanding influence over all the intermediate duration.
And thus the simplest dictate of conscience,
and the most sublime discovery of religion
point to one and the same object—"Jesus
"delivered for our offences, and raised again
"for our justification,"—Jesus coming " in
"the clouds of heaven with power and great
"glory."

5. The resurrection of Christ, and the
glory which immediately followed, convey to
us some idea of a spiritual and glorious body.
He had given, before his passion, various ex-
hibitions of his power over the corporeal frame.
He fasted forty days and forty nights. He
walked on the surface of the waters. On
the mount of transfiguration " his face did
" shine as the sun, and his raiment was white
" as

"as the light." But the sensible form of his body was still the same, and equally discernible from every other, whether at the marriage supper of Cana in Galilee, or in the agony of the garden of Gethsemane, in the splendour of Tabor, or the ignominy of mount Calvary. After the resurrection, his body assumes other properties, and exercises other powers. He becomes visible and invisible at pleasure. He changes place with the rapidity of thought. He is in the midst of the disciples, though the doors are shut. And yet it is not a spirit. "Behold," says he, "my hands and my feet, that it is I myself. "Handle me, and see: for a spirit hath not "flesh and bones as ye see me have."— "While they beheld, he was taken up, and "a cloud received him out of their sight." "So also is the resurrection of the dead. It "is sown in corruption, it is raised in incor- "ruption; it is sown in dishonour, it is "raised in glory; it is sown in weakness, it "is raised in power: it is sown a natural "body, it is raised a spiritual body. There "is a natural body, and there is a spiritual "body." What a motive have we here,

men and brethren, to maintain a " converfa-
" tion in heaven, from whence we look for
" the Saviour the Lord Jefus Chrift; who
" fhall change our vile body, that it may
" be fafhioned like unto his glorious body,
" according to the working whereby he is
" able even to fubdue all things unto him-
" felf."—" Beloved, now are we the fons of
" God, and it doth not yet appear what we
" fhall be: but we know, that when he fhall
" appear we fhall be like him; for we fhall
" fee him as he is."

Thus have I endeavoured, through much
weaknefs, and frequently in much fear and
trembling, to adduce a feries of evidence of
the truth and divine original of Chriftianity,
to which God himfelf ftill continues to give
witnefs; evidence arifing out of its fpirit, its
native tendency, and its bleffed effects. I have
attempted to fhew; That the Gofpel of Chrift
is the true and only religion of nature, as exhibiting the moft fatisfactory and confiftent
view of the character and moral perfections
of the Supreme Being; as prefenting the moft
univerfal adaptation to the faculties of the human

man understanding, and to the natural and reasonable expectations of the human heart, through the various changing scenes of the life which now is; as the great interpreter of the mystery of Providence; as the grand cement of human society; and as the only satisfactory demonstration of the life and immortality after which we pant, and without which our present transitory, fluctuating, miserable existence were an enigma not to be resolved. How far I have succeeded it would ill become me to conjecture. But if any thing suggested in the course of these Lectures, has been so happy as to lay hold on the heart and mind of so much as one young person, in danger of being drawn aside by the error of the wicked one; if any known truth has been set in a new light, recalled to the memory, or impressed on the heart and conscience; if the religion of the blessed Jesus has been effectually recommended to the information, the esteem, the comfort of one precious soul, then an object has been attained, of more value than the discovery and conquest of a Continent. If we have failed, it is from want of ability, not from the weakness of the cause, and the attempt is harmless though unsuccessful.

I feel it incumbent on me, before I descend from this place, thus publicly to express my humble and thankful acknowledgements to Almighty God, for his gracious support through the labours of the season; and the rather, that at one period they were threatened with interruption, if not final termination, by severe and dangerous bodily infirmity. Hitherto the Lord hath helped. May spared, prolonged life, and restored health be more zealously and affectionately devoted to his service.

To you, my friends, I stand deeply indebted, for attendance so regular, for attention so patient, candid and serious, and for encouragement so liberal and affectionate. May the bountiful Giver of all good recompense to you and yours, a thousand fold, in temporals and in spirituals, the kindness which ye have shewn to the preacher.

My particular thanks are due, to the Gentlemen who formed this design, from motives
so

so laudable, and who have conducted it with so much wisdom, firmness, spirit and perseverance. O had the execution realized their conceptions, what a treasure would the world have possessed! But they have expressed their satisfaction in terms the most encouraging; and it becomes not me to undervalue, what they have been pleased to approve. May their zeal and industry in every good cause, be owned of God, and crowned with success; and may their labours of love for the benefit of others, be transformed into showers of blessings, to water and enrich themselves and their families.

Will my Brethren, in the ministry of the Gospel, be pleased to accept my warmest acknowledgements for their countenance, assistance and support, throughout the whole process of this undertaking? Their friendship has been so unfeigned, their co-operation so generous, their sympathy so truly Christian, that I must have a heart of marble not to feel, and feeling, not to express it. But in doing me honour, have they not discovered a spirit which reflects the highest honour on themselves?

selves? A spirit exalted above all that is mean and selfish; a spirit that can rejoice in a brother's acceptance, and overlook a brother's infirmities. This accordingly strengthens the obligation laid upon me, and I trust I shall carry a sense of it with me to the regions of perfect purity and friendship. If our names shall descend to posterity, I shall deem it a high honour for mine to descend in such company. In the mean time, may the blessing of the most High God descend, and rest, on their persons, their families, and their flocks, to cause them to abound in every temporal comfort, and in all spiritual and heavenly attainments in Christ Jesus.

My Friends, we have a common debt of gratitude to discharge to the Rev. Dr. REES, and the Office-bearers of his Church, for granting us, in a manner so truly liberal, the use of this comfortable and commodious place, of worship. In your name and my own, render them sincere and hearty thanks; with kindest wishes, and fervent prayers for the continuance and increase of their union, comfort and prosperity. May grace, mercy and peace

peace from God the Father, and the Lord Jesus Christ, be multiplied to them, and to all who love our Lord Jesus in sincerity and truth; and may the multitude of them that believe, be of one heart and of one soul.

If I have omitted the due acknowledgement of any person or circumstance, which ought to have been noticed, it proceeded not from wilful neglect, and will be, by the candid, imputed to human frailty, not to deliberate unkindness: if I have fallen into error, or been guilty of misrepresentation, the same candour, I trust, will be extended, when I solemnly declare, that, in no one instance, did I mean to deceive or to misrepresent.

Brethren, farewell. We are dropping each other by the way; but we are journeying to our Father's house, and shall arrive every one in his order. Let us not fall out by the way, but endeavour to render what remains of the road smoother, and more pleasant to each other, by looks, and words, and acts of mutual cordiality and devout affection. Let us make it appear that we believe the gospel, by breath-
ing

ing its spirit, and by reducing its precepts into practice. He who doeth the will of God, the same shall know of the doctrine whether it be of God. "And the peace of God, "which passeth all understanding, shall keep "your hearts and minds through Christ "Jesus:" to whom with the Father and the Holy Spirit, be all honour and glory, world without end. Amen.

FINIS.

*PUBLISHED BY THE SAME AUTHOR.*

### IV.

### STUDIES OF NATURE,

A Translation from the French of JACQUES-BER-
NARDIN-HENRI DE SAINT PIERRE,

In five Volumes Octavo, containing five interesting Engravings. Price in Boards 1l. 10s. To be had of the Translator, and of C. Dilly, Poultry.

### V.

### SERMONS, PREACHED AT DIFFERENT PLACES AND ON VARIOUS OCCASIONS,

Collected and re-published in their respective order, in two Volumes Octavo, Price in Boards, 12s. To be had of the Author, and of Murray and Highley, No. 32, Fleet-street.

### VI.

### SAURIN's SERMONS,

A Translation from the French,

Forming a 6th Volume to those formerly translated by the Rev. ROBERT ROBINSON, of Cambridge. Price 6s. Boards, to be had of the Translator, and of Joseph Murgatroyd, Chiswell-street.

### VII.

### THE INTELLECTUAL AND MORAL DIFFERENCE BETWEEN MAN AND MAN.

A Sermon preached on Occasion of the Death of the late Rev. JOHN FELL; a new Edition, being the Third, printed uniformly with this Volume, for the Accommodation of such as may wish to bind them up together. Price 1s. 6d. To be had of the Author, and of R. Good, 65, Bishopsgate Without.

*PUBLISHED BY THE AUTHOR OF THE
LAST EIGHT LECTURES.*

I.

SACRED BIOGRAPHY,

In 6 vols. Octavo, a new Edition, being the Fourth. Price 1l. 16s. in Boards; to be had of the Author, and of Murray and Highley, No. 32, Fleet-street.

II.

LAVATER's ESSAYS ON PHYSIOGNOMY,

A Translation from the French,
In Imperial Quarto, containing upwards of Eight Hundred capital Engravings; in forty-one Numbers, at 12s. each. To be had of the Translator; of T. Holloway, the Engraver, Newington-Green; and of Murray and Highley, No. 32, Fleet-street.

III.

THE LETTERS OF EULER TO A GERMAN PRINCESS,

(THE PRINCESS D'ANHALT-DESSAU, NIECE TO FREDERICK II. KING OF PRUSSIA,)

On different Subjects in Physics and Philosophy, in two large Volumes Octavo.
A Translation from the French, with many plates; Price 16s. To be had of the Translator, and of Murray and Highley, No. 32, Fleet-street.

www.ingramcontent.com/pod-product-compliance
Lightning Source LLC
Chambersburg PA
CBHW022109290426
44112CB00008B/611